ADULT READING SERIES

Challenger

Teacher's Manual

FOR BOOKS 1 - 4

COREA MURPHY

Dr. Bob Lambach

About the Author

Corea Murphy has worked in the field of education since the early 1960s. In addition to classroom and tutorial teaching, Ms. Murphy has developed language arts curriculum guides for public high schools, conducted curriculum and effectiveness workshops, and established an educational program for residents in a drug rehabilitation facility.

Ms. Murphy became interested in creating a reading series for older students when she began working with illiterate adults and adolescents in the early 1970s. The **Challenger Adult Reading Series** is the result of her work with these students.

In a very real sense, these students contributed greatly to the development of this reading series. Their enthusiasm for learning to read and their willingness to work hard provided inspiration, and their many helpful suggestions influenced the content of both the student books and the teacher's manuals.

It is to these students that the **Challenger Adult Reading Series** is dedicated with the hope that others who wish to become good readerswill find this reading program both helpful and stimulating.

A special note of gratitude is also extended to Kay Koschnick and Christina Jagger of New Readers Press for their work and support in guiding this series to completion.

ISBN 0-88336-874-9

EACH ONE TEACH ONE

© 1986, 1991
New Readers Press
Publishing Division of Laubach Literacy International
Box 131, Syracuse, New York 13210

Printed in the United States of America

Cover design by Chris Steenwerth

9 8 7 6 5 4 3 2

Table of Contents

Book 4

Answer Keys

Introduction to the *Challenger* Series

Challenger Adult Reading Series is an eight-book program of reading, writing, and reasoning skills designed to meet the needs of adult and adolescent students. It takes students from the beginning stages of reading to the critical reading, writing, and reasoning skills associated with the latter ninth grade level. The first four books in this series emphasize "learning to read." Beginning with the fifth book, the emphasis shifts to "reading to learn."

Each book in this controlled vocabulary series contains twenty lessons, plus reviews. Each lesson includes a reading selection and a variety of exercises and activities.

The reading selections in the odd-numbered books are generally fiction pieces. Books 1 and 3 contain light-hearted stories about adult characters who get caught up in a variety of situations. Most reading selections in Books 5 and 7 are minimally adapted well-known works of fiction.

The reading selections in the even-numbered books are engaging nonfiction pieces. The selections in Books 2 and 4 are generally similar to topics found in encyclopedias. Most selections in Books 6 and 8 are adaptations from highly-respected works of nonfiction. These selections enable students to broaden the scope of their knowledge.

Preceding each reading selection in the odd-numbered books is a word chart that introduces new words according to a specific phonics principle. In Books 1 and 3, these words appear frequently in both the reading selections and the exercises. In Books 5 and 7, the words from these charts are the basis for dictionary work and other word study exercises.

The wide variety of exercises and activities helps students develop their reading, writing, and reasoning skills and increase their basic knowledge. Comprehension exercises based on the reading selections focus on the development of literal, inferential, and critical reading skills. Also, the comprehension exercises in Books 5 through 8 introduce or reinforce various concepts associated with literary understanding.

Word study exercises are designed to increase the students' vocabulary and further develop their reading and reasoning skills. These exercises vary from simple word associations to classifying, sequencing, and categorizing exercises, analogies, vocabulary reviews, activities which emphasize using context clues, those which require using dictionaries and other reference materials, and several types of puzzles.

Students are eased into writing. Early in the series, exercises focus on writing at the sentence level and are designed to simultaneously improve spelling, sentence structure, and students' skill in expressing themselves clearly. Most lessons in Books 5 through 8 include at least one exercise in which the student must write responses in complete sentences or brief paragraphs. The individual lesson notes in this manual offer suggestions of topics to be considered for additional writing assignments. Although *Challenger* is primarily a reading series, teachers should encourage their students to understand that writing is an essential aspect of literacy.

The review lessons of Books 1 through 5 contain indexes of the words introduced in the preceding lessons. Word indexes are included in the Teacher's Manuals for Books 6 through 8. These indexes can be used in developing various reinforcement activities and vocabulary reviews.

The books also include periodic reviews. The last review in each book can be used as a diagnostic tool to determine the appropriate placement for students using this program. An accuracy rate of 85% or better on the final reviews indicates that a student is ready for the next book.

Significant Educational Features

Wide Learning Suitability/ Minimal Instructional Needs

This series has been tested successfully with students in many different types of instructional settings:

- Secondary remedial reading programs
- Secondary special education programs
- Adult volunteer literacy programs
- ABE, pre-GED, and GED programs
- Community college reading programs
- Educational programs in correctional institutions
- Tutorial programs for employees who wish to develop literacy skills in order to advance in their chosen occupations

Because both adults and older teens develop their skills more effectively when they assume a high degree of responsibility for their learning development, the lessons in the *Challenger* series have been designed so that they can be completed by students with only minimal instruction from the teacher.

An Integrated Approach

These books integrate reading, writing, and reasoning activities. The words introduced in each lesson provide the organizing principle for this integration. Through frequently seeing and using these words in reading, writing, and reasoning activities which are repeated in design but varied in content, students are better able to understand and apply what they have learned to a variety of situations. The thoroughness of this integrated approach enables students to begin each new lesson with greater mastery and confidence.

Sequenced Skill Building

Each lesson builds upon skills and content which students have worked with in previous lessons. Students experience a sense of progress because they quickly learn to apply their skills to new situations.

Students are continually challenged by the increased breadth and difficulty of each lesson, through which their reading progress is reflected. Generally, each reading selection is slightly longer than the previous one. In addition, the content, vocabulary, and sentence structure in the reading selections gradually become more sophisticated and demanding. The exercises, too, capitalize on students' increasing proficiency. Building on students' current skill level, the exercises gradually expand the students' knowledge in a spiral-like fashion—both broadening and deepening their abilities in the various skill areas.

Highly Motivating Material

For the past ten years, this series has been used with adult and adolescent populations for which it is designed. Students comment that many characteristics of this reading program help to hold their interest in their efforts to become more proficient readers. The characteristics they most frequently cite include:

- the exceptionally motivating reading selections
- the mature presentation and diversity of material
- the information presented in each lesson
- the emphasis on using reasoning powers
- the challenge of increasingly difficult materials
- the success and confidence the *Challenger* books generate

Comprehensive Teacher's Manuals

The comprehensive teacher's manuals offer practical suggestions about procedures and techniques for working with students. Individual lesson notes in the manuals present objectives, guidelines, and suggestions for specific activities in each lesson.

Answer Keys

Complete answer keys for each lesson in the first four books are found in both the *Teacher's Manual for Books 1-4* and in the *Answer Key for Books 1-4*. The *Answer Key for Books 5-8* contains the answers for those books. In addition, the individual teacher's manuals for *Challenger* 5, 6, 7, and 8 contain answer keys for each of those books.

> Although it is recognized that there are students of both sexes, for the sake of clarity and simplicity, we chose to use the pronouns *he, him,* and *his* throughout this book.

SCOPE AND SEQUENCE: BOOK 1

Phonics — Lesson	1	2	3	4	5	6	7	8	9	10	11	12	13	14	15	16	17	18	19	20	R1	R2
1. Recognize long vowel sounds: (CV and CVC¢)	★	★	★	★	★	☆	☆	★	☆	☆	☆	☆	☆	☆	☆	☆	☆	☆	☆	☆	☆	☆
(CVCC)						✩				☆						☆				☆	☆	
2. Recognize short vowel sounds: (VC and CVC)	★	★	★	★	★	☆	☆	★	☆	☆	☆	☆	☆	☆	☆	☆	☆	☆	☆	☆	☆	☆
(CVCC)				★	★	★	★	★	★		☆						☆		☆		☆	☆
3. Recognize sounds for y	☆		☆	★		☆	☆		★		☆			☆			☆	☆	☆	★		☆
4. Recognize sounds for vowel groups: ee					★				★	☆								☆	☆			★
ay, ey, oy, uy									★													
ai, ie, oa, oi, ou, ue										☆							☆	☆	☆			
ea (as in eat and head)													☆	☆			☆	☆	☆			
oo (as in food and foot)												★	★				☆					
5. Recognize r-controlled vowel sounds: ar, are, or, er, eer, ir, ur											★	★	★									
air, oar, oor												★	★									
ear (as in ear and bear)													★									
our (as in sour and four)													★	★								
6. Recognize vowel sounds followed by l: al, el, ild, ol, ul, ull														★								
7. Recognize vowel sounds for single consonants	★	★	★	★	★	☆	☆	★	☆	☆	☆	☆	☆	☆	☆	☆	☆	☆	☆	★	☆	☆
8. Recognize sounds for initial consonant blends: st, sk										★					★							
bl, cl, fl, gl, pl, sl																★	☆					
br, cr, dr, fr, gr, pr, tr, str																	★					
sm, sn, sp, sw, thr, tw																		★				
chr, sc, scr, shr, spl, spr, squ																			★			
9. Recognize sounds for final consonant blends: nd, nt, ck, mp						★	☆	☆		☆					☆	☆	☆					
ng, nk, st, sk							★			☆							☆					
st, sk			★												★							
10. Recognize silent consonants: kn, wr, mb, ght, tch										★							☆					
11. Recognize sounds for digraphs: ch, sh																	☆		☆			
th, wh																		★				
dge																						
12. Recognize sounds for c and g																				★		
13. Mark long and short vowel sounds													☆							★		

Word Analysis — Lesson	1	2	3	4	5	6	7	8	9	10	11	12	13	14	15	16	17	18	19	20	R1	R2
1. Recognize verb endings: -ed, -ing		☆	☆	☆	☆	☆	☆	☆	☆	☆	☆	☆	☆	☆	☆	☆	☆	☆	☆	☆	☆	☆
-s	☆			☆	☆	☆	☆	☆	☆	☆		☆	☆	☆	☆	☆	☆	☆	☆	☆	☆	☆
2. Recognize noun endings: -s	☆	☆	☆	☆	☆	☆	☆	☆	☆	☆		☆	☆	☆	☆	☆	☆	☆	☆	☆	☆	☆
-'s	☆	☆	☆	☆	☆	☆	☆	☆	☆	☆		☆	☆	☆	☆	☆	☆	☆	☆	☆	☆	☆

KEY: ★ = Primary emphasis   ☆ = Secondary emphasis   ✩ = Integrated with other skills

Skills Chart

KEY: ★ = Primary emphasis ★ = Secondary emphasis ☆ = Integrated with other skills

Word Analysis, cont.	1	2	3	4	5	6	7	8	9	10	11	12	13	14	15	16	17	18	19	20	R1	R2
3. Recognize contractions for:																						
not					☆	☆	☆	☆	☆	☆	☆	☆	☆	☆	☆	☆	☆	☆	☆	☆	☆	☆
is							☆				☆	☆	☆	☆	☆	☆	☆	☆	☆	☆	☆	☆
am											☆	☆	☆	☆						☆		
will															☆		☆			☆		
had												☆										
are																☆		☆	☆			☆
have																		☆				
would																			☆			
4. Recognize abbreviations:																						
Mr.	☆				☆			☆	☆	☆	☆	☆	☆	☆	☆	☆	☆	☆	☆	☆	☆	☆
Mrs., Ms.					☆	☆	☆	☆	☆		☆	☆	☆	☆	☆	☆		☆	☆	☆		
Dr.																☆	☆			☆		
5. Recognize other word endings:																						
-y, -ly									★			☆	☆									
-er											★											
-ful, -less														★								
6. Recognize common word beginnings: un-, re-														★					★			☆
7. Distinguish words that look similar/rhyme	★	★	★	★	★	★	★	★		★		★	★		★	★	★		★	★	★	★
8. Form compound words																★		★				

Vocabulary	1	2	3	4	5	6	7	8	9	10	11	12	13	14	15	16	17	18	19	20	R1	R2
1. Learn unfamiliar vocabulary	☆	☆	☆	☆	☆	☆	☆	☆	☆	☆	☆	☆	☆	☆	☆	☆	☆	☆	☆	☆	☆	☆
2. Identify synonyms								★	★					★	★						★	★
3. Identify antonyms								★		★			★	★							★	
4. Identify word associations										★	★		★						★			
5. Learn/review common expressions														★						☆		★

Comprehension	1	2	3	4	5	6	7	8	9	10	11	12	13	14	15	16	17	18	19	20	R1	R2
1. Decode words accurately when reading aloud	★	★	★	★	★	★	★	★	★	★	★	★	★	★	★	★	★	★	★	★	★	★
2. Pronounce word endings when reading aloud	☆	☆	☆	☆	☆	☆	☆	☆	☆	☆	☆	☆	☆	☆	☆	☆	☆	☆	☆	☆	☆	☆
3. Group words appropriately when reading aloud	☆	☆	☆	☆	★	★	☆	★	★	★	★	★	★	★	★	★	★	★	★	★	★	★
4. Interpret punctuation correctly when reading aloud	☆	☆	☆	☆	★	★	★	☆	★	★	★	★	★	★	★	★	★	★	★	★	★	★
5. Identify words using phonics and context clues	☆	☆	☆	☆	★	★	☆	☆	★	★	★	★	★	★	★	★	★	★	★	★	★	★
6. Read silently	★	★	★	★	★	★	★	★	★	★	★	★	★	★	★	★	★	★	★	★	★	★
7. Follow oral directions	☆	☆	☆	☆	☆	☆	☆	☆	☆	☆	☆	☆	☆	☆	☆	☆	☆	☆	☆	☆	☆	☆
8. Improve listening comprehension	☆	☆	☆	☆	☆	☆	☆	☆	☆	☆	☆	☆	☆	☆	☆	☆	☆	☆	☆	☆	☆	☆
9. Discuss stories	★	★	★	★	★	★	★	★	★	★	★	★	★	★	★	★	★	★	★	★	★	★

Comprehension, cont.

Lesson	1	2	3	4	5	6	7	8	9	10	11	12	13	14	15	16	17	18	19	20	R1	R2
10. Develop literal comprehension skills:																						
– Recall details	★	★	★	★	★	★	★	★	★	★	★	★	★	★	★	★	★	★	★	★	★	
– Locate information in the story	★	★	★	★	★	★	★	★	★	★	★	★	★	★	★	★	★	★	★	★		
11. Develop inferential comprehension skills:																						
– Infer word meanings from context clues		☆	☆	☆	☆	★	★	★	★	★	★	★	★	★	★	★	★	★	★	★	★	★
– Infer information from the story	☆	☆	☆	☆	☆	☆	☆	☆	☆	☆	☆	☆	☆	☆	☆	☆	☆	☆	☆	☆	☆	
– Use context clues to predict correct responses	★	★	★	★	★	★	★	★	★	★	★	★	★	★	★	★	★	★	★	★	★	★
– Classify words under appropriate categories																	★			★		★
12. Develop applied comprehension skills:																						
– Relate reading to personal experience	☆	☆	☆	☆	☆	☆	☆	☆	☆	☆	☆	☆	☆	☆	☆	☆	☆	☆	☆	☆	☆	
– Draw conclusions	☆	☆	☆	☆	☆	☆	☆	☆	☆	☆	☆	☆	☆	☆	☆	☆	☆	☆	☆	☆	☆	
13. Recognize number words													★					★	★	★	★	
14. Learn/review basic factual information																		★	★			

Writing

Lesson	1	2	3	4	5	6	7	8	9	10	11	12	13	14	15	16	17	18	19	20	R1	R2
1. Write legibly	★	★	★	★	★	☆	☆	★	☆	☆	☆	☆	★	☆	★	☆	☆	★	☆	★	☆	☆
2. Copy words accurately	★	★	★	★	★	★	★	★	★	★	★	★	★	★	★	★	★	★	★	★	★	★
3. Copy sentences accurately	★	★																				
4. Spell words with greater accuracy					★	★	★	★	★	★	★	★	★	★	★	★	★	★	★	★	★	★
5. Form new words by adding the endings:																						
-ed					★	★	☆															
-ing					★	★																
-y									★													
-er											★											
-est															★							
6. Change the *y* to *i* before adding:																						
-er											★											
-est																						
7. Write number words															☆			★				
8. Use *a* and *an* appropriately								☆				☆				☆					☆	
9. Compose sentences																				★		

Note: Specific suggestions for additional writing assignments appear in the individual lesson notes for Book 1 and in Chapter 7 of this manual.

Study Skills

Lesson	1	2	3	4	5	6	7	8	9	10	11	12	13	14	15	16	17	18	19	20	R1	R2
1. Complete exercises:																						
fill-in-the-blank		☆	☆	☆	☆	☆	☆	☆	☆	☆	☆	☆	☆	☆	☆	☆	☆	☆	☆	☆	☆	☆
matching								☆	☆	☆	☆	☆	☆	☆	☆	☆	☆	☆	☆		☆	☆
yes/no questions				☆																		
writing sentences								☆				☆			☆					☆		
true/false questions																				☆	☆	☆
multiple choice questions																						☆
analogies																						
2. Apply reasoning skills:																						
context clues	☆	★	☆	☆	★	☆	☆	★	★	★	★	★	★	★	★	★	★	★	★	★	★	★
process of elimination					★			☆	☆	★	★	★	★	★	★	★	★	★	★	★	★	★
3. Use word indexes to check spelling					☆	☆	☆													☆		

KEY: ★ = Primary emphasis   ★ = Secondary emphasis   ☆ = Integrated with other skills

SCOPE AND SEQUENCE: BOOK 2

Phonics

Lesson	1	2	3	4	5	R	6	7	8	9	10	R	11	12	13	14	15	R	16	17	18	19	20	R
1. Use phonic skills to decode unknown words	★	☆	★	★	★	★	★	★	★	★	★	★	★	★	★	★	★	★	★	★	★	★	★	★
2. Recognize long and short vowel sounds	☆	☆	☆	☆	☆	★	☆	☆	★	☆	★	☆	☆	☆	☆	☆	☆	☆	☆	★	★	☆	★	★
3. Identify long and short vowel sounds	★	★	★	★	★		★	☆		★			★											
4. Identify silent *e*	★																							
5. Recognize/contrast *r*-controlled vowel sounds		☆	☆	☆	★		☆	☆	☆	★	★	☆		★		☆	☆		☆	☆	☆	☆	☆	
6. Recognize vowel sounds preceding *l*			★		☆					★								☆					☆	★
7. Contrast *ow* (as in *cow* and *slow*)													★											
8. Recognize *aw* words									★									☆						
9. Contrast *oo* (as in *food* and *foot*)							☆	☆						☆	☆								☆	
10. Contrast other vowel sounds											★	☆						☆						
11. Recognize sounds for single consonants, consonant blends, and digraphs	★				★	★		★		★	★	★	★	★	★	★	★	★	★	★	★	★	★	★
12. Contrast sounds for single consonants, consonant blends, and digraphs	☆	★	★	★	★	★	★	★	★	★	★	★	★			★	★	★	★				★	
13. Recognize sounds for *c* and *g*	☆	☆	☆				☆	☆	☆	☆	☆	☆	☆	☆	☆			☆	☆				☆	☆
14. Recognize silent consonants and vowels	☆	☆							☆	☆		☆						☆						
15. Identify silent consonants and vowels											★							☆						

Word analysis

Lesson	1	2	3	4	5	R	6	7	8	9	10	R	11	12	13	14	15	R	16	17	18	19	20	R
1. Use syllabication to decode words	☆	☆	☆	☆	☆	☆	☆	☆	☆	★	☆	★	☆	☆	☆	☆	☆	☆	☆	☆	☆	☆	☆	★
2. Recognize abbreviations and contractions	☆	☆	☆	★	☆	☆	☆	☆	☆	☆	☆	☆	☆	☆	☆	☆	☆	☆	☆	☆	☆	☆	☆	☆
3. Distinguish words that look similar/rhyme	★	★	★	★	★	★	★	★	★	★	★		★		★	★	★	★		★		★	★	
4. Recognize noun endings												☆					☆		☆		☆			
5. Recognize verb endings											☆													
6. Recognize other word endings									★					★		★			★	★			★	
7. Recognize common word beginnings								☆										☆			☆		☆	
8. Divide compound words									☆	☆									★					
9. Form compound words							☆		★	☆													☆	

Vocabulary

Lesson	1	2	3	4	5	R	6	7	8	9	10	R	11	12	13	14	15	R	16	17	18	19	20	R
1. Learn unfamiliar vocabulary	★	★	★	★	★	★	★	★	★	★	★	★	★	★	★	★	★	★	★	★	★	★	★	★
2. Infer word meanings from context clues	★	★	★	★	★	★	★	★	★	★	★	★	★	★	★	★	★	★	★	★	★			☆
3. Identify antonyms				★				★	★			★		☆						★	★	★	☆	☆
4. Identify synonyms											☆										★		★	★
5. Complete word associations					☆		★			★									★			★		★
6. Complete analogies	☆	☆			☆																		☆	
7. Learn/review idiomatic expressions/common sayings														★				☆				☆	☆	
8. Learn/review collective nouns																☆								

KEY: ★ = Primary emphasis   ★ = Secondary emphasis   ☆ = Integrated with other skills

Comprehension

Comprehension	Lesson	1	2	3	4	5	R	6	7	8	9	10	R	11	12	13	14	15	R	16	17	18	19	20	R
1. Follow oral and written directions		✩	✩	✩	✩	✩	✩	✩	✩	✩	✩	✩	✩	✩	✩	✩	✩	✩	✩	✩	✩	✩	✩	✩	✩
2. Group words appropriately when reading orally		✩	✩	✩	✩	✩	✩	✩	✩	✩	✩	✩		✩	✩	✩	✩	✩	✩	✩	✩	✩	✩	✩	✩
3. Interpret punctuation correctly when reading orally		✩	✩	✩	✩	✩	✩	✩	✩	✩	✩	✩	✩	✩	✩	✩	✩	✩	✩	✩	✩	✩	✩	✩	✩
4. Identify words using context clues & phonics skills		✩	✩	✩	✩	✩	✩	✩	✩	✩	✩	✩	✩	✩	✩	✩	✩	✩	✩	✩	✩	✩	✩	✩	✩
5. Recognize title as topic of reading selection		★	✩	✩	✩	✩	✩	✩	✩	✩	✩	✩	✩	✩	✩	✩	✩	✩	✩	✩	✩	✩	✩	✩	✩
6. Improve listening comprehension		☆	☆	☆	☆	☆	☆	☆	☆	☆	☆	☆	☆	☆	☆	☆	☆	☆	☆	☆	☆	☆	☆	☆	☆
7. Discuss the reading passage		✩	✩	✩	✩	✩		✩	✩	✩	✩	✩	✩	✩	✩	✩	✩	✩	✩	✩	✩	✩	✩	✩	✩
8. Relate reading to illustrations		✩	✩	✩	✩			✩	✩	✩	✩	✩		✩	✩	✩					✩			✩	✩
9. Develop literal comprehension skills:																									
– Recall details		★	★	★	★	★	✩	★	★	★	★	★	✩	★	★	★	★	★	✩	★	★	★	★	★	✩
– Locate information in the reading passage		★	★	★	★	★	✩	★	★	★	★	★	✩	★	★	★	★	★	✩	★	★	★	★	★	
10. Develop inferential comprehension skills:																									
– Infer word meanings from context clues		✩	✩	✩	✩	✩	✩	✩	★	★	★	★	★	★	★	★	★	★	✩	★	★	★	★	★	✩
– Infer information from the selection				✩				✩	✩	✩	✩	✩	✩	✩	✩	✩	✩		✩	✩	✩	✩	✩		
– Draw conclusions based on selection															✩	✩		✩						✩	
– Use context clues to predict correct responses		✩	✩	✩	✩	✩	✩	✩	✩	✩	✩	✩	✩	✩					✩	✩				✩	✩
– Classify words under topic headings		★	✩	✩	☆			☆	☆							☆									
– Determine topic headings for words																✩									
11. Develop applied comprehension skills:																									
– Relate reading to personal experience		✩	✩	✩	✩	✩	✩	✩	✩	✩	✩	✩	✩	✩	✩	✩	✩	✩	✩	✩	✩		✩		
– Draw conclusions based on personal experience		☆	✩	✩	✩	✩	✩	✩			✩	✩		✩	✩	✩		✩	✩	✩	✩	✩			✩
12. Learn/review basic factual information		✩								☆	✩	✩	✩	☆					☆			☆		✩	✩
13. Reorder words into meaningful sentences						✩	✩	✩						✩								✩			
14. Sequence events accurately																	✩	✩							

Writing

Writing	Lesson	1	2	3	4	5	R	6	7	8	9	10	R	11	12	13	14	15	R	16	17	18	19	20	R
1. Write legibly		☆	☆	☆	☆	☆	☆	☆	☆	☆	☆	☆	☆	☆	☆	☆	☆	☆	☆	☆	☆	☆	☆	☆	☆
2. Copy words accurately		✩	✩	✩	✩	✩	✩	✩	✩	✩	✩	✩	✩	✩	✩	✩	✩	✩	✩	✩	✩	✩	✩	✩	✩
3. Capitalize words appropriately		☆	☆	☆	☆	☆	☆	☆	☆	☆	☆	☆	☆	☆	☆	☆	☆	☆	☆	☆	☆	☆	☆	☆	☆
4. Spell words with greater accuracy		✩	✩	✩	✩	✩	✩	★	✩	★	✩	✩	✩	✩	✩	✩	✩	✩	✩	✩	✩	✩	✩	✩	
5. Use homonyms correctly		✩	✩	✩	✩	✩		✩				✩												✩		
6. Spell number words accurately			☆	★			✩								✩										
7. Form new words by adding the endings: -y / -er													✩		✩					☆					
8. Change y to i before adding -er, -est, -ly																✩			✩						
9. Unscramble words/sentences													✩					✩				✩		✩	
10. Write sentence answers to questions		✩	✩	✩	✩	✩	✩	✩	✩	✩	✩	✩	✩	✩	✩	✩	✩	✩	✩	✩	✩	✩	✩	✩	✩

Note: Specific suggestions for additional writing assignments appear in the individual lesson notes for Book 2 and Chapter 7 of this manual.

KEY: ★ = Primary emphasis ✩ = Secondary emphasis ☆ = Integrated with other skills

Study Skills		1	2	3	4	5	R	6	7	8	9	10	R	11	12	13	14	15	R	16	17	18	19	20	R
Lesson																									
1. Increase concentration		★	★	★	★	★	★	★	★	★	★	★	★	★	★	★	★	★	★	★	★	★	★	★	★
2. Complete reading comprehension questions requiring:	single words answers	☆	☆	☆	☆	☆		☆	☆	☆	☆	☆			☆	☆	☆	☆		☆	☆			☆	☆
	phrases	☆	☆	☆	☆	☆			☆	☆	☆	☆	☆	☆	☆	☆	☆	☆	☆	☆	☆	☆	☆	☆	
	complete sentences	☆	☆	☆	☆	☆	☆	☆	☆	☆	☆	☆	☆	☆	☆	☆	☆	☆	☆	☆	☆	☆	☆	☆	☆
3. Complete exercises:	fill-in-the-blank	☆	☆	☆	☆	☆	☆	☆		☆	☆	☆	☆	☆	☆	☆	☆	☆	☆	☆	☆	☆	☆	☆	☆
	matching	☆	☆	☆	☆	☆			☆		☆		☆	☆	☆	☆		☆	☆				☆		☆
	multiple choice						☆			☆			☆				☆			☆					☆
	analogies									★										★			★		★
4. Apply reasoning skills to exercises:	context clues	★	★	★	★	★	★	★		★	★	★	★	☆	☆	☆	☆	☆	☆	☆	☆	☆	☆	☆	☆
	process of elimination	★	★	★	★	★	★		★	★	★	★	★	☆	☆	☆	☆	☆	☆	☆	☆	☆	☆	☆	☆
5. Use a globe or atlas				☆	☆			☆			☆	☆													
6. Use an encyclopedia					☆																				
7. Use word indexes to look up correct spelling		☆	☆	☆	☆	☆	☆	☆	☆	☆	☆	☆	☆	☆	☆	☆	☆	☆	☆	☆	☆	☆	☆	☆	☆

KEY: ★ = Primary emphasis   ★ = Secondary emphasis   ☆ = Integrated with other skills

SCOPE AND SEQUENCE: BOOK 3

Phonics — Lesson	1	2	3	4	5	6	7	8	9	10	11	12	13	14	15	16	17	18	19	20	R
1. Use phonics skills to decode unknown words	★	★	★	★	★	★	★	★	★	★	★	★	★	★	★	★	★	★	★	★	★
2. Recognize long and short vowel sounds	☆	☆	☆	☆	☆	☆	☆	☆	☆	☆	☆	☆	☆	☆	☆	☆	☆	☆	☆	☆	☆
3. Recognize sounds for vowel combinations: *ai, ee, ēa, ĕa, ui*								★													
oa, ou, oi, oo									★												
au										★											
r-controlled vowel combinations											★										
4. Recognize sounds for consonant blends: *st*		★																			
bl, br, cl, cr, fl, fr			★																		
gl, gr, pl, pr, sl, str				★																	
dr, tr, thr, sc, sk, sw					★																
sm, sn, sp, scr						★															
5. Recognize sounds for digraphs: *ch, sh*		★				★															
th, wh						★															
6. Recognize sounds for *c* and *g*	☆												★								
7. Recognize vowel sounds preceding *l*												★									
8. Recognize silent consonants							★			☆				☆							
9. Recognize *r*-controlled vowel sounds											★				★						
10. Recognize *gh* and *ght* words														★							
11. Recognize *ow* sounds (as in *cow* and *slow*)																★	☆				
12. Contrast vowel and consonant sounds																					☆

Word Analysis — Lesson	1	2	3	4	5	6	7	8	9	10	11	12	13	14	15	16	17	18	19	20	R
1. Use syllabication to decode words	★	★	★	★	★	★	★	★	★	★	★	★	★	★	★	★	★	★	★	★	★
2. Recognize abbreviations and contractions	☆	☆	☆	☆	☆	☆	☆	☆	☆	☆	☆	☆	☆	☆	☆	☆	☆	☆	☆	☆	☆
3. Divide compound words	☆	☆	☆	☆	☆	☆	☆	☆	☆	☆	☆	☆	☆	☆	☆	☆	☆	☆	☆	☆	☆
4. Form compound words					☆	☆		★				☆									
5. Divide words into syllables			★	☆				☆					☆	☆	☆						
6. Combine syllables to form words									☆		☆					☆					
7. Recognize common word endings: -er	☆																				
-est		☆																			
-y																					
-ly					☆	☆															
-ful and -less											☆										
-en							★		☆	☆											
8. Recognize common word beginnings: re-											☆										
in-												☆									
mis-													☆								
de-																☆					
ex-															★	★					
com-, con-																★	★	★			
un-																	★	★			
dis-, im-, in-																★	★	★			
up-, down-, over-, under-																			★		

KEY: ★ = Primary emphasis ★ = Secondary emphasis ☆ = Integrated with other skills

Vocabulary

Lesson	1	2	3	4	5	6	7	8	9	10	11	12	13	14	15	16	17	18	19	20	R
1. Learn unfamiliar vocabulary	★	★	★	★	★	★	★	★	★	★	★	★	★	★	★	★	★	★	★	★	★
2. Infer word meanings from context clues	★	★	★	★	★	★	★	★	★	★	★	★	★	★	★	★	★	★	★	★	★
3. Identify definitions/descriptions of terms	☆	☆	☆	☆				☆		☆		☆	☆		☆	☆	☆	☆		☆	☆
4. Identify synonyms					★						★									☆	
5. Identify antonyms						★														☆	☆
6. Distinguish between synonyms and antonyms							★	★						★							
7. Complete analogies													☆				★				
8. Complete word associations									★	★											

Comprehension

Lesson	1	2	3	4	5	6	7	8	9	10	11	12	13	14	15	16	17	18	19	20	R
1. Follow written directions	★	★	★	★	★	★	★	★	★	★	★	★	★	★	★	★	★	★	★	★	★
2. Identify words using context clues	★	★	★	★	★	★	★	★	★	★	★	★	★	★	★	★	★	★	★	★	★
3. Read stories independently		★	★	★	★	★	★	★	★	★	★	★	★	★	★	★	★	★	★	★	
4. Complete exercises independently	★	★	★	★	★	★	★	★	★	★	★	★	★	★	★	★	★	★	★	★	★
5. Improve listening comprehension	☆	☆	★	★	★	☆	★	★	★	★	☆	★	★	★	★	★	★	★	★	★	★
6. Group words appropriately when reading orally	★	★	★	★	★	★	★	★	★	★	★	★	★	★	★	★	★	★	★	★	★
7. Interpret punctuation correctly when reading orally	☆	★	★	★	★	☆	★	★	★	★	★	★	★	★	★	★	★	★	★	★	
8. Develop literal comprehension skills:																					
- Recall details	★	★	★	★	★	★	★	★	★	★	★	★	★	★	★	★	★	★	★	★	★
- Locate specific information	★	★	★	★	★	★	★	★	★	★	★	★	★	★	★	★	★	★	★	★	
9. Develop inferential comprehension skills:																					
- Infer word meanings from context clues	★	★	★	★	★	★	★	★	★	★	★	★	★	★	★	★	★	★	★	★	★
- Infer information from the story	★	★	★	★	★	★	★	★	★	★	★	★	★	★	★	★	★	★	★	★	
- Use context clues to predict correct responses	★	★	★	★	★	★	★	★	☆	★	☆	★	★	★	★	★	★	★			
- Summarize the story											☆										
- Draw conclusions based on story				★	☆				☆	☆	☆	☆		★	★			☆		☆	★
- Predict outcomes				☆									★	★							
- Classify words under topic headings											☆							☆			
10. Develop applied comprehension skills:																					
- Relate reading to personal experience				★		★		★	★	☆	★	★		☆	★	★	★		★		
- Draw conclusions based on personal experience			☆	☆	☆	☆			☆		☆	☆	★		☆	☆					
11. Learn/review basic factual information																☆			★		

Literary understanding

Lesson	1	2	3	4	5	6	7	8	9	10	11	12	13	14	15	16	17	18	19	20	R
1. Distinguish between fiction and non-fiction	★	☆	☆	☆	☆	☆	☆	☆	☆	☆	☆	☆	☆	☆	☆	☆	☆	☆	☆	☆	
2. Identify/interpret characters' actions, motivations, and feelings	★	★	★	★	★	★	★	★	★	★	★	★	★	★	★	★	★	★	★	★	
3. Identify/interpret plot	★	★	★	★	★	★	★	★	★	★	★	★	★	★	★	★	★	★	★	★	
4. Relate title to content of story						★	★						★								
5. Identify/interpret setting (place)						★	★	★									★		☆		☆

KEY: ★ = Primary emphasis   ★ = Secondary emphasis   ☆ = Integrated with other skills

Writing

Writing	Lesson	1	2	3	4	5	6	7	8	9	10	11	12	13	14	15	16	17	18	19	20	R
1. Write legibly		☆	☆	☆	☆	☆	☆	☆	☆	☆	☆	☆	☆	☆	☆	☆	☆	☆	☆	☆	☆	☆
2. Copy words accurately		★	★	★	★	★	★	★	★	★	★	★	★	★	★	★	★	★	★	★	★	★
3. Capitalize words appropriately		★	★	★	★	★	★	★	★	★	★	★	★	★	★	★	★	★	★	★	★	★
4. Spell words with greater accuracy		★	★	★	★	★	★	★	★	★	★	★	★	★	★	★	★	★	★	★	★	★
5. Form new words by adding the endings: *-ing*		✬																				
-est			☆																			
-y				☆																		
-ly						☆	☆															
-ful, -less								☆	✬													
6. Change the *y* to *i* before adding *-er, -est*					☆																	
7. Unscramble words										☆		☆						☆	✬			✬
8. Write sentence answers to questions		★	★	★	★	★	★	★	★	★	★	★	★	★	★	★	★	★	★	★	★	★

Note: Specific suggestions for additional writing assignments appear in the individual lesson notes for Book 3 and Chapter 7 of this manual.

Study Skills

Study Skills	Lesson	1	2	3	4	5	6	7	8	9	10	11	12	13	14	15	16	17	18	19	20	R
1. Increase concentration		★	★	★	★	★	★	★	★	★	★	★	★	★	★	★	★	★	★	★	★	★
2. Skim story to locate information		★	★	★	★	★	★	★	★	★	★	★	★	★	★	★	★	★	★	★	★	★
3. Complete exercises:																						
– Reading comprehension questions		☆	☆	☆	☆	☆	☆	☆	☆	☆	☆	☆	☆	☆	☆	☆	☆	☆	☆	☆	★	★
– Fill-in-the-blank		☆	☆	☆	☆	☆	☆	☆	☆	☆	☆	☆	☆	☆	☆	☆	☆	☆	☆	☆	☆	☆
– Matching		☆	☆	☆	☆	☆	☆	☆	☆	☆	☆	☆	☆	☆	☆	☆	☆	☆	☆	☆		☆
– Multiple choice														☆								
4. Apply reasoning skills to exercises: context clues		★	★	★	★	★	★	★	★	★	★	★	★	★	★	★	★	★	★	★	★	★
process of elimination		★	★	★	★	★	★	★	★	★	★	★	★	★	★	★	★	★	★	★	★	★

KEY: ★ = Primary emphasis   ✬ = Secondary emphasis   ☆ = Integrated with other skills

SCOPE AND SEQUENCE: BOOK 4

Phonics

Lesson	1	2	3	4	5	R	6	7	8	9	10	R	11	12	13	14	15	R	16	17	18	19	20	R
1. Use phonic skills to decode unknown words	★	★	★	★	★	★	★	★	★	★	★	★	★	★	★	★	★	★	★	★	★	★	★	★
2. Identify long and short vowel sounds	☆	☆		☆												☆								
3. Recognize sound for -le			☆									☆												
4. Identify silent letters									☆				☆	☆										
5. Distinguish sounds for g										☆														

Word Analysis

Lesson	1	2	3	4	5	R	6	7	8	9	10	R	11	12	13	14	15	R	16	17	18	19	20	R
1. Use syllabication to decode words	★	★	★	★	★	★	★	★	★	★	★	★	★	★	★	★	★	★	★	★	★	★	★	★
2. Divide words into syllables	☆	☆	☆	☆	☆			☆				☆				☆				☆				☆
3. Combine syllables to form words											☆		☆											
4. Recognize common word endings: -er	☆	☆											☆											
-y			☆																					
-ing				☆		☆																		
-est, -ness, -ship, -ment													☆											
-ful																				☆				
-less																					☆			
5. Recognize common word beginnings														☆										
6. Form compound words																★								
7. Recognize singular and plural forms									★	☆							☆							

Vocabulary

Lesson	1	2	3	4	5	R	6	7	8	9	10	R	11	12	13	14	15	R	16	17	18	19	20	R
1. Learn unfamiliar vocabulary	★	★	★	★	★	★	★	★	★	★	★	★	★	★	★	★	★	★	★	★	★	★	★	★
2. Infer word meanings from context clues	★	★	★	★	★	★	★	★	★	★	★	★	★	★	★	★	★	★	★	★	★	★	★	★
3. Identify definitions/descriptions of terms	★	★	★	★	★	★	★	☆	★	★	★	★	☆	★	★	★	★	★	★	★	★	★	★	★
4. Produce definitions/descriptions of terms	★																★		☆	★				
5. Learn/review idiomatic expressions/common sayings																				★				
6. Identify synonyms		★				★						★		★			★							
7. Identify antonyms		★				★						★		★										
8. Distinguish between synonyms and antonyms																							★	
9. Complete word associations		★		★				★		★											★			
10. Complete analogies																								
11. Complete double crostic											☆		☆											
12. Learn/review multiple meanings and pronunciations																								
13. Learn/review abbreviations																		☆				☆		

Comprehension

Lesson	1	2	3	4	5	R	6	7	8	9	10	R	11	12	13	14	15	R	16	17	18	19	20	R
1. Identify words using context clues	★	★	★	★	★	★	★	★	★	★	★	★	★	★	★	★	★	★	★	★	★	★	★	★
2. Read selections independently	★	★	★	★	★	★	★	★	★	★	★	★	★	★	★	★	★	★	★	★	★	★	★	★
3. Complete exercises independently	★	★	★	★	★	★	★	★	★	★	★	★	★	★	★	★	★	★	★	★	★	★	★	★
4. Improve listening comprehension	☆	☆	☆	☆	☆	☆	☆	☆	☆	☆	☆	☆	☆	☆	☆	☆	☆	☆	☆	☆	☆	☆	☆	☆
5. Group words appropriately when reading orally	☆	☆	☆	☆	☆	☆	☆	☆	☆	☆	☆	☆	☆	☆	☆	☆	☆	☆	☆	☆	☆	☆	☆	☆
6. Interpret punctuation correctly when reading orally	☆	☆	☆	☆	☆	☆	☆	☆	☆	☆	☆	☆	☆	☆	☆	☆	☆	☆	☆	☆	☆	☆	☆	☆

KEY: ★ = Primary emphasis   ☆ = Secondary emphasis   ☆ = Integrated with other skills

Comprehension, cont.

Lesson	1	2	3	4	5	R	6	7	8	9	10	R	11	12	13	14	15	R	16	17	18	19	20	R
7. Develop literal comprehension skills:																								
- Recall details	★	★	★	★	★	★	★	★	★	★	★	★	★	★	★	★	★	★	★	★	★	★	★	★
- Locate specific information	★	★	★	★	★	★	★	★	★	★	★	★	★	★	★	★	★	★	★	★	★	★	★	★
- Sequence events																			★					
8. Develop inferential comprehension skills:																								
- Infer word meanings from context clues	★		★	★	★	★	★		★	★	★	★	★	★	★	★	★	★	★	★	★	★	★	★
- Infer information from the reading		★	★	★	★	★			★	★	★		★	★	★		★		★		★	★	★	
- Draw conclusions based on reading		★		★				★													★	★	★	
- Use context clues to predict correct responses			★		★	★	★		★			★				★		★		★		★	★	
- Determine topic headings for words					★									★										
- Classify words under topic headings						★						★	★									★		
- Determine cause and effect relationships															★									
9. Develop applied comprehension skills:																								
- Draw conclusions based on personal experience	★			★	★				★	★	★		★	★	★	★				★			★	
- Relate reading to personal experience			★		★				★	★	★	★	★	★					★					
- Sequence events					★					★														
10. Learn/review basic factual information	★	★	★	★	★	★	★	★	★	☆	★	★	☆	★	★	★		★	☆	★	☆		★	★
11. Locate/infer information from a menu																								★

Writing

Lesson	1	2	3	4	5	R	6	7	8	9	10	R	11	12	13	14	15	R	16	17	18	19	20	R
1. Write legibly	☆	☆	☆	☆	☆	☆	☆	☆	☆	☆	☆	☆	☆	☆	☆	☆	☆	☆	☆	☆	☆	☆	☆	☆
2. Copy words accurately	★	★	★	★	★	★	★	★	★	★	★	★	★	★	★	★	★	★	★	★	★	★	★	★
3. Capitalize words appropriately	★	★	★	★	★	★	★	★	★	★	★	★	★	★	★	★	★	★	★	★	★	★	★	★
4. Spell words with greater accuracy	★	★	★	★	★	★	★	★	★	★	★	★	★	★	★	★	★	★	★	★	★	★	★	★
5. Form new words by adding the endings: -er	★	★																						
-y			☆	☆																				
-ing																								
6. Change f to v to form plurals							☆																	
7. Change the y to i before adding: -er, -est, -ness									☆				☆											
-ly																		☆	☆					
8. Unscramble words										★	★		★	★	★	★		★		★			★	
9. Write sentence or paragraph answers to questions	★	★	★	★	★	★	★	★	★	★	★	★	★	★	★	★	★	★	★	★	★	★	★	★

Note: Specific suggestions for additional writing assignments appear in the individual lesson notes for Book 4 and Chapter 7 of this manual.

Study Skills

Lesson	1	2	3	4	5	R	6	7	8	9	10	R	11	12	13	14	15	R	16	17	18	19	20	R
1. Increase concentration	★	★	★	★	★	★	★	★	★	★	★	★	★	★	★	★	★	★	★	★	★	★	★	★
2. Skim passage to locate information	★	★	★	★	★	★	★	★	★	★	★	★	★	★	★	★	★	★	★	★	★	★	★	★
3. Apply reasoning skills to exercises: context clues	★	★	★	★	★	★	★	★	★	★	★	★	★	★	★	★	★	★	★	★	★	★	★	★
process of elimination	★	★		★	★	★	★	★	★	☆	★	★	★	★	★	★	★	★	☆	★	★	★	★	★
"intelligent guessing"	★					☆	★	★	★	☆	☆	★	☆	★	☆	★	★	☆	☆	★	☆	★	★	★
4. Use a dictionary to look up word meanings		☆	☆	☆	☆	☆	☆	☆	☆	☆	☆	☆	☆	☆	☆	☆	☆	☆	☆	☆	☆	☆	☆	★
5. Use an atlas or globe														☆	☆									

KEY: ★ = Primary emphasis   ★ = Secondary emphasis   ☆ = Integrated with other skills

1. Introduction to Book 1

Book 1 is designed for adolescent and adult students reading at or below the second grade level. In order to use this book, students should already be able to recognize, pronounce, and write most letters of the alphabet. One hundred per cent accuracy is not necessary. For example, a student may confuse *b* and *d, m* and *n,* and *p* and *q.* These difficulties can be addressed as the student confronts them in the lessons. Also, the student does not need to know alphabetical order.

Printing need not be stressed over cursive writing or vice versa. Thus, if the student asks, "Should I print or write?" tell him to do whichever is more comfortable. The student, however, should be able to both print and write his name. If the student does not know how to do this already, set aside some instructional time for practice. Students who need this practice appreciate it because so many forms require both printed names and signatures.

The emphasis in Book 1 is on phonics principles, oral reading, appropriate homework exercises, and the development of a good working relationship between you and the student. Procedures and techniques for these areas of emphasis are explained in later chapters.

Book 1 includes the following significant features:

- The student is introduced to basic phonics principles. These not only give him the tools he needs to develop into a good reader but also enable him to progress more rapidly than a random introduction of words would allow.

- All words are introduced gradually and reviewed frequently in different contexts so the student rapidly learns to sight read them or sound them out with minimal difficulty.

- The student reads all the stories aloud in your presence to establish correct reading patterns. In addition, all words in the word charts, which appear at the beginning of each lesson, are sounded out in class to develop greater accuracy.

- You discuss each story with the student rather than having him write out answers to comprehension questions. Written comprehension questions at this stage of the student's development are usually a source of needless frustration and tend not to contribute to reading progress. Oral discussion, on the other hand, gives you the opportunity to establish good reading patterns, become aware of the student's strengths and weaknesses, and develop a good working relationship with the student.

- A word index listing all words that have been introduced appears after every fourth lesson. These indexes provide the student with a spelling guide and you with a tool for reinforcing the lesson objectives.

- Two review lessons appear at the end of Book 1. After having previewed each exercise with you, the student should be able to complete the lessons with at least 75% accuracy. A lower score indicates the need for more review before the student begins Book 2.

The student does not have to be able to sight read or sound out all the words in Book 1 prior to beginning Book 2. He should, however, be able to sight read or sound out at least 70% of the words listed in the final index with minimal help from you.

When the student has finished Book 1, he has been introduced to approximately 1500 words and is able to read, with your assistance, a story of approximately 400 words with relative ease.

How much time does a student need to complete Book 1? The answer to this question depends on his efforts and the amount of instructional time available. Generally speaking, a student who has one-hour lessons four times a week and consistently completes his homework can finish Book 1 with the desired accuracy in eight weeks. But this will depend on how many sessions a student needs to complete each lesson and the appropriate reinforcement activities, as well as how many interruptions are encountered.

2. Preparing to Teach

Each of the twenty lessons in Book 1 includes a word chart, a story, and reading/writing exercises. Each word chart focuses on a specific phonics principle. The stories, which contain many words from the word charts, give the student experience with typical reading situations. The exercises present the words in other formats to help the student become more familiar with them. The exercises do not contain comprehension questions based on the stories because, for Book 1 students, oral discussion of the stories is preferable.

Scheduling the Reading Class

Beginning readers progress best when their classes meet for one hour five times a week at a regularly scheduled time. A schedule in which the student has his reading class only two or three times a week or at different times each week can work, but often progress is slower than for the student who works with a teacher at the same time each day.

It is important that the student realize the need for daily, regularly scheduled lessons. You might think that students wouldn't raise the issue in traditional school programs in which they are scheduled for reading in just this manner. But a perennial request is, "Since we work hard all week, can't we just take it easy on Friday?" On an occasional basis, this is reasonable. As a rule, it is not. Three days away from the lesson work is too long a break for the beginning reader. Just remind the student that, as painful as it sometimes feels, five lessons a week will contribute greatly to his reading progress.

In some institutions, the student has the option of deciding how often he wishes to attend reading class. This student, too, needs to be reminded how important daily, regularly scheduled reading classes are in helping him to achieve his goal. If the student chooses to attend class on a highly infrequent basis, tell him politely but frankly there is little point in his attending at all because he's not giving himself a chance to make any progress.

In volunteer programs, scheduling a student for daily reading classes is often impossible. In this type of learning situation, try to schedule your student for at least two classes a week. If only one class a week is possible, encourage the student to get a friend or someone in his family to help him complete the exercises in each lesson, which are usually assigned as homework.

The Lesson Format

After the first class, which of course involves no homework review, the procedure for each lesson is basically the same. The overview below gives you an idea of what happens during each class. Detailed procedures for this work appear in later chapters of this manual.

1. First the student reviews the work in the previous lesson. This includes correcting the exercises, pronouncing the sounds in the word chart and completing a random review of the words in the chart. The student also rereads any sections of the story he found difficult. In early lessons, the student often rereads the entire story.

2. The student pronounces the sounds and words in the word chart of the new lesson and does a random review.

3. The student completes the story segment of the new lesson. This includes becoming familiar with the Words for Study (which you usually pronounce for the student), reading the story aloud with your assistance, and briefly discussing the story with you.

4. The student completes reinforcement activities to practice words and sounds that continue to give him difficulty.

5. The student previews the exercises, which are usually assigned as homework.

Following this general procedure on a fairly consistent basis helps the student. He tends to work much better when he has a sense of routine. Modifications in the procedure should be made only when they will enhance the student's reading development.

Most students initially feel overwhelmed by the amount of work covered during each lesson. Remind the student that *all* new situations give rise to a panicky feeling. Taking a few moments to have the student recall his first days on a job or how he felt when he first moved to an area may help him realize that these "stagefright" feelings will not last forever.

By the third or fourth lesson, the average student is able to finish all the work in a one-hour class period. For students who are obviously struggling, schedule two class periods per lesson and gradually increase the workload as his work shows improvement.

Keep in mind that improvement is not to be confused with mastery. These lessons should not be seen as achievement tests but as opportunities to move the student smoothly toward his reading goal. The student does not have to be able to sound out all the words by himself or read the story fluently in order to go on to the next lesson. Mastery will come with consistent practice in working with the phonics rules and the words provided in each lesson of Book 1.

Do not expect to know from the outset how much time to allot for each segment of the lesson. Each student is so different that understanding exactly how to pace the lessons takes time. By paying attention to the student's responses and rate of accuracy, you will gradually learn how to schedule the lesson so that the student improves his reading skills in a relaxed but efficient manner.

Preparing the Lessons

In preparing the lessons, develop the habit of following this procedure:

1. Familiarize yourself with the lesson the student is to work on that day.
2. Skim the appropriate lesson notes in Chapter 9 of this manual for suggestions to help you teach the lesson.
3. Review any notes you took after the preceding class in which you jotted down words or phonics rules the student needs to review. The practice of teacher notetaking is discussed in the introduction to Chapter 8 of this manual.
4. Decide which reinforcement activities you want to use and complete any preparation needed for this segment of the lesson. Suggestions for reinforcement activities are listed in Chapters 6 and 7. For some activities, the only preparation necessary is deciding whether or not they will benefit the student.

You will find that preparing for the lesson takes very little time and that the results are highly worthwhile. Because of this preparation, the lessons proceed in a smooth and orderly manner, and the student learns good work habits from you.

Occasionally everything may seem to go wrong even though you have painstakingly prepared the lesson, and you wonder why you bothered preparing anything in the first place. Then, too, you may have days when you've had no time to prepare, and everything runs smoothly. On these occasions, you may wonder if preparation is really all that necessary. Both types of situations occur, but they are the exceptions rather than the rule. Chalk the first type up to experience and forget it; enjoy the second type and continue to prepare the lessons.

Last and most important, you need to prepare yourself mentally and emotionally for the class. If possible, take several minutes before the student's arrival to unwind from the previous activities of the day. If this is not possible, take a few minutes at the beginning of class to sit quietly and compose your thoughts. At first, the student will probably think you are crazy, but you will be surprised how soon he, too, starts using this time to prepare himself to work.

As a general rule, how well the lesson goes is determined by how relaxed and focused you are on the work. As the teacher, your main function is to serve as a smooth bridge between the student and the lesson material. Although teaching theory and technique are extremely important, your own patience and concentration determine how helpful this "bridge" is.

The Teacher-Student Relationship

Making sure that you are relaxed for the lesson also contributes to the development of a good working relationship with your student. In some learning situations, a student has enough motivation or self-confidence to succeed in spite of any relationship he may have with a teacher. But this is rarely the case with the adult or adolescent beginning reader, who relies heavily on your support and encouragement.

To appreciate more fully the beginning reader's situation, it may be helpful to spend a few moments reflecting upon your own life. Most of us, as adults, have developed the habit of avoiding or faking those situations in which we feel inadequate. Instead, we tend to stick with routines that are familiar and give us some sense of security.

The adolescent or adult learning how to read has entered into a situation in which he can neither avoid nor fake his way through the material. And he must be admired for having put himself in a situation in which he has to reveal so much of himself to a complete stranger— the teacher. Unless he is extremely motivated or thick-skinned, he must feel a sense of support from you or he will drop out because exposing his lack of knowledge just gets too painful after a short while.

In addition, learning how to read *is* hard work. No matter how much progress is being made, virtually all students experience a sense of frustration and futility at one time or another. Your encouragement will help him to stick with it when he's ready to throw in the towel.

Suggestions for a Good Working Rapport

Use these suggestions to help you consider how to best develop a good working relationship with your student. Keep in mind that they are only suggestions.

- Strive for naturalness in your voice and mannerisms. Some teachers unconsciously treat beginning reading students as if they were invalids or victims of a ruthless society. A condescending or pitying approach does not help the student attain his reading goals.
- Greet the student pleasantly and spend a few minutes in casual conversation before you actually begin work. As a rule, do not allow this conversation to exceed three minutes. Occasionally, the student is too upset to concentrate, and he needs a shoulder to lean on far more than he needs to improve his reading skills. In terms of helping the student attain his reading goal, *occasionally* should be defined as once in every 12 to 15 classes.
- Participate fully in this pre-lesson conversation and listen attentively to the student's remarks. Often you can later refer to these remarks when you are explaining some aspect of the lesson such as vocabulary words. In these instances, the student quickly grasps the meaning of the word, and he appreciates the fact that you actually listened to what he said earlier.

- Use a phrase such as "Shall we get started?" to indicate it is time to begin the lesson. Consistently using transitional statements helps the student feel more comfortable with both you and the class routine. Too, we all have our lazy streaks, and the reading student is no exception. If he finds that he can chitchat his way through half the lesson time, he will often do just that. Who wouldn't?

- In a tutorial situation, work from the student's book rather than your own. This practice conveys a "we're-in-this-together" spirit, which contributes to a good working relationship. Also, if your attention is focused on the student's book, directing the work is much easier.

  Using the student's book works well with up to three students. You can either sit with a different student each time or move from one to another according to the students' needs. With more than three students, it is expedient to use your own book.

- If possible, work at an uncluttered table rather than at desks. Try to have straight-backed, cushioned chairs for both you and the student since physical comfort makes developing a good relationship easier. If permissible, allow the student to drink beverages during the lesson. Adults, especially, find this helps them to concentrate better on the work and feel more at ease. Generally speaking, neither smoking nor eating during class is a good idea. If the student rushes into class with a sandwich because he hasn't had time to eat, allow him to eat it during the pre-lesson conversation or ask him to wait until after class.

- Be sure to use positive reinforcement during the lesson. This practice is discussed in detail in Chapter 3.

- Develop the habit of wishing the student a good day or a good evening as he leaves the class. This is especially important if both you and the student have had a rough session. The student, particularly the adolescent, needs to know that you don't carry personal grudges. Even if he leaves with a murderous look in his eye, he will be paying attention to how you end the lesson.

Classroom Supplies

For each class, the student needs to bring his reading book, his composition book, and a pen or pencil. The use of the composition book—a slim, loose-leaf binder with wide-lined paper—is discussed in Chapter 7.

You need your own reading book (if you are not working from the student's book), any notes and reinforcement activities pertaining to the lesson, a few sheets of blank paper on which to write phonics clues, and a pen. A pen is recommended because the student can spot your marginal notes and corrections more easily. Avoid red ink as it is frequently associated with too many bad memories.

An alphabet chart with both printed and written upper case letters is helpful. This chart can be either a poster prominently displayed in the classroom or an insert for the student's composition book. When the student cannot remember how to form a certain letter, simply remind him to refer to the chart.

If possible, have a globe, a set of encyclopedias, and a dictionary within easy reach.

Most students find the globe fascinating. The first time this resource fits naturally into the work is in Lesson 4 in which Cape Cod is mentioned. Finding the location of Cape Cod on the globe can easily lead into a brief discussion during which both you and the student locate your town or city, places of birth, places you've been, and so forth. In addition to helping the student learn more about geography, the globe also provides one of the many comfortable ways in which you and the student can become better acquainted. If a globe is not available, try to get hold of an atlas.

The encyclopedia and the dictionary are valuable resources because they provide pictures and additional information about many of the words introduced in the lessons. Have the student do as much of the research as he can, but help him when he needs it.

These small research experiences help the student feel comfortable using books he tends to find intimidating. Through practice in using encyclopedias and dictionaries, the student slowly but surely gains confidence in his ability to find answers to his questions.

A Final Note on Preparation

Be prepared, especially in the early lessons, to look for symptoms of eyestrain. Among the common symptoms are rubbing the eyes, excessive blinking, and opening the eyes wider than necessary during reading.

If you suspect the student has a visual problem, ask him if he has had an eye examination within the past three years. If he has not, tell him that he must have one because he is going to be doing a great deal of reading. Help him make the necessary arrangements if he is unable to do so on his own. And firmly remind him that seeing is far more important than reading.

A Summary of Do's

1. Do try to schedule as many daily, one-hour classes each week as possible.
2. Do develop a consistent lesson format.
3. Do give yourself time to decide the lesson format that will work best for your student.
4. Do take time to prepare for each class.
5. Do insist that your student have an eye checkup if he shows symptoms of eyestrain.
6. Do develop a good working relationship with your student because it is essential to his reading progress.
7. Do make sure that the environment in which you teach is as conducive to good learning as possible.
8. Do give yourself a few moments to relax before each class.

3. The Word Chart

A word chart appears at the beginning of each lesson in Book 1. The words in the chart illustrate the particular phonics principle being studied and also appear in the story and exercise segments of the lesson.

Initially, many students feel overwhelmed by the number of words in the chart and often want to know if they have to memorize all these words. This reaction is understandable since the chart does contain a lot of words. Assure students that they don't have to work at memorizing any of them. They naturally learn to sight read these words because they see them so often in the stories and exercises.

Students also often want to know why they have to learn these particular words. Briefly repeat that many of these words appear in both the story and the exercises. By studying the words first, students usually find the work in the other parts of the lesson easier.

Giving Explanations

In remedial reading instruction, the teacher's ability to give sound and timely explanations is a vital part of working with students. Thus it is necessary to spend some time discussing this technique before going on to the other aspects of the word chart.

Use the following guidelines to help develop a procedure for giving explanations. These suggestions pertain not only to the word chart but also to other segments of the lesson.

- Have a sound explanation for everything you present. These explanations should reflect how the lesson work contributes to reading improvement. When presented with such explanations, the student gains greater trust in both you and the procedures and throws himself more wholeheartedly into the task of learning to read.

  Students seem to demand explanations for practically everything only when they sense a teacher is unsure of what he is doing. If you take time to think through the reasons for the lesson material, you will be better able to convey a genuine sense of authority, and the student will no longer demand that valuable learning time be sacrificed for numerous explanations. In short, the student begins to trust your judgment.

- When students ask why they have to do something, remarks such as "Because I say so," or "Because it's in the book," do not satisfy them. In moments of extreme exasperation, such remarks are expedient because they allow you to release frustration, and they give the student a comforting glimpse that you are working just as hard as he is.

  Generally speaking, however, emotionally charged remarks both anger and discourage the student. When you take the time to point out how the work contributes to his reading progress, the student usually works harder and more efficiently.

- Do not expect the student to understand immediately and thoroughly all explanations. Most of us can make better sense of explanations after we have experienced situations in which they apply. The reading student is no exception. For example, as he begins to sound out new words successfully, he begins to understand the explanation for using a phonics approach to reading. Too, relevant repetition is what ultimately enables the student to thoroughly understand the explanation. You have many opportunities to repeat explanations throughout this series.

- Explanations should be brief and to the point. Elaborate or unnecessary explanations break the student's concentration and may be confusing. As a rule of thumb, regard any explanation that exceeds three or four sentences as too elaborate. Regard any explanation that doesn't pertain specifically to the lesson objectives as unnecessary unless the student requests one.

  This last suggestion is especially helpful for word chart work, which is usually the most difficult section of the lesson for students. In word chart work, explanations should be restricted to sounding out and knowing the meanings of the words. For example, in Lesson 3, if the student wants to know why Coke is capitalized, briefly explain that he'll be reading a sentence about two people drinking Cokes in one of the exercises and that product names are always capitalized. If the student doesn't ask, don't call it to his attention.

- Courteously discourage the student who asks for too many explanations about specific items in the lessons. The pace of the lesson needs to be smooth. When the student asks for an explanation that obviously will not contribute toward completing the task at hand, kindly suggest to him that an explanation will make more sense when he encounters the rule.

  Because of the nature of our language, the student may ask questions for which there are no easy answers. For example, in Lesson 10, many students want to know why the words contain silent letters. Do not get involved trying to explain the evolution of the English language. Simply tell him that if he concentrates on the patterns, he will be able to sound out and spell many of these words in no time. Then proceed to the next word on the chart.

  Be patient. As you learn more about a student's needs and abilities, you naturally develop a sense of when to offer an explanation. Keep in mind, however, that the student does need explanations for such general questions as: "Why do I have to sound out these words?" "Why do I have to read this story?" and "How are these exercises going to make me read better?" He also needs to have a sense that you know what you are doing, but this does not entail taking away valuable time from the lesson to explain every step.

Using a Phonics Approach

For teachers who are not familiar with phonics methods and/or grew up when the sight-reading method was in vogue, reviewing the reasons for the emphasis on phonics in these lessons may be helpful.

A phonics approach is used because it is an effective and efficient way to teach adolescent and adult students how to read. Although not all words in the English language can be decoded using phonics, enough words do adhere to phonics principles to make this approach worthwhile.

By learning some basic, simply presented phonics rules, the student has the necessary tools for reviewing forgotten words and sounding out new words. These tools enable the student to develop confidence in his ability to handle increasingly difficult material.

A third reason for the phonics approach in Book 1 is that it provides an orderly framework for the introduction of new words, and learning thrives on order.

You should use the phonics method that works best for both you and the student. For example, if you have been trained to start decoding with the initial sound of the word and have experienced success with this method, continue to use it for the phonics work in this book.

In some cases, especially in working with adolescents, the student is so entrenched in a particular phonics method that it is advisable for you to adapt yourself to his method, even if it differs from your own. Too much valuable time is lost trying to implement another phonics approach.

The key to success with a phonics approach is consistency. Stick with whatever phonics method you decide works best for both you and the student. Don't teach some word charts by having the student start with the initial sounds and other word charts by starting with the vowel sound.

The Recommended Phonics Approach

If neither you nor the student has any preference for a particular phonics method, have the student begin sounding out the word by saying the vowel sound. Experience indicates that this phonics method is highly successful with both adolescents and adults. The long *a* work in Lesson 4 is the basis for illustrating how this particular method is used.

1. The student says the guide sound.
2. You ask the student to state how he knows that words containing this guide sound have a long *a* sound. (The student has studied the silent *e* rule in previous lessons.)

3. The student covers up everything in the first word except the *a* and says the vowel sound.
4. The student uncovers the letter to the right of the vowel and says the vowel sound plus this letter. For example, if the word is *Dave*, the student says *āv*.
5. The student uncovers the first letter of the word and says *Dāv*. Sometimes the student makes two distinct sounds, *D-āv*. In these instances, you tell him, "Say it fast," and the student says *Dāv*.
6. The student then uncovers the *e* so that he sees the entire word. If necessary, the student again reviews the function of the silent *e*.

In early word chart work, the student may have difficulty putting the sounds together and following the direction, "Say it fast." Assist the student by either saying the sounds and having him repeat them or saying the sounds as he is making them. Much patience is required from both of you for this work. Remember there is a light at the end of the tunnel, for the average student soon demonstrates an ability to sound out words in this way with much less assistance from you.

As the student becomes more proficient, less time will be spent on each word. In the early lessons, however, do not rush this work. Solid phonics patterns that will help the student move much more quickly in later lessons are being established.

Beginning with the vowel sound helps the student to develop the habit of taking his time. Too often, the beginning reader identifies the initial sound in the word and then guesses the rest. And, far too often, he is wrong. By emphasizing the vowel sound, adding the end sound, and then working on the initial sound, the student pronounces words with much greater accuracy. Additionally, he becomes more adept at correctly pronouncing vowel sounds which, for many students, are the most difficult. As one student remarked, "I feel like I have more of a chance if I do the hardest part of the word first."

Another advantage to the phonics method is that it stresses using a problem solving approach to decoding. The initial pressure most students feel to get the right answer, which usually means blurting out the first word that comes to mind, gives way to patiently discovering how to say the word. This, in turn, helps students develop the major asset they bring to the classroom—their intelligence.

Sounding Out Words on the Word Chart

The following procedure is recommended for helping the student to sound out words in the word chart.

1. The student sounds out the guide sound for the words in the first column. For this step, you need to experiment a bit to see how the student prefers to work with guide sounds. Some students find it helpful to know that they can say all the guide sounds before they actually go to work on sounding out the words. Other students prefer

to work with one guide sound and its corresponding words before proceeding to the next guide sound.

2. The student sounds out the words for the guide sound. Again, you need to observe the student. If this work seems to put too much strain on the student, he should sound out only half the words for each guide sound. You can help the student sound out the remaining words as he encounters them later in the lesson.

3. The student reviews the words he has sounded out and the corresponding guide sound before he goes on to the next guide sound. Each time the student is ready for the next guide sound, he reviews only the guide sound and corresponding words immediately preceding the new guide sound.

4. The student does a brief random review of the entire chart. This random review should last only a minute or two. If the student has forgotten a word, help him to sound it out. If the student becomes frustrated over having forgotten a word, remind him that the emphasis of this work is on learning to sound out words, not memorization. He is not expected to remember all the words, and he should not feel upset.

Use these three techniques for the random review.

- Have the student sound out or sight read a column of words he has studied. This gives him the opportunity to hear the distinct guide sounds in fairly rapid succession and reinforces his ability to distinguish among these sounds.

- Point to the words at random and have the student sight read or sound them out. Make sure that you alternate words that are difficult for the student with those which give him no special trouble.

- Say one of the words and have the student locate it on the chart. If the student has difficulty locating the word, tell him to study the guide sounds as you repeat the word, giving extra emphasis to the guide sound. After the student has found the row in which the word appears, repeat it until the student locates it. The student should sound out any incorrect words he points to so that he can hear the difference between this word and the one you are saying. Of the three random review techniques, students generally enjoy this last one the most.

Using Cue Words

A student can use cue words, words he already knows, to help him sound out new words. But cue words should not be introduced until the student demonstrates some ability to use a phonics method to sound out the words. If introduced too early, cue words tend to confuse the student more than they help him.

The words you select should be short, common words which the student can learn to sight read quickly rather than having to expend a great deal of effort memorizing them. When first introducing the student to words which

will become his cue words, do give them extra emphasis during the random review and reinforcement activities.

The suggested time for you to think about establishing cue words is Lesson 11, which focuses on r-controlled vowels. Because these vowel sounds are difficult for most students to master, you want to emphasize certain words in this lesson which the student can use as cue words in later work.

The following example illustrates how a student benefits from using cue words. The student, who has been trained to start with the vowel sound when decoding a new word, is working on Lesson 15. When he encounters the word *choose* on the word chart, he tells the teacher he can't remember the sound for *oo*. The teacher says nothing but instead writes *zoo* in the margin of the book and underlines the *oo*. Because the student can sight read this word and has seen it used before as a cue word, he correctly pronounces the sound for *oo* and decodes *choose* with no further difficulty.

Cue words are particularly helpful for the following phonics principles: r-controlled vowels, vowel combinations, and vowels followed by the letter *l*. For all other phonics principles, the teacher needs to be sensitive to the student's decoding strategies in deciding whether or not to establish cue words. For example, suppose the student is stuck on the *tch* sound in *switch* in Lesson 18. Some students immediately recall that the *t* is silent upon seeing the cue word for this sound written in the margin. Other students find it more helpful if the teacher simply draws a line through the *t* to indicate that it is silent.

Develop a general set of cue words by choosing one word for each sound. It is important to use the same cue word for all situations in which the student can't figure out that particular sound. Occasionally you may want to use a special cue word for a particular student. For example, one student was given *Joan* as the cue word for the sound for *oa* instead of the usual choice, *boat*, because his wife's name was Joan and that cue word worked better for him.

Phonics and the Sight Word Reader

Because most students who use Book 1 can read only a few words on the word chart, they tend to respond to phonics instruction as conscientiously as they can. As they become more comfortable with various sounds and the method you use for pronouncing the words, they are able to decode with increased accuracy and speed.

Often this is not the case with the student who knows at least half the words on the early word charts. Because this student can sight read some words, he doesn't understand why he should have to spend so much time learning how to sound out "a few" missed words here and there. This student also fails to recognize that the word charts become increasingly difficult. Without some basic phonics skills, the student's 50% accuracy rate in the early charts invariably drops to 30 or 40% in the later charts.

Concentrate on phonics rules in the early lessons in spite of the student's resistance. Briefly explain that he is going to *review* basic sounds and that he will learn a method he can use only when he needs to. In other words, he isn't going to have to sound out words that he can already sight read. Remind the student as often as necessary that he really will be able to see improvement in his reading because he knows how to use a phonics method.

Refer to the following guidelines in planning your chart work for this student.

- Have the student read the words in the order in which they appear on the chart.

- When the student misses a word, teach him the guide sound and then have him sound out the word. Use the phonics method in which the student starts with the vowel sound because this type of student, more than any other, tends to guess the words based on the initial consonant sound.

- After the student has finished the word chart and the random review, have him review all the sounds emphasized in the lesson, even if they gave him no difficulty.

- Reinforcement activities should focus on those sounds and words which gave the student difficulty. Usually this type of student has the most trouble with short vowel sounds.

Variations in Pronunciation

Another issue that confronts the teacher in helping a student to sound out words is what to do when the student's way of saying a word does not conform to standard English pronunciation.

Don't even consider commenting on the student's pronunciation unless you are certain it is unacceptable. Check in a good dictionary. A number of words have more than one acceptable pronunciation. The word *aunt*, introduced in Lesson 4, is a good example. Less obvious, perhaps, is the *wh* digraph, which is formally studied in Lesson 18. This digraph can be pronounced either as *w* or *hw*. Many other words that have more than one acceptable pronunciation can be found in our language.

Occasions arise in which you use one acceptable pronunciation and the student uses another. In these instances, try to use the student's pronunciation during any word chart or word study work. This courtesy helps the student to sound out the word more efficiently. Also adopt the student's pronunciation in subsequent stories or exercises. In all other situations, pronounce the word as you normally would. The student benefits from learning that many words have more than one acceptable pronunciation.

You also need to be familiar with regional speech patterns. If everyone in a particular geographic area pronounces a word one way, then you should consider this to be the acceptable pronunciation, even though the dictionary does not acknowledge it.

The third thing that you may need to consider presents a truly difficult situation. Sometimes a student pronounces a word differently from both the dictionary and society in general because everyone in his immediate environment says the word this way. In this situation, introduce the student to the correct pronunciation and explain to him that this pronunciation is considered the standard one. Have the student practice saying the word a few times so that he gets used to saying it.

As a general policy, correct a student's pronunciation only if you think such corrections will be helpful. In other words, unless the student shows a desire to learn the standard pronunciation, don't force the issue. Also, avoid making these types of corrections on days when the student is having more difficulty than usual with the lesson.

Under some circumstances, you should emphasize the standard pronunciation even if the student resists. If you know the student has a career goal that involves working with the public, remind him that standard speech patterns make a good impression on most people and that changing pronunciation habits is not as hard as he may think.

If the student's pronunciation is hindering his reading progress, encourage him to use a standard pronunciation. For example, many students tend to ignore *-s* and *-ed* endings. Explain that if he develops the habit of paying attention to these endings and pronouncing them, both reading and spelling work will be less difficult for him. Also, knowledge of these endings and the ability to use them correctly will be helpful on the High School Equivalency Exam. Because passing this test is a long term goal for many reading students, they become more committed to learning these endings.

Teaching Unfamiliar Vocabulary

The student should also learn the meanings of unfamiliar words. Before beginning any work on the word chart, tell the student that he should let you know when he is unfamiliar with the meaning of a word he has just sounded out. Most students readily comply with this request.

A few students, however, are too embarrassed or stubborn to admit they don't know the meanings of some words they are studying. But they reveal their lack of knowledge either by puzzled facial expressions when they have just sounded out an unfamiliar word or through using the word inappropriately in later segments of the lesson. Gently remind students that their reading will progress more smoothly if they tell you when they are unfamiliar with a word.

Sooner or later most students want to know why they have to learn the meanings of words that they do not use. Explain that they will be seeing many of these words in the lessons, and knowing what the words mean will make this work easier. Also, no one really knows when he's going to have use for a particular word. Even though we may not use certain words now, knowing what they mean can be helpful later on.

The student does not need to know the precise definition for all the words on any given word chart. And at this stage of his development, he also needn't be troubled with multiple meanings. For example, many students do not know the meaning of *fume* in Lesson 5. You can give a sentence clue for this word: "The fumes at the gas station make me feel sick to my stomach." Or if you choose to tell the student the meaning, simply say, "A fume is gas that usually has a smell." This gives the student a general idea of what the word means. To point out that *fume* also means "to complain angrily" only confuses the student unless he is already familiar with this meaning.

Generally, the student isn't confused by sentence clues in which an ending has been added to the unfamiliar vocabulary word. Note that, in the above example, the plural form of *fume* was used. But students are often confused by sentence clues in which negative words are used. For example, many students do not know the meaning of *cope*, which is introduced in Lesson 2. Avoid a sentence clue such as, "Sometimes I can't cope with all this work." The word *can't* throws the student off in his attempt to infer the meaning of *cope*. A sentence clue such as, "You sure cope well with all the homework I give you," is much more helpful.

Whether you give the student sentence clues or definitions of the vocabulary words, develop the habit of speaking with expression. In fact, be as dramatic as your sense of decorum will allow. This not only makes learning new words more enjoyable but also provides a short breather from the hard work of sounding out all the word chart words.

How you choose to teach the meaning of unfamiliar words should be determined by how easily the student sounds out words. Use the following guidelines to help you decide the best procedure for your student.

- If the student has minimal difficulty sounding out the words on the chart, make up simple sentences for the words he doesn't know and have him infer the meanings. When possible, make up sentences that pertain to the student's circumstances and interests. After the student correctly infers the meaning of the word, have him make up a sentence in which he uses this word.

- If the student has some difficulty sounding out the words but is still able to progress fairly smoothly through the chart work, make up sentences for some of the words and simply tell him the meanings of the others. Use sentences for those words that you think the student can grasp the meaning of most easily. Have the student occasionally make up his own sentences for the words.

- If the student is having a great deal of difficulty sounding out the words, give brief meanings for all but one or two words the student is unfamiliar with. Use sentences for those words that you think the student can grasp the meaning of most easily.

The Need for Positive Reinforcement

For many students, the word chart is the most difficult and tedious part of the lesson. Students usually develop a liking for the stories because they enjoy actually reading. Also, they usually find the exercises enjoyable because they have completed a concrete piece of work and are curious to know how many of their answers are correct. The typical reading student is hard-pressed to find anything good to say about the word chart, even though he slowly begins to see that this work is the foundation for rapid reading progress.

Because the word chart is so demanding, the teacher needs to be more conscious than usual of the value of positive reinforcement. Develop the habit of saying "Good" or "Right" after each correct response. Even if the student makes an error, the situation usually presents an opportunity to say something positive. For example, in Lesson 1, when you point to the word *rude* during the random review, the student may say *rule*. As you point out the *d*, you can say, "You've almost got it, but let's review this letter."

Your supportive remarks should be brief and spoken in a natural voice. Keep in mind that excessive praise is ultimately as counterproductive as no praise at all. Words of encouragement should stress the notion of progress because the student is progressing as he completes each lesson. After all, regardless of how much trouble the student has had, by the end of just the first lesson, he has studied 70 words and read a complete story. The average adolescent or adult is able to accomplish this in a one-hour session—no small feat!

When to Start the Story

Does a student have to know all the words listed on the chart before he can proceed to the story? The answer is *no*. If he can sound out or sight read half the words, he is ready to start the story. A student has many opportunities for additional practice with most of the word chart words in the story, the exercises, and the reinforcement activities. Also, words that usually give students trouble appear frequently in later lessons. Keep in mind that a student's skill in reading increases as he encounters these words in the context of the stories and exercises.

A Summary of Do's and Don'ts

1. Do make sure the student understands how a phonics approach helps him to improve his reading.
2. Do use the phonics method that works best for both you and the student and practice consistency in using this method.
3. Do offer the student as much positive reinforcement as you can when he is sounding out the words on the chart.

4. Do establish cue words for the student to use in later lessons.

5. Do have the student begin the story segment of the lesson even if he can sound out or sight read only 50% of the words with minimal assistance from you.

6. Don't waste valuable time explaining points that have no real bearing on the lesson objectives.

7. Don't let the student talk you out of using the phonics approach because he thinks he doesn't need it.

8. Don't expect the student to memorize any of the words listed on the chart.

9. Don't correct the student's pronunciation unless it will contribute to his reading progress or meet his personal needs.

10. Don't hold the student responsible for either precise definitions or multiple meanings of words.

One Final Reminder

The student does *not* need to sound out all the words on the word chart in order to begin the story. If this work is too difficult, he should sound out only half the words for each guide sound. You can help the student sound out the remaining words as he sees them in the story, the exercises, and the reinforcement activities.

4. The Story

The story segment of the lesson is comprised of three parts: the Words for Study, the story, and the oral discussion of the story. As mentioned earlier, the student is not required to write answers to comprehension questions in Book 1 because experience indicates that oral discussion is more beneficial at this stage of reading development.

Until the student is thoroughly familiar with the lesson routine, use a standard, transitional sentence to indicate the shift from working on the word chart to reading the story. A simple statement such as, "Now you're going to see many of the words you have just studied in the story," is sufficient. Such a brief transitional sentence helps the student understand the relationship between the word chart and the other segments of the lesson in which he is actually thinking about and reading the words he has studied.

Words for Study

The Words for Study section contains words which the student has not yet formally studied but which appear in the story and exercises. They are listed in the order in which they appear in these two segments of the lesson.

Explain to the student that he will see these words in the current story and exercises. They are listed separately because they cannot be easily sounded out. (Actually some of the words can be sounded out, but the student has not yet studied the phonics rules that apply to these words. It is not necessary to mention this information unless the student asks about it.) Do tell the student that most of these words are used so often in the lessons that he will easily learn to sight read them.

In the early lessons especially, many students can sight read most of the words in Words for Study. By all means, let the students do so. In some cases, students can easily sight read a word, but fail to pronounce the ending. For example, some students working on the Words for Study in Lesson 4 say *look* instead of *looked*.

Make sure the student pronounces these endings when he reads the Words for Study. If he wants to know why this is important, tell him that the word appears this way in the story, and he will read the story more accurately if he pays attention to endings. Briefly explain that, as he moves through the book, he will learn how these endings affect the meaning of words. For now, it's important that he just get used to pronouncing them whenever they appear.

If a student does not know how to pronounce a word in the Words for Study, simply say it and have the student repeat it a few times. It is not recommended that the student sound out any of these words until Lesson 9. Prior to Lesson 9, the student has enough practice sounding out words in the word chart. He needs a short break from this work because he will probably have to sound out many of the words again as he encounters them in the story and exercises. The Lesson 9 notes in Chapter 8 of the teacher's manual include suggestions for sounding out the Words for Study.

As you did with the words on the word chart, spend a minute or two reviewing the Words for Study by pointing randomly to the words and asking the student to say them. Or say a word and have the student locate it and repeat its pronunciation. Make sure that you alternate difficult words with those which give the student no trouble.

General Procedures for Reading the Story

Because you want to establish good reading patterns in Book 1, all first readings of the story should take place in class. Developing good reading patterns is much easier when on-the-spot correction is available. And fewer opportunities exist for sloppy or incorrect reading habits to take root. You can assign second readings for homework.

A student may want to know why he has to read the story aloud when people usually read to themselves. Explain that by hearing him read aloud you can learn what gives him difficulty and help him. He will have many opportunities to read silently in Book 1 as he completes the exercises. Be sure to emphasize that you are there to help him. Many reading students need to be reminded of this fact frequently because they often have a history of poor teacher-student relationships. Most students come to enjoy oral reading once they are familiar with the punctuation discussed later in this section and understand that you are not going to make fun of their mistakes.

Begin the story by having the student read its title. Briefly explain that the title gives him a general idea of what the story is about and helps to focus the reader's attention. By the third lesson, the student usually has no difficulty remembering to read the title.

Now for the harder part. After the student has read the title, you need to use a procedure for the oral reading and story discussion that works well for your student. Be patient. Often you need to work with a student for four or five lessons before you discover his strengths and weaknesses. The guidelines below suggest procedures for dealing with particular types of students.

Good Decoding/Good Concentration Students

- Have the student read the entire story, assisting him in sounding out or recalling words when he makes errors. If a word he missed appears in the Words for Study, the student often remembers it if you simply point to its location in the Words for Study. If he doesn't remember, tell him the word.
- Discuss the story after the student has finished reading it. If the student cannot remember a particular detail,

indicate the appropriate paragraph, have the student reread it, and repeat the question.

- After the discussion, have the student reread either a difficult section or the entire story to reinforce accuracy and recall. If the student asks why he needs to reread the story, mention the importance of accuracy and gently remind him that progress in reading comes with much practice.

Good Decoding/Poor Concentration Students

- Take turns reading the sentences. As the student begins to see that he can handle the reading, he is usually willing to read all the sentences himself. As you did with the first type of student, assist him with words that give him difficulty.

- Discuss what is happening both when the student reaches the middle of the story and when he has finished it. If the student cannot recall a particular detail, indicate the appropriate sentence, have the student reread it, and repeat the question.

- After the discussion, have the student reread either specific sentences or small sections of the story that gave him difficulty in order to reinforce accuracy.

Poor Decoding/Good Concentration Students

- Have the student read the first paragraph twice—once for correct pronunciation and once for meaning. Assist him with words that give him trouble.

- After the second reading, discuss what is happening in the paragraph. If the student cannot remember a particular detail, indicate the sentence or word which gives the answer, have the student reread it, and repeat the question. Use this procedure for remaining paragraphs.

- Briefly review the entire story.

- After the discussion, point to the words and one or two sentences that gave the student trouble and ask him to reread them.

Poor Decoding/Poor Concentration Students

- Take turns reading the sentences. Assist the student with words that give him trouble.

- After every one or two sentences, no matter who has done the reading, ask the student to tell you what is happening. Usually the student responds correctly. If not, have him reread the sentence and phrase your question more specifically so that you are virtually giving the student the answer.

  After reminding the student a few times that sentences always give some kind of information, read two or three sentences before asking him a question.

  If the student cannot recall a particular detail, indicate the word which gives the answer, have him reread it, and repeat the question.

- After reading the story, do not ask the student to summarize what happened or review any difficult words unless you are certain that the student can respond correctly. Difficult words can be reviewed in the exercises and reinforcement activities.

Unfortunately, no student fits neatly into any of these four categories on a consistent basis. Take this into consideration in pacing the work. For example, even a rapidly improving student can have a lousy lesson. In this situation, omit the second reading of the story. Or perhaps the poor decoding/poor concentration student is working on a lesson in which everything goes smoothly. When this occurs, he can usually reread the entire story without too much stress. As you become increasingly familiar with the student's skills, you will naturally develop a knack for appropriate changes in the procedure.

The Need for Accuracy

To establish good reading patterns, the student must read the story accurately. This does not mean that he must read the entire story without making a mistake. Accuracy means that errors are corrected, with or without assistance from you, and that the student rereads as much of the story as his skill and concentration allow. Mistakes made during the rereading are also corrected.

If the student becomes frustrated because you insist on accuracy, gently remind him that reading the words correctly from the beginning will make reading easier for him later on. In most instances, the student develops an appreciation for high standards. The student who merely finishes a story, making mistakes here and there, may feel satisfied; but the student who knows that he has read every word in the story correctly experiences a real sense of accomplishment.

The need for accuracy demands consistent support and patience from the teacher. To help the student accept the fact that you correct him quite often, pay special attention to your voice and gestures. Your voice should convey a sense of considerate detachment. In other words, you are there to help the student correct errors that you, in no way, condemn him for making.

Because so many students are sensitive about their lack of skill in reading, they tend to regard any sign of impatience on your part as a form of condemnation. To counteract this tendency, speak calmly and naturally. Also avoid such gestures of impatience as pencil-tapping, foot-tapping, and other unnecessary movement that can be easily misinterpreted.

To a large extent, let your pen do the talking. As the student becomes more proficient with phonics rules, he can often read an entire story without you having to say a word. You need only to make a few helpful marks or indicate trouble spots with your pen and write a cue word or two in the margin.

The less talking you do, the better the student can recognize his progress. Through this "silent treatment" and speaking in a calm voice when you do talk, the student begins to regard his mistakes simply as items that need correction rather than as indictments.

Dealing with Oral Reading Difficulties

The following suggestions address some of the difficulties students are apt to encounter when reading the story aloud.

Ignoring Punctuation Signals

All students are able to respond appropriately to the punctuation in the stories with a little practice. Many students are already familiar with these signals. But if an explanation is necessary, use the following guidelines.

- Because the student is concentrating hard on his reading, offer explanations only when necessary. For example, if the student does not let his voice drop at the end of the sentences in Lesson 1, you should teach him the purpose of periods.

- If you need to explain a piece of punctuation, stop the student when he gets to the end of a sentence and say, "Good reading. But before you go on, there's something I want you to take a look at." Try to keep all interruptions supportive and casual. You don't want the student to dread these interruptions because then he won't learn from them.

- Point to the punctuation and ask the student if he knows what it's called. If he doesn't, pronounce it, and have the student repeat it.

- Briefly explain the purpose of the punctuation. For example, for quotation marks, all you need to say is, "These marks tell you that a person in the story is talking." Explanations should pertain to the purpose punctuation serves. Students have an opportunity to learn basic rules for punctuation as they are writing.

- Read the sentence so the student can hear how punctuation guides the voice. For some students, you will also need to read the sentence as if the punctuation were not there. Through hearing the difference, the student understands how punctuation helps the reader. Reading the sentence these two different ways is especially helpful for students who have trouble responding correctly to commas.

- Have the student read the same sentence until he responds correctly to the punctuation.

- Introduce poor decoding/poor concentration students to only the period and question mark in the early lessons unless they ask for an explanation of other punctuation. These other marks should be introduced gradually. Introduce punctuation marks to all other students as they demonstrate a need to know their function in oral reading.

- All students occasionally forget to respond to punctuation. During the early lessons, point to the missed piece of punctuation and ask, "What does the (name of the signal) tell you?" Unless the student is really struggling with the story, have him reread the sentence, so he can respond to the signal correctly. In later lessons, you need only to point to the ignored piece of punctuation.

Ignoring Word Endings

The most troublesome endings for students are *-ed*, *-s,* and *-ing.* Teach the student how to pronounce these endings and any others as he encounters them in the Words for Study and the story. Remind him to pronounce these endings whenever he fails to do so. A helpful way to do this is to draw a line with your pen under any missed ending and have him reread the word. Occasionally remind the student that pronouncing these endings will make his reading more accurate and help him in later work.

Avoid explanations that pertain to grammar. Many endings are emphasized more specifically in the exercises. If a grammatical explanation is needed, save it for the exercises. Keep in mind that the story segment of the lesson should focus exclusively on accurate reading, appropriate expression, and comprehension.

In some cases, students mispronounce endings because they are used to saying these endings differently in their everyday speech. Refer to the discussion of pronunciation in Chapter 3 of the manual for suggestions on how to handle this issue.

Mispronouncing and Forgetting Words

In general, the student should correct his errors. If his concentration seems to be flagging, provide occasional corrections to help him. For words the student can sound out, use the same procedure you did when working with the word chart. Tell him the correct pronunciation of all other words. If the word occurs for the first time in the current lesson, the student can often recall it if you point it out on the word chart or in the Words for Study. When appropriate, writing cue words neatly in the margin is also helpful.

As you did with word endings, use your pen to underline troublesome letters or mark silent letters, but avoid overmarking. Generally five or six marks per story is enough. Too many marks discourage the student. Make a mental note of other words or sounds that give the student frequent trouble and emphasize them in your reinforcement activities.

In helping the student to pronounce correctly words he has missed, avoid using context clues. Sounding out the words is enough for him to handle. He has many opportunities to learn about context clues in the exercises.

Skipping Words

Oral reading helps the student develop the habit of reading *all* the words in each sentence. When he occasionally skips a word, indicate that word with your pen and have the student read it before he continues.

Sometimes the student loses the sense of the sentence when he skips a word and then corrects himself. Most students quickly develop the habit of rereading the entire sentence from the beginning. This practice should be encouraged only when the student doesn't know what he's reading about. Discourage the student who wants to start a sentence over every time he makes a mistake.

Also discourage the student from using his finger to indicate his reading place. Although this practice is helpful in the very early lessons, it often becomes a habit that hinders the student's progress in later lessons.

But if a student skips entire lines frequently, have him mark each line by putting his finger under the first word at the left and moving it down the page, line by line, as he reads. Students who frequently skip lines often need glasses, so suggest that they have an eye examination.

Misreading Little Words

Surprisingly enough, usually the short words give students the most trouble. Often a student asks, "What difference does it make if I read *on* instead of *in*? I still know what's happening in the sentence." A helpful response is to ask the student what the sentence, "John is *in* the car," means. After the student has correctly explained this, ask him what "John is *on* the car," means. Usually the student sees the point. This type of explanation can be used for all prepositions and most other words as well.

Assessing Comprehension through Oral Discussion

Discussing stories orally rather than requiring the student to write out answers to comprehension questions is recommended for several reasons.

First, oral discussion helps develop good teacher-student relationships. Even though the discussion and dialogues are brief and to the point, the teacher and student become better acquainted with each other, and this contributes to a good working relationship.

Second, oral discussion helps the teacher become more aware of the precise nature of the student's strengths and weaknesses. This information is particularly useful in making decisions about reinforcement activities. For example, if a student frequently has trouble understanding the sequence of events, the teacher can print simple sentences about daily activities on separate index cards and have the student put the cards in order as a reinforcement activity.

Third, oral discussion helps the student who suffers from the "right answer" syndrome. This student becomes so upset when he doesn't get the right answer that he often has trouble concentrating on the rest of the work. Brief, informal discussions about the story are far less threaten-

ing for this student than writing out answers to comprehension questions.

Last, oral discussion frees the student from having to look through the story for the right answer. For the beginning student, skimming does not contribute to accuracy and genuine comprehension. In oral discussion work, the teacher can guide the student's attention to the part of the story containing the answer if such assistance is necessary.

General procedures for helping the student to comprehend the story are outlined in the discussion of the four basic types of students which appears earlier in this chapter. Refer to these procedures as you plan this work and make appropriate modifications as the student shows improvement.

If the student remembers previous stories, that's fine. If he doesn't, this in no way interferes with his understanding of the story he is currently working on. Occasionally, information from previous stories makes reading the current story more enjoyable. In these instances, you can provide the information.

Literal Level Questions

Literal level questions deal with the most basic kind of comprehension—remembering what the author has said. The answers to literal questions can always be found in the reading selection. The student does not need to interpret information or apply what he has read to knowledge he already possesses.

When asking the student literal level questions, start with a general rather than a specific question. The student who worries too much about getting the right answer especially appreciates this. An example of a general question is, "What does this sentence tell you?" Or if the student has read a paragraph, ask, "What happened in this paragraph?"

The advantage of the general question is that students almost always give an acceptable answer, and the oral discussion is off to a good start. More specific questions can follow in which the student is asked about the character's names, problems, and activities.

Using the story in Lesson 1 as an example, specific questions include: "How did Bob get to work? How did Bob feel about his job? What did Bob do after Mr. Jones fired him?" In any story, if a student is unable to answer a specific question, help him to locate the answer according to the procedures listed for the four types of students.

From the very first lesson, gently establish a pattern for precise answers. Students will give precise answers to specific questions simply because this type of question demands a precise answer. But they may well need help in developing the habit of answering general questions with precision. The following dialogue illustrates how the teacher can encourage the student to give precise answers. This student, reading according to the poor decoding/poor concentration procedure, has just completed the first two sentences in Lesson 1.

Teacher: What happened in these two sentences?
Student: Some guy overslept.
Teacher: Good. What's his name?
Student: Bob.
Teacher: So what happens to Bob because he overslept?
Student: He was late for work.
Teacher: Right. Now let's move on to the next sentence.

Through these brief dialogues, the student learns two things about reading which most beginning readers initially don't realize: sentences give information and each sentence builds on information given in preceding sentences. You do not need to formally teach these concepts. As you help the student develop precision in his answers, he begins to see for himself that reading communicates information in an orderly fashion.

This level of precision is not required for every detail of the story. Most students become precise enough in their answers to let you know they understand what they have read. For the student who continues to demonstrate that he has only a vague idea of what the story is about, use the dialogue model once or twice during the story reading. You can fill in any other necessary details.

Applied Level Questions

Applied level questions help the student see that reading can be enjoyable and worthwhile. Through this type of question, the student is encouraged to relate the story to his own experience and thoughts. Using Lesson 1 as an illustration, examples of appropriate applied level questions are: "Do you think someone should be fired for being late for work? Do you think it was really a good thing that Bob was fired since he hated his job so much? Do you think Bob is a responsible person?"

In general, ask one applied level question for each story. The dialogues which these questions generate should last only a few minutes. Occasionally, when the student seems especially interested in a particular topic, the dialogue time can be extended. But this should not become a regular pattern because it tends to break the student's concentration, and completing the lesson becomes more difficult.

Brief as they are, these applied level question dialogues can be either highly productive or highly devastating moments. Because they affect the overall quality of the teacher-student relationship, consider the following guidelines in planning this discussion.

- Be impartial. Applied questions have no value if you are closed to the student's opinions. Students have an uncanny ability to detect teacher biases, so you want to avoid applied questions that pertain to your pet theories. For example, if you have an ironclad definition of what constitutes a responsible person, do not ask the student, "Do you think Bob is a responsible person?" Rather ask

an applied level question for which you can listen to the student's answer in an unbiased manner.

- Be willing to help the student respond to the question. Many students are simply not used to anyone asking them what they think. They need some help in learning how to express their thoughts. For this type of student, the dialogue might go something like this:

Teacher: Do you think Mr. Jones was right in firing Bob?
Student: I don't know.
Teacher: Would you have fired Bob if you were the boss?
Student: No, I would have given him another chance.
Teacher: If you were talking to Bob, how would you handle the situation?
Student: Well, I think that as long as a person is doing his job, he should be able to come to work whenever he wants.
Teacher: So it wouldn't matter if a worker was late or not?
Student: No. As long as he's doing what he's supposed to do, what's the difference?
Teacher: That's interesting. Maybe in the next story, Bob will get a job working for a boss who thinks like you. We still have some time left. Let's use it to practice some of the words you studied today before we preview the homework.

- Be willing to help the student develop a thought. Some students have little difficulty expressing their thoughts, but they may need help in thinking through their ideas and elaborating on them. You want to encourage these students to explore their thoughts by asking a series of questions. The following dialogue illustrates how this technique works.

Teacher: Do you think Mr. Jones was right to fire Bob?
Student: Sure. You can't run a business with people showing up whenever they feel like it.
Teacher: Do you think he should have warned Bob first?
Student: He's the boss. He can do whatever he wants.
Teacher: Do you think Bob will have trouble getting another job?
Student: In times like these, he should have realized how lucky he was to have a job in the first place.
Teacher: Maybe he'll realize that in the next story. We still have some time left. Let's use it to practice some of the words you studied today before we preview the homework.

- In general, avoid expressing your opinion. Notice in both dialogues the teacher does not indicate what he thinks about Mr. Jones firing Bob. The neutrality is conducive to helping the student express and develop his own thoughts.

On an occasional basis, you should share your thoughts with the student. He benefits by being reminded that you also think about these questions and by hearing how you express and develop your thoughts. But keep your statements brief—the class period is the student's time.

Both literal and applied questions help the student respond to the reading selection. With practice, he learns to use information from the story to support his own thoughts. And he begins to see connections between the characters and situations in the stories and his own life experiences. In making these connections, reading becomes an enjoyable activity that helps the student think more clearly and motivates him to learn more.

The Necessity of Teacher Observation

It is fairly easy for teachers to observe the need for spontaneous modifications in the procedure, such as demanding less than usual from the student when he is having a rough day. But many teachers have a more difficult time closely observing a student's progress so they can accurately determine when he is ready for a more challenging pace.

Keep in mind that the procedure most conducive to accurate reading and rapid progress is the procedure for good decoding/good concentration students. No matter how gradual the implementation, this is an attainable goal for nearly all students working in Book 1.

There are two major pitfalls in remedial reading instruction that you want to avoid. First, do not concentrate on mistakes the student makes to the extent that you overlook his overall progress. By emphasizing errors, teachers can spend excessive amounts of time on troublesome words and phonics rules the student can learn more comfortably through working with them in future lessons. Too, any words of encouragement may begin to have a hollow ring because the student has been made abundantly aware of his reading difficulties.

Second, do not stick with an established procedure long after it has outlived its original usefulness. Procedures dealing with the general lesson format and the phonics approach should remain constant because they help the student feel more comfortable and develop efficient work habits. But modifying other procedures when the student is ready for a greater challenge will allow him to progress more rapidly.

The key to avoiding these pitfalls is teacher observation. For example, as you observe a poor decoding/good concentration student begin to sound out words more proficiently, discuss what happens in the story after the first reading and make the second reading the last step in the procedure.

To help you develop the habit of observing a student's progress, keep the following questions in mind as he reads the story. You will find that you naturally become more aware of a student's progress and perceive his mistakes in a proper perspective. These questions can help you observe the student's progress in other segments of the lesson as well.

- Can the student sound out more words with less help?
- Can the student sight read more words than in earlier lessons?
- Can the student follow punctuation signals with less help?
- Does the student take time to decode difficult words instead of blurting out what he hopes is the right word?
- Is the student correcting more of his own mistakes rather than waiting for the teacher to say something?
- Is the student showing increased mastery of words that have given him trouble in past lessons?
- Is the student reading the story with increased expression?
- Are the student's answers to questions about the story consistently more accurate?
- Is the student showing overall improvement in his patience and concentration?
- Is the student concentrating more on his work in spite of distracting personal problems?

By keeping these questions in mind as you work with the student, you become more attuned to his progress and are better able to make appropriate changes in the procedure. Introduce these changes gradually and wait until he demonstrates some degree of comfort and mastery before you make other changes.

Through observation and these increased demands, even poor decoding/poor concentration students are usually able to complete the story work according to the procedure outlined for good decoding/good concentration students by the time they have finished Book 1. For students already following the good decoding/good concentration procedure, modifications in the procedure are not recommended. Instead, offer these students more challenging reinforcement activities.

Some Final Thoughts

If anything inevitably wears down both the student and the teacher as the lessons progress and the stories become longer, it's zombie reading. No matter how much difficulty the student has with the story, he is capable—from the very first lesson—of interjecting some expression into his reading, even if it is simply letting his voice drop when he comes to a period. As the student gains confidence in reading aloud, encourage him to read with expression. This is not to say he should read as if he were trying out for a play. Expression can be defined as responding appropriately to punctuation and putting some life into reading.

Keep in mind that the story should be a source of enjoyment and satisfaction for the student. More attention should be paid to how accurately he is decoding than to details he does not remember. The student has many opportunities to work on the development of comprehension skills in both the exercises and the reinforcement activities. This work, in turn, helps him improve his comprehension skills.

Priority must be given to the reading skills which are emphasized in the lessons. Oral discussion provides a pleasant break from working so intensively on these skills, but it is only a break. Once the discussion of the story has ended, it is time to return to studying the words.

A Summary of Do's and Don'ts

1. Do pronounce all the words listed in the Words for Study that the student cannot decode. Wait until Lesson 9 before you encourage the student to sound out words that follow phonics rules he has studied.

2. Don't expect the student to sight read the words listed in the Words for Study after only one lesson. He has many opportunities to practice reading these words in future lessons and reinforcement activities.

3. Do schedule first readings of the stories as a class activity rather than homework. This will help you determine the student's strengths and weaknesses and plan appropriate reinforcement activities.

4. Do insist that the student accurately decode the words in each story.

5. Do encourage the student to observe the punctuation signals and read with some expression.

6. Do ask the student both general and specific literal level questions.

7. Do ask at least one applied level question for each story. As a general rule, limit discussion to two or three minutes. And keep an open mind about the student's responses.

8. Do avoid too much emphasis on comprehension of the story. Keep in mind that comprehension skills are addressed in other segments of the lesson as well.

9. Do use a procedure for oral reading and discussion that reflects the student's current skill level.

10. Do consciously monitor the student's progress so that you can accurately determine when he needs additional practice or is ready for a more demanding procedure.

5. The Exercises

Four purposes underscore the exercises which follow each story.

First, the student becomes more skillful in using the phonics method to sound out words. He grows in accuracy, patience, and confidence each time he practices this method.

Second, through seeing words repeated, he increases his sight vocabulary.

Third, he increases both his decoding and comprehension skills in the word study exercises included in each lesson. In these exercises, he works with word beginnings, word endings, compound words, and spelling rules.

Fourth, he develops his reasoning ability in exercises which require him to think, use context clues, and practice process of elimination. In addition, he applies what he already knows to new situations and discovers new information. Exercises in these lessons requiring these skills include synonyms and antonyms, categorizing and classifying, modified cloze exercises and answering general information questions.

Before proceeding further, more needs to be said about the last purpose mentioned above. Reasoning is emphasized in most exercises because many beginning readers think that reading is merely recognizing words. Often a student will say, "If I can already read these words, can I skip this section?" Occasionally a student is merely trying to get out of doing some work. More often, however, the student really doesn't understand that reasoning is the essence of reading.

As the teacher, your response is, "Even though you know the words, this exercise gives you a chance to review them and to think about them in a different way. Thinking is a big part of reading." Be sure the tone of your voice is warm and matter-of-fact. Too often, the student's associations with the word *think* are particularly unpleasant. He's heard, "Can't you think!" or "Don't you have a brain?" too many times.

Do not expect that the student will immediately grasp the significant relationship between reading and reasoning. Repetition is as important in understanding concepts as it is in learning to read words. Many opportunities occur throughout this series to use such phrases as "Reason it out," or "Think about it for a minute." Repeating these phrases helps the student to perceive the connection between reading and reasoning and understand its significance.

Previewing the Exercises with the Student

In Book 1, the student is *not* responsible for reading the directions that precede each exercise. The directions have been written for the teacher's benefit. The few students who are capable of reading the directions should do so during the preview segment of the lesson.

Explaining the directions is preferable to reading them to the student. After all, the student has just finished working on a lesson in which he has been introduced to many new words. Your oral explanation not only gives him a breather but also helps to strengthen his auditory skills. Like all other aspects of teaching, no hard and fast rules exist for this procedure. Monitor the student's reactions to decide which way of communicating the directions works best for him.

Allow enough time at the end of the class period for previewing the exercises. It is important that the student understand precisely what is expected of him, so don't rush this segment of the lesson. For the student who progresses smoothly through the lessons, five minutes is more than sufficient. The student who experiences more difficulty needs more time at first, but eventually he, too, can understand the nature of the assignment in this five-minute segment.

Use the following guidelines to assist you in previewing the exercises with the student.

1. In your own words, explain the directions for one exercise at a time.

2. If a column of words appears in an exercise, have the student pronounce the words. If a particularly troublesome word appears in one of the sentences, have him review this also.

3. If an example is provided, have the student read it.

4. Have the student complete one item in each exercise. If the student still seems confused, have him complete another item.

5. After all the exercises have been previewed, have the student tell you briefly what he is supposed to do in each one. If he forgets the procedure for any of the exercises, have him study his own examples to refresh his memory.

Assigning the Exercises

You should spend a few minutes during the first class talking about homework—which is how students will perceive the exercises no matter where or when they complete them.

Many students initially believe that attending class is sufficient. You may need to convince them that homework is important because it provides additional practice with the words they are studying and that this practice is just as important as class time. If students have trouble understanding this point, athletic practice is a helpful analogy. Do not expect students to remember why homework is important after having heard the reason only once. In addition to giving them support in completing the homework, remind them often of the relationship between this activity and improving their reading skills.

The following guidelines are designed to help you decide whether the exercises should be assigned as homework or in-class work.

- If the student is reasonably motivated and has a comfortable place to complete the work outside the classroom, assign the exercises as homework.
- If the student is reasonably motivated but has no place to complete the work, help him make arrangements to use a vacant room. If no other room is available, encourage the student to come to class early to complete the homework.
- If the student is poorly motivated, incorporate the exercises into the lesson time. Gradually introduce the concept of homework so that by the sixth lesson the student is completing at least some of the exercises on his own.
- If the student's reading class lasts an hour or more, have him start the exercises after he has completed the lesson work and taken a short break.

The diversity of students and learning situations is so great that you can't expect to know just how to assign the exercises before you even meet the student. Also don't expect your first decision to be necessarily the best one. Pay attention to how the situation unfolds. If modifications need to be made, first discuss with the student the problems that have arisen and then make the necessary modifications.

For example, one student who had been doing all the exercises with painstaking care at home suddenly started rushing her work, and her accuracy rate dropped from 85% to 60%. After the third time, the teacher asked what was happening. The student revealed that additional responsibilities at home worried her so much that she couldn't concentrate on her homework.

The teacher thought for a minute and then proposed that the student do only half the exercises for the next week. At that time they would see how things were going and, it was hoped, return to their former schedule. The student required two additional weeks to become accustomed to her new responsibilities but then was able to resume completing all the exercises as homework with 85% accuracy.

Several points from the above example may help you in your work with the students—particularly adult reading students, whose lives can be fairly complicated.

- The teacher did not respond immediately to the declining accuracy in homework. After all, everyone has a few bad days now and then.
- The teacher initiated the discussion about homework. Unless he's a chronic complainer, the student will usually not admit that he just can't cope with the work. Be sensitive to this and tactfully ask the student if he is having trouble with the work when things seem to go awry.
- The teacher thought before he suggested an alternative. Too often teachers feel pressure to make instant decisions. This is unfortunate because a hasty decision is often a bad one.
- The teacher did not ask the student for specific details about her new responsibilities. This is really none of the teacher's business. But a teacher should communicate his hope that all goes well with the student.
- The teacher assumed responsibility for modifying the homework schedule. Perhaps this seems authoritarian or contradictory to the principle that the student must assume responsibility for his learning. It's neither. Between the issues that confront him each day and learning to read, the student has his hands full. He depends on you to provide the structure for learning, and part of this structure involves making decisions about homework.
- Even though the teacher's initial plan had to be modified, the goal of returning to the former homework procedure with 85% accuracy was not abandoned. It is better to be too strict with timing at first and adjust it as necessary.

Doing the Homework

The following three sections are designed to help you anticipate and deal with problems that are apt to arise as students attempt to complete the exercises.

Letting Students Work Together

A major excuse students present to the teacher runs something like this: "I can always figure out these answers better when I'm working with you. Wouldn't it be better just to do all this work in class?"

The answer, of course, is *no*. In the beginning, when everything is new to the student, the exercises do seem to make more sense to him when the teacher is present for on-the-spot corrections. Reassure the student that the exercises become easier with practice. He is to do his best.

If possible, suggest that the student do his homework with someone else who is working in the same book. They can help each other sort out the difficulties that arise. If no one else is working in the same book, perhaps a relative or friend can help.

Sometimes teachers fear that if the student works with somebody else, he will fall prey to mindlessly copying the answers offered by his "partner-in-crime." Occasionally this happens. Then you and your student should have a little talk. But more often than not, the student's improvement is accelerated for several reasons.

- The student's recall is improved because he both says and hears the words aloud more often.

- The opportunity to help another student with pronunciation and offer explanations reinforces both his recall and his understanding of the material.

- Working with another student lessens the student's embarrassment over his inadequate reading skills. He becomes more confident and takes increased pride in his work.

- The student starts perceiving himself as a student. Working with his mind becomes more and more natural to him.

Helpful Study Hints

One concern often expressed by the student is the inability to concentrate on homework. Suggest that the student be patient. Becoming accustomed to the kind of concentration this work demands takes time. Again, an athletic analogy is helpful. For example, ask the student how he feels after jogging or playing basketball when he hasn't exercised for a while.

Sometimes a student tries to complete the homework right after a full day's work or just before going to bed or while he is fulfilling other responsibilities. Suggest that he schedule a definite, 30-minute study time in quiet surroundings and at times when he is not exhausted. Many students find that getting up one half hour earlier is the best solution. They are not disturbed, and their minds are surprisingly alert.

You may also need to mention the following considerations for, quite possibly, he has never given them any thought.

- Is he using proper lighting?
- Does he sit at a table or desk?
- Is his studying posture a good one—neither too tense nor too relaxed?
- Is he minimizing noise distractions? Some students work better with the sound of a radio or human voices in the background, but most are seriously distracted by noise.
- Is homework his only activity during study time? Some students are convinced that they can manage two activities simultaneously—for example, completing the exercises and cooking dinner. Students, especially during the early stages of reading, should attempt to establish a schedule that allows them to concentrate exclusively on homework.

Not all of these suggestions need to be made during the student's first lesson. Indeed, if they are all mentioned at this time, the student will undoubtedly feel overwhelmed. During the first lesson stress only the reason for doing the exercises. There will be many opportunities during later classes to mention the other factors involved in good homework habits.

Make sure that these factors are presented in the form of suggestions. You are not stating policy; you are simply encouraging the student to think about how he can best achieve his reading goal within the circumstances of his life. He'll get the point.

Reminders to the Student

Mention the following reminders as the situation warrants. If the situation warrants *all* the reminders, pray for patience and suggest one that addresses the student's biggest stumbling block. Unless the student is exceptionally motivated or thick-skinned, too many reminders at one time can have a devastating effect.

- The student is to complete *all* homework items. Sometimes a student skips an item because he doesn't know the answer. Tell him to answer all questions to the best of his ability. Not only does learning thrive on corrected mistakes, but also much is to be said for the art of intelligent guessing.

- The student is to spell his answers correctly. Spelling errors in original writing are understandable. But because the words needed to answer the questions almost always appear in the same exercise, encourage him to develop the habit of checking his work for accuracy. Occasionally a student will protest that he wants to see if he can spell the words without looking at them. Support this practice and tell him he still needs to check for accuracy and make any necessary corrections.

- The student is to write his answers legibly. Most students quickly develop good handwriting practices. In instances of careless writing, don't struggle to read what he has written. Simply have him write more neatly and remind him that both you and he must be able to read his writing.

- The student need not complete the items in an exercise in order. Sometimes the student completes the first six or so items, and the rest are blank. His explanation is that he couldn't figure out the next answer, so he decided to wait until he could get help in class. Encourage the student to work by process of elimination. Most students need to be taught this method.

Process of elimination first comes into play in Exercise 4 of Lesson 8. If your student is not familiar with this technique, spend a few minutes teaching it. Make sure that he can say *process of elimination* and understands what *to eliminate something* means. If the student finds it easier to draw a line through each choice as he eliminates it rather than use the preferred check mark, that's fine. Just make sure his line doesn't obliterate the word in case he needs to make corrections later.

- The student need not complete the exercises in order. But the student should be encouraged to complete one exercise before starting the next one. Too much skipping around is counterproductive to concentration and grasping the point of the exercise.

- The student needs to check over his homework after he has finished all the exercises. Because he is using process of elimination and completing the exercises in a sequence that may differ from the original, beginning readers tend to overlook items. Checking for thoroughness corrects this tendency.

Use discretion in timing these homework suggestions and reminders. If the student is having an unusually rough day, the most important reminder you can give him now is how well he was able to put aside the concerns of his rotten day and concentrate on the lesson. The student's reply is often, "Yeah, but look at all the mistakes I made." Your response is, "Yes, but you stuck with it."

Above all, remind the student of the progress he is making. When the student is particularly discouraged, do this in a concrete way. For example, show him how many pages of work he has completed, or have him look at the previous Word Index to see how many words he has studied. Or have him look at his composition book to see all the writing he has done. (The composition book is discussed in Chapters 6 and 7 of this manual.)

Correcting the Homework

Be sure you allow enough time to go over the homework with the student. You will need to allot more time for reviewing the homework if the student has found an exercise particularly difficult. Also, more time may be required as the exercises increase in number and complexity. You will probably need to observe the student and try out a few different schedules before you hit on the pace that works best for your student. But once you establish the appropriate pace, consistency promotes good concentration and effective learning.

Of all the lesson segments—the word chart, the story, and the exercises—the exercises should be covered most thoroughly. All the homework should be corrected. Remember that many patterns are being established. If the student develops the habit of doing something incorrectly, he will have a hard time unlearning the procedure.

As the student, wearing a horror-stricken look, watches your corrections appear all over the pages, he wonders what on earth he has gotten himself into. Be sure to explain why everything is being corrected. Even though reading students are overly sensitive to having their mistakes pointed out, they eventually adapt to this procedure. Adolescents seem to need more help from you in this regard. If you get complaints, remind the student that mistakes are part of learning and that corrections make learning more worthwhile.

Consider the following suggestions as you go over the homework.

- If the error involves only one or two words, have the student correct it.
- If extensive revision is needed, such as in a sentence, the teacher should do it. Unless the student is exceptionally capable, extensive revision is too much for the beginning reader.
- The student should reread all corrected work to reinforce accuracy.
- Use a pen so the corrections will be easier to see. Encourage the student to work in pencil to make erasing easier. If a student insists upon using a pen, make sure you use a different color. As mentioned before, avoid red.

Corrections involving concepts not yet studied don't require explanations. For example, if the student omits a comma, have him put it in the correct place. The first time this situation occurs, find out whether or not the student knows anything about commas. If he knows the pronunciation of *comma* and can recognize them, simply tell him that he will be studying commas later on. If the student is unaware of commas, have him say the word a few times and practice making this mark. After he has inserted the comma in his sentence, mention that he will be studying them later; for now, he is just getting used to using them.

Corrections involving a previously studied concept should be reviewed. For example, if a student who has completed the exercise in Lesson 5 on *-ed* endings spells *robed* for *robbed* in a sentence, briefly review this rule. In this way, the student begins to relate the exercises to other learning situations.

The student should read everything except the directions as he goes over his homework with you. Thus, if he is going over a fill-in-the-blank exercise, he should read the entire sentence. This method provides additional practice with the individual words, context clues, and oral reading.

Also, make sure the student reads his own responses. Some students, as they correct an exercise which required them to choose the correct answer from a list, pause when they get to their answers, and read the answer from the list rather than their own handwriting. Discourage this habit from the outset. The student needs to become comfortable reading his own writing.

For the first ten lessons, the student should aim for 70% accuracy. Eighty per cent accuracy is a reasonable expectation for the remaining ten lessons. Neither the student's sentence writing nor the occasional exercise in which everything goes wrong should be included in this average.

If the student scores below these levels more often than not, divide each lesson into two class sessions and increase the number of reinforcement activities. Suggestions for these activities appear in the next chapter. Keep in mind the goal of one lesson per class session. With the reinforcement activities and appropriate homework suggestions, the student should be able to complete one lesson per class with the desired accuracy by the tenth lesson.

Too often, going over homework is nothing more than a dry, mechanical routine in which the student simply reads his answers. Not only does this deprive the student of practice with the words and concepts he's been studying, but also it is unfair. Consciously or unconsciously, the student's efforts are being slighted if the homework critique is being done in a dreary, "what's-the-answer-to-number-2" style.

Take your time and enjoy this part of the lesson. If opportunities arise for brief tangents in which items are related to life experiences, take advantage of them. Keep in mind that, with the exception of the first lesson, correcting the homework is the first activity. Both the student and you have an hour of hard work ahead, so strive to make the homework critique a relaxed introduction to the new work which lies just ahead.

When a Student Doesn't Do His Homework

If the student neglects to complete the exercises once in every eight lessons or so, don't worry. Just remind him of the importance of homework and the need to be as consistent as he possibly can.

If the student neglects to do his homework in general, don't worry about this either. Homework is the student's responsibility. This does not mean you are off the hook. You are the one with the alternative plans, reminders, and suggestions about homework. Part of your job is to communicate this information and assist the student in finding a workable solution. But, when all is said and done, it is the student's job to complete the work.

If your student is an adult, you have two choices if you see that reminders are getting you nowhere. You can incorporate all the exercises into lesson time and accept the reality that the student will make only minimal progress. Or you can ask your student, "Are you sure you really want to work on your reading?"

If the answer is "yes," review once again the importance of homework. Then arrive at a mutually agreed upon oral contract in which the student has sufficient time to develop the habit of producing work or else the class will be terminated. If the answer is "no", encourage the student to keep his goal in mind for a time when he doesn't have so many other priorities and wish him a gracious farewell.

If the student is an adolescent, solicit the support of a parent, counselor, or friend of the student whom you believe would be helpful in this situation. Be sure the focus is on the issue of homework and not the student's personality. Do not expect immediate results just because you have gone out of your way to help the student. Keep at it. If you give up, you can be certain the student will too. If you find an ally to help you work with this student, be sure to keep him informed of the progress as well as the setbacks.

On the Very Worst Days

Now, of course, when a person is discouraged, he often resorts to self-pity for some sort of illusory solace. The reading student is no exception. You have him look at the Word Index for encouragement, and he says, "Yeah, but I still don't know how to read some of these words." You have him skim his composition book for a sense of accomplishment, and he says, "Yeah, but you practically rewrote these sentences for me."

Don't lose your patience. After all, if being impatient is a problem for the student, you're not going to help matters any by losing your temper. Conversely, don't pressure yourself to adopt the tone of a gentle saint unless, of course, you happen to be one. Always strive for naturalness, especially in these situations.

In a kind and firm voice, remind the student that most learning requires this kind of hard work, that *all* students face these "what's-the-use" moments and learn to work toward their goals in spite of their frustration. The moments of pain are counterbalanced by moments of accomplishment and growth. Once he realizes his situation is not unique, his personal sense of failure is diminished, and he moves with strengthened confidence toward his goal of literacy.

Do not hesitate to use occupational or daily living examples to reinforce the value of the suggestions and reminders. For example, accuracy is a work habit personnel managers look for. Process of elimination is helpful in resolving problems that confront us during the course of a day. This training of intelligence is not something that stops at the classroom door, and the student may need to have you point this out.

A Summary of Do's and Don'ts

1. Do make sure the student knows why he is doing the exercises.
2. Do strive to have the student complete the exercises as homework.
3. Do remember that resistance to homework is natural and should be handled in a reasonable, supportive manner.
4. Do make sure the student knows exactly what he is supposed to do.
5. Do maximize learning by correcting all work.
6. Don't rush through the homework review.
7. Don't assume that the student already knows good study habits and procedures.
8. Don't give the student too many suggestions, reminders, or explanations at one time.
9. Don't expect the student to remember a concept or rule after having heard it only a few times.
10. Don't expect any procedural changes you make to be successful immediately.

6. Reinforcement Activities

As the term suggests, these activities are designed to reinforce the student's understanding and retention of the lesson material. Using reinforcement activities is particularly helpful in three types of situations.

Those students who find the work extremely difficult benefit from spending only half the class period on the actual lesson. Use the remaining time for two or three reinforcement activities which address areas of weakness. As a student demonstrates improvement in his ability to handle the work, gradually decrease the time spent on reinforcement activities and increase the lesson time.

Other students, because of high motivation and/or good sight reading ability, do not need to spend the entire period on the lesson. From time to time, having such students start the next lesson is a good idea. In most instances, however, this extra time is better spent on reinforcement activities. Writing exercises and spelling reviews are especially beneficial.

All students and most teachers occasionally need a break in the routine. When this happens, have the student complete the segment of the lesson he is working on. Then proceed directly to an appropriate reinforcement activity. Your schedule may be thrown off a bit, but it's worth it. Just make sure that you leave enough time at the end of the class period to preview the homework.

The suggestions in this section are based on activities that students have found both helpful and enjoyable. This list is by no means complete. Take some time to develop your own "bag of tricks." Through talking with other teachers, skimming puzzle magazines, and using your own imagination, you will soon have reinforcement activities for a variety of skills. Students, too, often recall helpful activities from their earlier schooling. In fact, many of the suggestions which follow come from students.

Word Index Activities Requiring No Preparation

A word index including all words the student has studied to that point appears after every four lessons in Book 1. In planning reinforcement activities, use the word index that most immediately precedes the current lesson. For example, if you are planning an activity to go along with Lesson 11, use the word index following Lesson 8 to assist you in selecting the words you wish to emphasize.

In addition to being a source for many reinforcement activities, the word index is also a reminder of accomplishment. Most students enjoy seeing all the words they've studied presented in this format. They also enjoy noticing that each index is much longer than the preceding one.

The following activities are suggestions for using the word index which require no preparation on your part.

Word Review

Have the student pick any column in the word index and pronounce all the words. The student should mark the words he can't sight read or sound out with relative ease. After the student has completed the entire column, review the troublesome words. Most students can sustain concentration on this activity for two or three columns before their attention begins to fade.

Guess the Word

Have the student pick a column. Then select a word from that column and give the student a clue for the word. Have the student find the word in the column and pronounce it. For example, if the student has picked the *L* column in the word index following Lesson 4, your clue might be, "I am thinking of a place where people go to swim." The student finds *lake* and pronounces it.

If you know that your student is familiar with a nearby lake, use this information. For example, you might say, "Michigan is the name of a . . ." If the student responds with *state*, remind him that he is to use the column and find a word beginning with *l*. Try to give clues pertaining to the student's environment since this association makes retention easier.

Guess the Word: Student Edition

The teacher picks the column, and the student selects the word and provides the clue. If a student can't think of a clue for a word, suggest that he pick another word. As students get better at this game, their clues naturally become more sophisticated; there is no need to teach the art of giving good clues.

Three Little Words

The word index can also be used to reinforce word associations and phonics principles. In this game, the teacher picks the column and decides on the topic. Using the first column of the word index following Lesson 8, the teacher might say, "In the first column, find three things that people or animals can eat." Allow the student ample time to locate *beef, beet,* and *bone*; if he seems frustrated, direct his attention to the **B** section of the column.

If you wish the student to review a phonics principle, indicate a particular column and say, for example, "Find three words that have a silent *e*." Be sure that the student does not simply point to the words; he should also pronounce them.

In working with the above word index activities, keep these suggestions in mind:

- Five minutes is reasonable for each activity. If you wish to use the word index for an extended period of time, vary the activities to avoid exceeding the student's attention span.

- A student who finds the lessons particularly difficult should use only half a column for each reinforcement activity.

- Even though the student is developing the habit of skimming in some of these activities, avoid teaching this reading skill at this point. You may want to encourage the student to let his eyes go down or up a column of words in an orderly fashion, but additional explanation is unnecessary.

- Give the student all the support he needs to complete the activity successfully. For example, if he has found two words in the Three Little Words activity but cannot find the third, give him a hint. All reinforcement activities should be presented as games rather than tests.

Word Index Activities Requiring Preparation

The following activities require preparation on your part. If your schedule does not allow you time for this, simply focus on the activities that can be totally conceived and completed during the class period.

It is recommended that you try to schedule some preparation time for reinforcement activities—even if it is only on an occasional basis.

Taking time to prepare these activities serves several purposes. First and foremost, these activities help the student.

Second, in constructing an activity, you are actually doing homework just as the student does. It is easy to forget what it's like to have to do homework in addition to fulfilling other daily responsibilities. And because we forget, we are sometimes too rigid in our expectations of what the student should be able to accomplish. By spending time now and then to design a reinforcement activity, we are more likely to appreciate just what the student is going through as he confronts his homework.

Third, the student appreciates your taking time to prepare an activity. Quite often the student is also more motivated to participate in the activity if you have designed it for him. But don't hold your breath waiting for compliments.

Flash Cards

Having the student read series of neatly printed words on 3 by 5 inch index cards is an excellent way to reinforce specific phonics skills and develop sight vocabulary. If time allows, give the student a stack of index cards and a list of words, and have him make his own cards. Otherwise, you should make the cards.

Use the flash cards for five to ten minutes. Some students, especially male adolescents, enjoy flash card activities in a Beat the Clock format using an egg timer. Not only do they like to see how many correct answers

they can produce before the time runs out, but also they enjoy keeping a chart of their improvement.

Use the following suggestions to help you develop flash card activities.

Phonics review. If a student has trouble mastering a particular phonics principle, this activity is extremely helpful. Do not use flash cards which pertain to a particular phonics principle until the student has formally studied it. Thus in most cases, you need merely to print the words that appear in a particular word chart. Take some time, however, to skim the word index that precedes the lesson you're working on for other pertinent words.

For example, while doing Lesson 14, the student may benefit from working with flash cards pertaining to vowel sounds preceding the letter *l*. In addition to using words that appear in the word chart for this lesson, you might also use *all, call, felt, girl, hole, role, well,* and *will*, which appear in the word index following Lesson 12.

It is not necessary to use all the words studied to date for this type of review. Twenty words illustrating a particular phonics principle are sufficient. Continue to use the set of phonics flash cards until the student can sound out the words or sight read them with minimal difficulty.

Categories. For this activity, you need fifteen flash cards. Again, refer to the appropriate word index to make sure you are using words the student has studied. Think of three categories, and then select five words the student has studied and can associate with each category.

To begin this activity, simply lay out the fifteen cards in neat rows, five cards across and three cards down. Have the student pronounce the words on all fifteen cards. Then tell the student the first category. For example, you might say, "Now, I want you to put all the words that name the parts of the body in the first row." After the student has done this correctly, go on to the second category. After he has completed this category, have him figure out the category for the remaining five words. Give clues if necessary.

Here is an example of how the flash cards are initially arranged for a student who has completed Lesson 5. The three categories are: Parts of the body, People, and Words which relate to money. Note that some words are plural. This gives the student additional practice with this ending.

aunts	bums	feet	hip	save
bank	dimes	friends	men	taxes
bet	face	heel	nose	women

Make a sentence. In this activity, each flash card contains a single word. Be sure to include words the student finds troublesome. If the word is especially difficult, use it in two or three sentences.

Also include capitalization and punctuation signals on the flash cards. The student quickly learns to use these clues while figuring out the correct arrangement. As the student's skill increases, increase the complexity of the sentences. Here is an example of index cards for a student to arrange after he has completed Lesson 14. Bear in mind that this student has completed similar activities many times during previous reinforcement sessions.

computer's   he   Jack   laugh.   minute
mistake,   saw   started   The   the   to

Before he begins, the student should pronounce any words you think may give him trouble. After he forms a sentence, he should read it. Notice that the sentence, "The minute Jack saw the computer's mistake, he started to laugh." relates to the story in Lesson 14. Correlating the story with the Make a sentence activity helps the student to focus his thinking.

What's the order? For this activity, entire sentences are printed on index cards. The teacher lays out five cards on which he has written one sentence per card. After the student has read the sentences, he is to put these sentences in the order that makes the most sense. Here is a set of cards designed for the student who has completed Lesson 4.

I had so much fun that I got home very late.
I phoned a friend to see if he wanted to go.
I rode on a bus to the park.
My friend refused to go.
I wanted to go to the park.

After the student has put the sentences in a sensible order, he should read them again. Occasionally, the student's ideas about the proper order differ from the teacher's. If the student can reasonably justify his sequence, consider it correct.

Matching. This activity requires five sentences and ten cards. Write the sentence beginnings on five cards and the sentence endings on the remaining cards. After the student has arranged the cards so that he has five complete sentences, he should read them. The student needs to read the fragments before he begins to arrange them only if he has great difficulty in sounding out or sight reading the words. The following example can be used for a student who has completed Lesson 13.

1. Andy wanted to celebrate because
2. Jack always put on a hat when he went out because
3. Mack really needed to take time and relax more because
4. Joan wasn't asked to go to the party because
5. Linda wanted to take a course at the high school because

A. he was starting to lose his hair.
B. she wanted to learn more about reading.
C. he had just won a new television set.
D. he was always losing his temper.
E. her friends knew she was out of town.

Go fish. This game reinforces both pronunciation and sight vocabulary. To prepare it, cut 26 index cards in half to make 52 smaller cards. Choose thirteen words, and write each word on four separate cards. As an example,

you might consider using these words for a student who has completed Lesson 6: *cute, feel, feet, hug, huge, know, phone, rule, talk, what, which, won't,* and *would.*

Most students recall having played this game during childhood. If not, explain that the object of the game is to get more books, or sets of four identical cards, than any other player. He gets books by asking his opponent for cards which match the set he wants to complete. For example, he may say, "Do you have any cards with the word *huge*?" If the opponent has no *huge* cards, the student asking for the card draws the top card from the face-down stack. If he happens to pick a card on which *huge* is printed, he gets another turn.

This game is more appropriate for a group of two or three students. The number of cards dealt to each player at the beginning of the game is determined by how many students are playing and how much time they have. Hands of seven to nine cards generally work well.

Individualized Exercises

Sometimes a student has difficulty with a particular skill. In spite of the fact that he has many opportunities to master this skill in Book 1, he may need additional practice.

For example, a student may have trouble with the silent letter combinations appearing in Lesson 10. Try designing a short exercise in which some of these silent letter words are used. Use the word index and the types of exercises that appear in Book 1 to help you. The highly motivated student is usually willing to complete this material for homework. Just be sure he understands what you want him to do. The less motivated student can complete the exercise during the time you've scheduled for reinforcement activities.

A Note to the Teacher

Because it takes time to prepare flash cards and individualized exercises, develop a system to organize and store these teaching aids for future use. Some students ask if they can take home sets of flash cards. This, of course, is for you to decide; but requesting that the student stay five or ten minutes after class to copy his own set is highly recommended. Also make sure that you file away at least one copy of any individualized exercise you create.

Additionally, do not pressure yourself to come up with something new every time you plan a reinforcement activity. It takes a few years to develop a solid file of reinforcement activities. And if you have neither the time nor energy to prepare an activity, just use one that requires no advance preparation.

Games and Other Activities

The following activities require no special preparation other than deciding whether or not they will benefit the student.

Spelling Quizzes

Spelling quizzes not only help students recall phonics rules and words with greater accuracy; they also help students become more comfortable in testing situations. But for the beginning student, spelling quizzes should be administered sparingly, perhaps after every four or five lessons. Students who demonstrate a knack for spelling derive greater benefit from a more challenging activity. And students who have decided difficulty with spelling often feel so defeated by spelling quizzes that it is advisable to emphasize correct spelling in less threatening situations—such as the lesson exercises and sentence writing.

Use the following suggestions in planning for spelling quizzes.

- Organizing principles such as *r*-controlled vowel words, days of the week, or numbers can be used. This type of organization is especially helpful for poor spellers.

- Have the student make all corrections to the right of the misspelled word. This way, both you and the student can easily spot troublesome items, and you can incorporate them in future reinforcement activities. Make sure the student develops the habit of drawing a line through the incorrect item to minimize the chance of confusing it with the correct version.

- Have the student keep all his spelling quizzes in one section of his composition book. This practice helps the student recall troublesome words quickly and provides an efficient way to monitor progress.

- If the student is a good speller, select fifteen words to dictate. After the student has completed the quiz, have him make any necessary corrections and read the corrected list. If he completes his homework on a consistent basis, tell him to study the troublesome words for homework and quiz him on these words at the beginning of the next lesson.

- If the student is a poor speller, select ten words to dictate. After each word, have the student make any necessary corrections and read the corrected word. Once the student has completed the quiz, have him read each word. Do not ask the student to study these words for homework unless you think he will benefit from a retest.

Silly Sally

This oral activity, based on a children's game called Crazy Grandma, uses many words the student has not yet formally studied. Thus the student soon realizes that many words adhere to phonics rules, and he comes to understand better the value of a phonics approach to reading.

For this activity, tell the student that he is going to review a phonics principle and that "Silly Sally" likes words that follow this principle but doesn't like words that don't. Then give the student three or four sentences which contain both a word that "Silly Sally" likes because it follows the principle and a word that she doesn't like because it does not follow

that principle. By that time, the student should have grasped the phonics principle and be able to make up his own sentences. For example, in a review of the long vowel sounds, your sentences might include:

- Silly Sally likes s<u>oa</u>p, but she doesn't like s<u>u</u>ds. (Note that the word which completes the *doesn't like* part of the sentence contains no long vowel sound.)
- Silly Sally likes Dave, but she doesn't like Dan.
- Silly Sally likes to boast, but she doesn't like to brag.

After each sentence, have the student explain the reason for Silly Sally's preference by stating the long vowel sound in that word. In addition to reinforcing long vowel sounds or any other phonics principle, the student also has some practice with word associations.

Word Scrabble

This activity, too, reinforces phonics skills. Twenty-six Scrabble tiles, one for each letter of the alphabet, are needed for this activity. With the letters exposed, the tiles should be placed in front of the student. As long as you keep the words simple, the student need not have studied all of them prior to playing. He should, however, be familiar with the phonics principle that underlies the words. Here is an example of how this game can be played with a student who has completed Lesson 9.

- Place the *y* tile to the right of the *a* and have the student make the sound for *ay*.
- Tell the student to listen carefully to your clue and then figure out what letter or letters need to be placed before the *ay* in order to make the correct word. For example, "I would like to come over to your house, but I don't know the . . ."
- After the student puts the *w* tile before the *ay,* he says *way.*
- The student is able to respond correctly to clues pertaining to *hay* and *ray* even though he hasn't yet studied these words. But avoid words with consonant blends at this point unless you think the student can easily figure out the answer. Consonant blends are not formally studied until Lesson 15.
- Vary the Word Scrabble game according to the student's needs. For example, you may give clues for missing vowels (*ball, bell, bill, bull*) or for consonant endings (*cop, cod, cob*). As the student's proficiency increases, the number of words and the nature of the clues can become more challenging.

Hangman

To play this game, you need paper and a pencil. Think of a secret word and draw short lines on the paper, one line for each letter of the word. Next to the lines, draw a gallows with a rope extending from the crossbeam.

Give the student a category for your secret word and have him guess a letter he thinks might be in the word. For example, if your secret word is *pretzel*, which appears in

Lesson 11, the category is snack food. The student may need to be reminded that all words have vowels, that *e* is the most commonly used vowel, and that vowels are a good starting point to figure out the answer.

Each time the student guesses a correct letter, write it on the appropriate line or lines. (The letter may appear more than once in the word.) Each time the student guesses a letter not appearing in the word, add one part of the body to the gallows. Begin with the head. The object of the game is to guess the secret word before the entire body is drawn. You and the student can decide the ground rules for the game. For example, if the student wants a lot of chances to guess the secret word, include facial features in your drawing, one feature per mistake.

Popular movie and song titles, athletic teams, and well-known phrases are sources for secret words. So are any specific words you want to review from the lessons. As long as the student is familiar with any key phonics principles appearing in the secret word, he can figure it out with little difficulty. For example, a student who has completed Lesson 11 on *r*-controlled vowels can easily figure out "The Star-Spangled Banner" even though he has not yet studied consonant blends.

Make sure that occasionally you and the student switch roles so that the student has the opportunity to "hang" you.

Magazine Games

Many puzzles and other activities can be found in puzzle magazines sold in most drugstores and supermarkets. A particular favorite with adolescents is "Word Find" in which listed words are to be found in a box of seemingly random letters. This game helps the student become more conscious of spelling and also improves his visual tracking and concentration. All you have to do is cross out any words on the list that are too difficult for your student to sound out or sight read.

Student-Requested Activities

From time to time, a student may need your help with something pertaining to his own needs, such as filling out a form or application or reading a letter or brochure. On an occasional basis, these are excellent reinforcement activities since they remind the student of the relevance of reading.

If the activity needs to be completed immediately, you may have to do most, if not all, the work. When time is not so crucial, however, allow the student to complete as much reading or writing as he can handle.

Some students develop the habit of bringing in a request more often than not. How you handle this situation will probably depend on the type of student you are working with.

If the student is an adult or older teen who has clearly defined learning goals which include being able to handle these outside reading and writing activities, then you should take these needs into serious consideration. Discuss with the student the fact that if he is to improve his reading skills, he must work regularly on the lessons and reinforcement activities. Then try to arrive at a mutually agreeable arrangement which allows time to deal with both the regularly scheduled work and the outside material that is important to him. Perhaps you can extend the amount of time you work with him. Or you may have to work out a schedule in which he covers the lessons and reinforcement activities at a slower pace.

If you suspect the student is bringing in outside materials to avoid working on a lesson, then you probably need to help him develop learning goals. Gently remind him, that, in the long run, his reading will progress more rapidly if he works through the lessons and reinforcement activities in an orderly fashion. If he is bringing in these materials simply to take up time, then he may call a halt to this practice. If the outside materials are truly important to him, then work with him to find a way of dealing with them. You may be able to work with him outside class, or if you are teaching in a traditional school setting, you may be able to refer him to a colleague, such as a guidance counselor, for assistance.

Student Writing

In addition to spelling work, the composition book is used for writing assignments. Because this reinforcement activity involves more explanation than the others, the topic of writing is discussed separately in the next chapter.

A Summary of Do's and Don'ts

1. Do make sure the scheduled lesson time is not sacrificed for reinforcement activities unless the student requires extra time to work on a specific problem area or needs a break. Because so many activities are games, the student—especially the adolescent—may try to talk you into shortening the lesson time and expanding the time for reinforcement activities. Explain that this, ultimately, hinders his progress.

2. Do plan and implement activities that address both the student's needs and sensitivities. For example, some students—particularly adults—think that flash cards are just for children. Take time to explain the value of this activity and gradually ease the student into it.

3. Do observe the student's concentration during these activities. If you notice his attention flagging, switch to another activity. Your ability to select and pace activities improves naturally with time and practice. Be patient.

4. Do have the student keep a composition book for his spelling and writing work. This book provides a sense of order and gives the student a sense of accomplishment.

5. Do occasionally develop your own reinforcement activities rather than relying solely on activities that

require no preparation. Remember to save your materials for future use.

6. Don't foster a "here's-some-more-hard-work" attitude toward the reinforcement activities. The student has just finished reviewing his homework, studying a lot of new words, and reading a story. He needs a little more informality from you for this segment of the lesson if the reinforcement activities are to benefit him.

7. Don't foster a "this-is-just-for-fun" attitude either. A student might not find the activities enjoyable. And you want the student who does find them enjoyable to recognize that pleasure and learning can go hand in hand.

8. Don't omit reinforcement activities for the student who is progressing smoothly through the lessons. Writing exercises and spelling tests are particularly helpful.

9. Don't ignore student requests. Discuss with him how the materials he brings to class contribute to his learning goals, and if he is serious about working with them, try to arrive at a mutually satisfactory arrangement.

10. Don't do all the work for a student when he brings in a request. For example, if a student has a letter he wants you to read to him, have him sight read or sound out as many words as he can. In this way, the student has a concrete example that learning to read is, indeed, a worthwhile goal.

7. Writing

Because the major purpose of this reading series is to help the student develop his reading skills, less emphasis has been placed on writing skills. Even though writing is an important skill, it is a distinct skill that requires a great deal of practice and instructional time. Some students, if they don't improve their reading skills fairly rapidly, soon regard reading as a hopeless goal and drop out mentally and perhaps physically. Writing is subordinated to reading so the pace of the lessons can respond to the need of some students for immediate results.

In Book 1, objectives pertaining to writing include legibility, accurate copying, and writing sentences. All students are expected to complete the activities and exercises pertaining to these objectives. If your students express a desire to do more or different kinds of writing, by all means, incorporate additional writing instruction and activities into the curriculum.

If you have a student who becomes discouraged when he learns that he must write sentences containing words he has just learned to read, try to allay his anxieties. The following list of reasons for writing may help.

Use this list judiciously. When a student wants to know why he has to write sentences as a reinforcement activity or for homework, give him a reason that pertains to his particular needs. For example, if the student is a poor speller, cite the first reason. Do not overwhelm the student by mentioning too many reasons at once.

- Writing helps to improve spelling.
- Writing helps a student to increase his sight vocabulary.
- It helps a student to remember definitions of words.
- It helps the student to formulate and express his thoughts more precisely. This type of thinking helps him to complete the exercises more rapidly.
- It develops the student's reasoning skills as he learns to monitor whether or not his writing makes sense.
- Knowing how to write sentences is part of what the student needs to know in order to develop skill in other types of writing he may want to do, such as letters and short paragraphs on job applications.
- Writing is a part of literacy. Even though this series emphasizes reading, to be literate the student must be able to write.
- Only through actually writing can the student see that he is able to write.

Guidelines for Writing Assignments

The writing assignment that students using Book 1 find most helpful and least threatening is to write original sentences using words they have studied in the lessons. Both the teacher and the student should be involved in selecting the words to be used.

The number of sentences and whether or not the student writes sentences as a reinforcement activity in class or as part of his regular homework assignment depends on the teacher's assessment. If a student is having a difficult time with the lessons in general, use sentence writing as a class activity. As a general guideline, consider having the student write four sentences, each of which contains one vocabulary word. This allows for ample time to complete the lesson and do one or two other reinforcement activities. As his reading and writing show considerable improvement, you can begin to assign him occasional sentence writing for homework.

The student who is progressing fairly smoothly through the lessons can be asked to write ten sentences on an occasional basis for homework. *Occasional* means no more than one writing assignment a week for the student who meets with the teacher on a daily basis. If the student meets less frequently with the teacher, more writing can be assigned. Be sure to avoid having the student write sentences on days when this is part of the current lesson.

Also keep in mind that completing the lesson exercises has priority over writing sentences. If the student's circumstances don't allow him time to complete both the exercises and the writing assignment for homework, restrict writing to the reinforcement segment of the lesson. As the student improves and needs less time to complete the exercises, he can then take on the additional responsibility of writing sentences for homework.

Generally speaking, writing should not be assigned as either a reinforcement activity or for homework until the student has completed Lesson 5. Before then, the student needs time to become comfortable with you, the lesson format, the class routine, and homework. If the student seems to have trouble adapting to the reading class, wait until he is more comfortable before you introduce writing.

The Composition Book

Both spelling quizzes and writing assignments should be kept in a composition book. A slim, loose-leaf binder with wide-lined notebook paper is recommended. This composition book enables both the student and the teacher to quickly review the student's progress. Additionally, the student develops a sense of pride in keeping his work in an orderly fashion. Encourage the student to keep all his spelling work in one section of the book and all his writing in another.

Have the student date his work. As the reading class progresses, most students enjoy looking back now and then at all the writing they've done. It is not uncommon to hear a student exclaim, "Wow, look at the baby sentences I was writing last September!"

As with the exercises, the student should correct each error in his original sentences. Because the student has become accustomed to this procedure in reviewing the exercises, he usually does not mind it. What he may balk at is hearing that he has to rewrite the sentences in correct form, preferably in ink, for homework. Whether or not the student chooses to print, write, or type both his initial sentences and the corrected versions is not important just so long as the revised work is as conscientiously accurate as possible.

Take some time to explain to the student that in rewriting his sentences, he gets used to writing standard English and seeing his work in correct form. More is said about this matter in the next section, Correcting Writing Assignments.

Experience indicates that most students like to keep their composition books in the following manner.

- On the first right-hand page, the student enjoys creating a title page. He should choose his own title. Just give him the help he needs with spelling and capitalization. Make sure the student's name appears on this page.

- On the back of the title page and all subsequent left-hand pages, the first drafts of writing assignments appear with their necessary corrections and a compliment from the teacher. Even though the teacher may need to read this compliment to the student, the student appreciates this reinforcement. And often he enjoys showing this comment to others.

- Opposite each first draft of a writing assignment, on the right-hand pages, the revised sentences appear. Encourage the student to use a pen for all his revision work. The revised sentences should also be corrected and accompanied by a compliment from the teacher.

Correcting Writing Assignments

Students enjoy learning the concept, *first draft*. They need to know that the pieces of writing they see in newspapers, magazines, and books are *not* first drafts, but the result of much revision and editing. The realization that anyone who writes also revises and edits makes these tasks more tolerable. Remind the student that this process becomes easier with practice.

The student needs to correct each error to establish patterns which apply both to future writing assignments and to reading. For example, adding an *s* to a plural noun helps the student to pay more attention to plural endings he encounters in the lessons.

The procedure is the same for correcting both the first draft and the revision.

1. The student reads the sentence.

2. In the order the errors appear, you explain any changes the student needs to make.

3. If the sentence contains one or two errors, the student makes the correction; otherwise, you should make them.

4. The student reads the corrected sentence.

5. If you think it necessary and if time permits, the student reads all his sentences after correcting them.

Dealing with Typical Writing Problems

The following six sections suggest ways of helping beginning student writers deal with problems they frequently encounter. Use these suggestions to help you plan your work with the student, but remember they are only suggestions.

Misspelled Words

If the student misspells a word he has previously studied, refer him to the correct spelling in the Word Index or a lesson. Encourage the student to use these resources in his writing.

If the student misspells a word he has not yet studied, tell him the correct spelling. If the student wonders what he is supposed to do when he wants to use a word he doesn't know how to spell, tell him to spell it the best he can and that he can make any necessary corrections in class.

Grammatical Errors

With teacher assistance, many students can correct most grammatical errors. For example, a student has just read his sentence using the word *yesterday*: "I wake up yesterday." Ask the student how he would say this if he were talking to a friend. Most students respond, "I woke up yesterday."

Have the student reread his sentence, distinguish between what he just said and what he's written, and make the correction. If the student doesn't know how to spell the correct word, have him say the word, paying attention to its pronunciation. If the student still has difficulty, spell the word for him.

Another reason for waiting until the student has completed Lesson 5 to start sentence writing is that you have time to familiarize yourself with your student's speech patterns. If you know that a student often uses the present tense of a verb when he should be using the past tense, simply state the correction and have the student make it on his paper.

Short Sentences

Most students do not have trouble writing complete thoughts. More often, students need to add more information to make the sentence more interesting.

Consider the following example written by a student working with the word *woman*: "I am a woman." Have the student read her sentence and ask her how she feels about being a woman. After a brief discussion, ask her to figure out a way of adding some of what she has just said to her sentence. Her revised sentence might be: "I am a woman, and I think men have a better life." The student may dictate the revision or she may revise it herself. Then have the student read her new sentence and compare it with the first draft to see how the revision gives the sentence more life.

Students who habitually write short sentences often find a word quota helps them develop more substantive sentences. For example, tell your student to try writing ten-word sentences. The word quota should be based on your assessment of the student's ability. Do not bother to establish one unless a student's sentences are chronically brief.

Run-on Sentences

This situation demands consummate tact on your part because, invariably, the student thinks he has written a terrific sentence and is dismayed to learn that he has to divide it into three or four shorter sentences. Respond by saying that his first draft would make perfect sense if someone listened to him read it. And that since he wrote the sentence, it undoubtedly makes sense to him. But by using commas and periods wherever necessary, he helps other readers to follow his thoughts more easily.

Revise the run-on sentence as necessary. Then to illustrate how punctuation helps the reader, read both the first draft and the revision to the student. Ask him to explain the difference between the two readings. After he has noted that your voice never stopped in the first reading, be sure to commend him for his effort and reassure him that learning how to use these punctuation marks correctly comes with practice.

Omitted Words

When reading their sentences aloud to the teacher, students are often surprised to see that they have omitted words. Remind the student that many writers have this problem because the mind can think faster than the hand can write. Suggest to the student that after he has written his sentences, he should read them to himself, pointing to each word as he encounters it. This strategy will help him learn to monitor his errors.

Teach the student how to use a caret (∧). Explain that writers use this mark to indicate where words need to be inserted in a sentence. Then show him how to insert the omitted words above the caret. Tell the student to use this mark whenever he omits something in his writing.

Confusing Sentences

After the student has read a sentence which falls into this category, tell him you don't understand what he's trying to express and ask him to explain what he meant. Once you understand his intent, start a more coherent version of his sentence at the bottom of the paper and have him finish it. How much writing you actually do should be determined by the student's skill and the complexity of the thought. After the student has read the revision, ask him if it matches what he meant. If not, work on the sentence until the revision accurately expresses the student's original idea. Make sure the original sentence is crossed out so that the student doesn't include it in his rewrite by mistake.

Recopying the Corrected Sentences

For the typical student, recopying the corrected sentences on the right-hand pages of the composition book is not an easy task. Generally speaking, the beginning writer is not used to any kind of extensive writing activity. He is also not used to having to spell so many words correctly at one time. Thus the student often regards copying as an excruciating task.

Students tend to fall into two categories. Fastidious students, overly anxious about the appearance of their revisions, usually tear up their papers whenever they make an error and start over again. Other students, unaware of the importance of concentration in copying, tend to copy their original errors as well as make new ones.

Have the student begin his first rewrite assignment during the last five minutes while you are jotting down words or activities you wish to stress in the next lesson. Observe the student's working habits.

If your student is fastidious, you will soon hear the sound of pages being angrily ripped out of the notebook. Explain that copying requires patience and practice and make appropriate suggestions from the guidelines below.

The second type of student usually has all his sentences written before the five minutes have elapsed. Take some time to go over his work with him. Invariably it contains many spelling errors and omissions. Explain that copying requires patience and concentration and ask him to recopy his sentences for homework.

Use the following guidelines to help you plan this recopying work. Explain the first three items before a student copies any revisions. Mention other items as necessary.

- Write legibly on the right-hand pages of the composition book. A pen is preferable to a pencil or typewriter.
- Observe both left and right margins. If the student's paper has no margin lines, have him draw them in with a ruler. The width of the margins is your decision. Explain that margins contribute to a neat appearance of the work and make copying easier.
- Number and skip a line between each sentence. This practice also contributes to a neater paper and easier copying.
- Read each sentence after copying it and take a few seconds to compare it with the corrected version on the left-hand page. In this way, the student learns to monitor his own errors.

- Draw a line through each misspelled word and write the correct spelling above. If the student notices he has made a spelling error immediately after writing a word, he should draw a line through it, write the word correctly next to the error, and then finish his sentence.
- Draw a caret and insert missing words as necessary.
- If an entire sentence is omitted, write it after the last sentence. The sentences do not have to appear in exactly the same order as they were written in the first draft.
- If an entire sentence is incorrect—for example, because it consists of the beginning of one sentence and the end of another—draw a line through it and write it correctly after the last sentence.

The student should probably recopy his work once more if he has made more than five errors. Because the practice of using margins is so new to most students, ignoring margins does not count as an error. Also, mistakes which the student has corrected himself do not count as errors. An error is any mistake that the student has completely failed to notice.

Situations do occur in which the student has noticed all his mistakes and corrected them properly. But he has made so many corrections in his revision that it looks no different from his first draft. Give the student some time at the end of the class period to write another revision.

Such detailed guidelines for recopying are necessary because the beginning writer usually needs a high degree of structure to complete an activity that is essentially foreign to him. Students may grumble at what they regard as unnecessary pickiness on your part; but in the long run, they usually appreciate these guidelines. Be sure that you equally appreciate the student's situation by giving him reminders about copying when necessary and complimenting him for completing a task which requires great patience and concentration.

A Summary of Do's and Don'ts

1. Do have the student keep an orderly composition book for all his sentence writing.
2. Don't assign any sentence writing until the student has had time to adjust to the class and your teaching style.
3. Do allow the student to help select the words he will use for writing the sentences.
4. Do make sure that all writing work is corrected.
5. Do keep in mind that revising and editing are difficult for most students and assist them in this work in whatever way you can.
6. Don't allow writing assignments to interfere with the student's lesson and other necessary reinforcement activities.

8. Using the Lesson Notes

As part of class preparation, you need to read only the notes for the lesson you are about to teach. Because you are already familiar with principles and procedures that pertain to all the lessons from reading the previous chapters in this manual, you have the necessary foundation for sound instructional practices. The lesson notes merely address some specifics.

Keep in mind that all the lesson notes are to be considered as suggestions based on the experience of other reading teachers. If you try one of the suggestions a few times and find it doesn't work, disregard it. For example, a few students are so overwhelmed by any work with contractions beyond learning how to read and pronounce them that any more said on this subject is counterproductive. Suggestions about contractions often appear in the lesson notes because most students can understand this information. If your student can't, ignore the suggestions until you think he is ready for them.

The Lesson Titles

The lesson titles appear mostly for the teacher's benefit. They provide a quick glimpse of the phonics principle emphasized in each lesson. The only terms appearing in the titles that are helpful to the student in his work are long and short vowels, consonants, silent letters, and the hard and soft *c* and *g*. The student does not need to know other terms which appear in the titles, such as *r*-controlled vowels, consonant blends, and digraphs.

Items of Primary and Secondary Emphasis

The items listed under **primary emphasis** require extensive teaching because the material involved is new to the student. In most cases, the items listed in this section deal with phonics principles and oral reading. Oral reading is to be construed as everything the student reads aloud— the words, the story, and the exercises. Oral reading always receives primary emphasis because the student is applying what he is learning to all parts of the lesson.

Items listed under **secondary emphasis**, on the other hand, are skills for which the student does not need instruction so much as he needs practice. For example, once the student has worked with context clues, he rarely needs to hear any more about how to discern meaning from context. He just needs practice in doing it. Occasionally, an item normally receiving secondary emphasis such as using context clues, is listed under **primary emphasis**. The reason for this is that more emphasis than usual has been given to a particular skill in order to review and assess the student's progress.

Story

You will notice that only a few of the lesson notes contain suggestions for dealing with the story segment of the lesson. Also, the notes contain no explanations for one of the items listed as receiving secondary emphasis in each lesson—story comprehension through oral discussion.

As the detailed discussion on the student's reading and comprehension of the story in Chapter 4 emphasizes, this segment of the lesson demands more flexibility on the teacher's part than any other. Students vary greatly in attention span, vocabulary, decoding skills, sight reading ability, and motivation. If you experience difficulty helping a particular student with the story reading and comprehension, take some time to review the procedures for helping various types of students discussed in Chapter 4. Even if your particular student seems to defy all categories, the suggestions provided may help you to develop your own procedures. Additional suggestions which apply to a specific story would probably be of little value.

Remember that the key to helping students make the greatest gains in the least amount of time is observation. Carefully monitoring your student's progress will help you to develop sound procedures for oral reading and comprehension.

Developing Your Own Notes

Develop the habit of keeping your own notes. Often you will hit upon an excellent way to present a certain skill or concept. Take some time to jot down your idea, especially if you know that you won't have the opportunity to use it again until a much later time. So much patience and concentration is called for in teaching reading that it's easy to forget these great ideas.

Also use notes to remind yourself of modifications, specific words, or reinforcement activities that you want to use with your student. This manual has emphasized many times how important good observation is. But often the teacher's ability to observe the student's progress is hindered when, in the middle of a lesson, he is frantically trying to remember what the student needs to review. Taking notes means that you really don't have to remember anything except, of course, to skim your notes just prior to the lesson. Your full attention can be on the student's work.

If you have a busy schedule, end the lesson five minutes early and write down any remarks or reminders about the student's work at that time. It certainly does not hurt the student to see that you, too, do work for this class.

9. Lesson Notes for Book 1

Lesson 1

The Long and Short Vowels

Primary Emphasis

- Long and short vowels
- Single consonant sounds
- Oral reading

Secondary emphasis

- Story comprehension (oral discussion)
- Legible handwriting
- Accuracy in copying material
- The silent *e* rule
- Using context clues

Chart

1. As you know, the word *a* is not pronounced as a long *a* when reading. *A* is the first word introduced because students can recognize it immediately and are off to a successful start. Generally, students pronounce *a* as a long *a* in the early lessons. Don't worry. As their skill in reading improves, students pronounce *a* as they would in conversation.

2. The silent *e* rule. The student first encounters the silent *e* when he sounds out the word *name*. Use the following procedure to help explain this rule.

   - After the student sounds out *name*, draw his attention to the fact that he did not pronounce the *e*.

   - Tell the student that any letter in a word that isn't sounded out is called a silent letter. Make sure the student knows what the word *silent* means.

   - Have the student notice that the final *e*'s are called silent *e*'s and that they are a signal to the reader that the vowel is long.

   - Reassure the student that it's not necessary for him to fully understand the silent *e* rule just now; he will get much practice using this rule in the lessons. For now, you are just introducing this rule because it is such a helpful one.

     Be prepared to repeat this explanation of the silent *e* rule as often as necessary. By the fourth or fifth lesson, students usually have no trouble using this rule to sound out new words.

3. Two different sounds are listed for the long *u* (*rule* and *use*). This discrepancy is a mild source of confusion for the student. An elaborate explanation is not necessary. If the student gives you a "this is impossible" look, reassure him that many things which seem strange now will, with practice, become manageable.

4. Do not expect the student to sound out the word *Eddie*. Either tell the student this word or help him sound out the first syllable and tell him the rest. Explain that Eddie is one of the characters in the story.

Words for Study

1. *o'clock*: After the student has said this word or you have pronounced it for him, point to the apostrophe and say, "This mark is called an apostrophe. You'll be seeing these a lot as you work through this book." There is no need to go into any detail.

2. *Mr.*: Most students recognize this word. If not, pronounce it and say, "Notice that it's spelled with a capital *M* and has a period after it." There is no need to go into any further detail about abbreviations or capitalization unless the student is curious and progressing smoothly through the work. Generally speaking, when instances of abbreviations or capitalized words occur in any of the lessons, draw the student's attention to the spelling of these words, but do not trouble him with explanations or rules.

Story

The word endings -*ed* and -*ing* appear in the story. Help the student pronounce these endings as he comes to them during the oral reading. There is no need for a phonetic or grammatical explanation. Do encourage the student to pronounce these endings correctly as this will help him with both spelling and specific exercises in later lessons.

Exercise 1: Copying Sentences

In sentence 4, the student encounters his first plural word, *rules*. After the student has read the sentence, and mistakes have been corrected, ask him, "Do you know the difference between *one rule* and *a lot of rules*?" Usually the student does. If not, give a brief explanation. It is not necessary to formally introduce the concepts *singular* and *plural*.

Exercise 2: Word Sounds

1. The student has not studied all the words in the left column. Help him to sound them out according to the method used with the word chart. Be sure to emphasize that, even in the first lesson, the student is able to apply what he has learned to new situations. This support not only bolsters the student's confidence but also helps him to recognize the value of a phonics approach to reading.

2. The student must use context clues in order to complete the items. Many students do not realize that they must consider the entire sentence in order to fill in the

blanks. Use the following guidelines to help you preview this exercise.

- Inform the student that he will be seeing many sentences like these in this book. The best way to figure out the answers is to read the sentence and say *blank* whenever a line appears.
- Read the first sentence to the student in the manner: "*Blank* did not have *blank* to go to the park."
- Have the student read the sentence in the same manner.
- Have the student reread the two words to be used in this sentence. Usually the student has no trouble deciding where to use *time* and *Tim* correctly. If he does have difficulty, however, have him read the sentence in the same manner again.
- Compliment the student for having figured out the answer and remind him that he will be using this procedure often in future lessons.

Note

At the end of the lesson, compliment the student in general for the work he has accomplished. If he seems overwhelmed by all this new material, remind him that this is the first lesson, that he has done very well, and that he will become accustomed to the work more quickly than he thinks is possible.

Lesson 2
More Work with Long and Short Vowels

Primary emphasis

- Long and short vowels
- Single consonant sounds
- Oral reading

Secondary emphasis

- Story comprehension (oral discussion)
- Legible and accurate handwriting
- The silent *e* rule
- Using context clues

Chart

1. Again, two different sounds are listed for the long *u*. A helpful reinforcement activity is to make flash cards for the nine long *u* words which the student has studied so far. Put no pressure on the student to sight read these words. Rather, encourage him to sound them out.

2. Because the student has not yet studied the digraphs *wh* and *ch*, do not expect him to sound out the words *which* and *when*. Either tell the student these words or help him to sound out the vowels and tell him the rest. Mention that the student will see these words in the lesson.

Words for Study

1. *without*: Mentioning the concept of compound words only confuses the student at this point. The concept is introduced in a later lesson.

2. *relaxed*: The form of all words appearing in the Words for Study is the same as those in the story. Again, encourage the student to pronounce this ending correctly.

3. *let's*: After the student has pronounced this word, point to the apostrophe and ask him if he remembers what this mark is called. If he doesn't, tell him. No additional explanation is necessary.

Story

The possessive words *Bob's* and *Dan's* appear in this story. Concentrate on pronunciation. Students understand what is being communicated; introducing the concept of possessives may confuse them.

Exercise 2: Word Sounds

Keep the following points in mind during your preview of this exercise.

- The student has not studied all the words in the left column. Help him to sound out the words. Again, support him in his effort to apply what he has learned to new situations.
- The student may not know what the word *cope* means. Remember that a student will not always admit difficulty with a definition. If you sense confusion, simply ask him if he knows the meaning of the word. Refer to the Vocabulary section of Chapter 3 in this manual for suggestions on teaching definitions.
- If the student has forgotten the procedure for working with context clues, remind him that the first sentence should be read as, "Mom needed a *blank* box for the roses." To help the student remember this procedure, have him read the sentence in the same way before he fills in the answer. Whenever necessary in subsequent previews, remind the student to say *blank* when he encounters the line in sentences involving context clues.

Lesson 3
More Work with Long and Short Vowels

Primary emphasis

- Long and short vowels
- Single consonant sounds
- Oral reading

Secondary emphasis

- Story comprehension (oral discussion)
- Legible and accurate handwriting
- Using context clues
- The silent *e* rule

Story

After the student reads the title, point to the apostrophe in *Eddie's* and ask the student what the mark is called. If he doesn't remember, remind him.

Exercises

No words in the exercises are new. In your preview work with the student, by sure he pronounces the -*s* and -*ed* endings correctly. Also continue to support his increased proficiency in sounding out words.

Lesson 4
Changing the First Consonant Sound

Primary emphasis

- Long and short vowels
- Single consonant sounds
- Oral reading

Secondary emphasis

- Story comprehension (oral discussion)
- Using context clues
- Legible and accurate handwriting
- The silent *e* rule

Chart

1. *refuse*: Cover the *re* and have the student say or sound out *fuse*. Have the student sound out the first syllable. Then have him say the word.
2. Because of the rhyme scheme used in this lesson, most students have little difficulty pronouncing the word sets. Spend more time than you ordinarily would in the random review of the chart so that the words will make a bit more of a lasting impression upon the student.

Words for Study

didn't: After the student pronounces *didn't*, review the word *apostrophe*. At this point, the student is ready for more detail about this punctuation mark. First ask the student if he knows what two words make up *didn't*. If he doesn't, tell him that *didn't* is another way of saying *did not*. Have him write *did not* on paper. Then ask the student to compare *didn't* with *did not* and find the difference. After the student has noted the missing *o*, explain that the apostrophe stands for this letter in *didn't*.

Whether or not you actually use the word *contraction* in your explanation should depend on your assessment of the student's ability to make sense of grammatical terms.

Some students are so intimidated by them that it's not worth mentioning. If the student seems to be struggling with the material in general, save your explanation of contractions until he's ready for it.

Exercise 1: Word Sounds

Some words in the left column are new to the student. Help him to sound out the words.

Note

By now, the pattern for legible and accurate handwriting should be well established. Thus it will no longer be mentioned in the list of objectives. This does not mean that writing has ceased to be important. Continue to have the student correct misspellings and items such as uncrossed *t*'s and open *a*'s.

Lesson 5
Changing the End Consonant Sound

Primary emphasis

- Long and short vowels
- Single consonant sounds
- Oral reading

Secondary emphasis

- Story comprehension (oral discussion)
- The ending -*ed*
- Using context clues

Chart

Some common vocabulary difficulties that occur in this lesson are *mute, muse, fuse, wed,* and *pod*. Because there may be more words that the student doesn't know, use the procedure for teaching definitions for only a few words. For the remainder, simply tell the student what the word means. For example, if the student does not know the meaning of the word *pod*, tell him that's what peas grow in. If the student grumbles about learning all these words he has no use for, gently remind him that:

- he will be seeing many of these words in later lessons.
- he just never knows when he is going to have use for a word.
- sounding out a word he's never heard of is quite an accomplishment.

Words for Study

1. *it's* and *don't*: Use the same procedure for teaching these contractions as you did for the word *didn't* in Lesson 4.
2. *Mrs.* and *Ms.*: After pronouncing these words, draw the student's attention to their spelling.

Exercise 1: Adding -ed

This exercise presents the student with his first formal spelling work. However, the teacher should be aware of two additional reasons for this exercise. The student has an opportunity to review eighteen words that he has studied, and he has practice using the -ed ending. Because some students have trouble correctly pronouncing this ending, this exercise is helpful. Do not expect the student to remember the spelling rules. He is merely becoming familiar with the fact that spelling rules exist. Concentrate instead on the pronunciation of the words. Use the following guidelines to help you preview this exercise.

- Tell the student that he is going to get some practice adding -ed to words he has studied. Unless the student asks for a definition, it is not necessary to discuss the meaning of past tense verbs.

- Have the student read *look*, note the -ed, and observe how the -ed has been added to *look* in the example.

- Have the student pronounce *look* and *looked* and note the difference in the pronunciation.

- Have the student read *last*, note the -ed, and write *lasted* on the line, using *looked* as a model. He is then to pronounce *last* and *lasted* and note the difference.

- After using this same procedure for the second and third columns, have the student add the -ed ending to *talk, joke,* and *pat* to make sure he understands how to complete this exercise.

- It is helpful for the student to recognize that he is dropping the final *e* in spelling the words in the second column and doubling the last letter for the third column words. However, don't explain these rules unless the student requests this information. The fact that he can pronounce the words correctly and perceive spelling patterns is enough.

- Make sure the student can pronounce the remaining words to be completed for homework.

Exercise 2: Word Sounds

None of the words at the left are new.

Lesson 6
Ending Consonant Blends

Primary emphasis

- Ending consonant blends: *nd, nt, ck, mp*
- Short vowel sounds
- Oral reading

Secondary emphasis

- Story comprehension (oral discussion)
- The ending -ed
- Using context clues

Chart

1. Because the words in each group rhyme, most students have little difficulty pronouncing them. Spend more time than usual in a random review of the chart.

2. Use the procedure for teaching definitions with only a few words. Simply tell the student the meaning of the remaining unfamiliar vocabulary words.

3. *can't* and *won't*: Use the same procedure as you did with the word *didn't* in Lesson 4.

4. No detailed explanation is needed of the sound for *y* in *lucky*. The student studies the sounds for *y* in Lesson 9.

Words for Study

Explain *wasn't* the same way you explained contractions in earlier lessons.

Story

Many instances of inflected endings appear in this story. Emphasize the correct pronunciation.

Exercise 2: Word Sounds

All the words at the left appear in the chart for this lesson.

Lesson 7
More Work with Ending Consonant Blends

Primary emphasis

- Ending consonant blends: *ng* and *nk*
- Oral reading
- Vowel review

Secondary emphasis

- Story comprehension (oral discussion)
- The ending -ing
- Using context clues

Chart

1. Again, because of the rhyme, students have little difficulty with these word groups. Extend the random review time.

2. The student should not be expected to sound out the *th* in *thing, thank,* and *think*. These three words are troublesome for most students. Have the student make up a few sentences for each of these words. Whether he does this orally or in writing depends on your assessment of his progress.

3. The student will not be familiar with the *wr* combination in *wrong*. Explain that the *w* is silent.

Exercise 1: Adding -ing

The student should experience no difficulty with this exercise. Be sure he notices he is using the same procedure here as he did with the ending -ed.

Exercise 2: Word Sounds

The student has not studied all the words at the left. Help him to sound them out by applying the same method used in the word chart.

Lesson 8
Review of Vowels and Consonants

Primary emphasis

- Long and short vowels
- Single consonant sounds
- Oral reading

Secondary emphasis

- Story comprehension (oral discussion)
- Using context clues
- *A* and *an*
- Matching synonyms
- Writing sentences

Chart

1. Extend the random review time.
2. Use the procedure for teaching definitions with only a few words. Simply tell the student the meaning of the remaining unfamiliar vocabulary words.

Words for Study

Spend some time with *were* and *where*. Point to one of the words and have the student use it in a sentence. Then do the same with the other. As an alternative procedure, use one word at a time in a sentence and have the student point to the word you are using.

Exercise 1: Word Sounds

Some words at the left are new to the student.

Exercise 2: Using *a* and *an*

Teach the difference between *a* and *an* during the preview. Make sure the student can correctly pronounce *an*. Some students confuse *an* and *and*. Use oral examples to explain the use of *an*. A helpful one is "Eddie ate *an* apple, but Bob ate *a* banana." If you remember the "Silly Sally" game, adapting it to the *a/an* rule helps the student. This game is explained in the chapter on reinforcement activities.

Exercise 4: Words That Mean the Same

The student is introduced to synonyms, matching, and process of elimination. Use the following guidelines for your work during the preview.

- Make sure the student can pronounce all the words.

- Avoid using the term *synonym*. At this point, the words *same thing* are easier for the student to understand.

- Have the student read the first item, which has been completed for him. Draw his attention to the check mark before *huge*.

- Have the student do one item on his own. Remind him to check off his choice after he's used it and to follow this procedure when he completes the exercise for homework.

- Tell him he does not have to complete the work in order. If he has trouble with a word, he can skip it and come back to it later. Casually mention that this method is called working by *process of elimination*. Emphasize this concept during the review period of the next class.

Exercise 5: Writing Sentences

The student encounters his first sentence writing. When he knows the new words, have him read the first question. After he thinks about it briefly, have him write his response. Assist him as necessary. His finished product should look something like "When it is time to quit, I relax." Or "When it is time to quit, I keep on working."

Note

Because this lesson contains more exercises and new material than previous lessons, allow more time to preview it.

Lesson 9
Vowel Sounds for *y*

Primary emphasis

- Vowel sounds for *y*
- *-y* as a suffix
- Words that end in *-ly*
- Oral reading

Secondary emphasis

- Story comprehension (oral discussion)
- Using context clues
- Matching synonyms

Chart

Make sure the student recognizes that days of the week are capitalized. Learning to spell the days is a good reinforcement activity. The student who is progressing well can also learn their abbreviations.

Words for Study

At this point, the student can begin to sound out some of these words. In this lesson, have him sound out *yet* and *what's*. Teach this contraction as you have the others.

Exercise 1: Adding -y to Words

Make sure the student can pronounce the examples. Have him note that the *y* in these words sounds like long *e*. Have him pronounce and complete *fussy, nosy,* and *sunny* during the preview session. If he still seems confused, he should also complete the next set during the preview.

Exercise 2: Words That End in -*ly*

Make sure the student can pronounce the sound for -*ly* and the words in the left column.

Exercise 3: More Words That End in *y*

Emphasize pronunciation rather than spelling in the note. Make sure the student can pronounce all the words in the left column.

Exercise 4: Words That Mean the Same

Review process of elimination during the preview. Have the student review the pronunciation of the words in the left column and complete the first two items (or any two items he wishes) to make sure he remembers how to do this type of exercise.

Lesson 10
Silent Letters

Primary emphasis

- Silent letters: *kn, wr, mb, ght, tch*
- Oral reading
- Using context clues

Secondary emphasis

- Story comprehension (oral discussion)
- Matching antonyms
- Word associations (choosing the unrelated word)

Chart

As the student works on sounding out these words, he may find it helpful to draw a line through the silent letters.

Words for Study

1. Many students find the chart work relatively easy but have trouble with these words when they appear in the story. Before the student reads the story aloud, review the chart words appearing in the story. For example, point to *match* in the first paragraph and have the student say it.

2. Even if you have worked with the definition of *numb* during the chart work, review its meaning. This helps the student to better understand the story.

Exercise 1: Word Sounds

Some words are new to the student.

Exercise 2: Word Opposites

Use the same procedure for antonymns as you did for synonyms. Include the term *process of elimination* in your explanation. Also, use the word *opposite* rather than *antonym*.

Exercise 3: Word Study

This is a new type of exercise for the student. Use the following guidelines for the preview.

- Explain that in each line he is going to see one word that does not fit with the rest.
- Have the student read the example and explain why *yesterday* is the right answer.
- After he has demonstrated an understanding of the directions and example, have him complete the second item. If he is still confused, have him complete the third item.
- Spot check words you think the student may have trouble either sounding out or sight reading. *Ant, guy,* and *fussy* sometimes cause difficulty.

Lesson 11
The *r*-Controlled Vowels

Primary emphasis

- The *r*-controlled vowels: *ar, are, or, er, eer, ir, ur*
- The endings -*er* and -*ier*
- Oral reading

Secondary emphasis

- Story comprehension (oral discussion)
- Using context clues

Chart

1. Students often have trouble distinguishing between the sounds for *ar* and *are*. The difference between the sounds for *er* and *eer* is also difficult for many students. Make sure the students know *car, care, her,* and *beer* well enough to sight read them. These cue words will help them in future lessons. For example, if the students can't sound out *dart* in Lesson 12, write *car* on the page and underline the *ar*. They should then be able to sound out *dart*. Review the cue words occasionally to reinforce retention.

2. Point out that the sound for *er, ir,* and *ur* is the same. This will help the student with words containing this sound.

Words for Study

I'm and *there's*: Teach these contractions as you did those in earlier lessons.

Exercise 1: Adding *-er* to Words

The student should experience no difficulty with this exercise. Be sure he notices that he is using the same procedure here as he did with the *-ed* and *-ing* endings.

Exercise 2: More Words That End in *-er*

Make sure the student can pronounce the words at the left.

Exercise 3: Changing the *y* to *i* and Adding *-er*

Use the following guidelines to preview this exercise.

- Point to *-er* in the directions and ask the student to say this sound. Tell him that he will be adding this sound to words he has already studied.
- Have the student sound out or sight read *handy*.
- Have him say *handy* and add the sound for *-er*. Then point to the example and ask him what he notices about the spelling. The student should have no trouble.
- After the student can pronounce the word *than*, have him read the sentence in which *handier* is used.
- Have the student pronounce *happy* and then write it with the *-ier* ending.
- Have the student write *happier* in the appropriate sentence. The student should have no difficulty noticing that *happier* makes no sense in the first sentence but does in the second.
- Review the pronunication of the remaining four words.
- Suggest that the student first spell the remaining four words and then use these words to complete the four sentences.

Exercise 4: Who Does What?

Make sure the student can pronounce all the words at the left. Encourage him to use the process of elimination to complete this exercise.

Lesson 12
Vowel Combinations

Primary emphasis

- Vowel combinations: *ai, ea, ie, oa, ue, oi, oo, ou*
- Using context clues
- Oral reading

Secondary emphasis

- Story comprehension (oral discussion)
- Writing sentences

Chart

1. Continue to establish cue words to help the student in future lessons. Recommended cue words are *rain, eat, head, pie, soap, blue, oil, food, foot,* and *out*. (The student has studied *out* prior to this lesson, but it is a helpful cue word for this particular sound for *ou*.)

2. Because the student has not yet studied initial consonant blends, tell him the pronunciations of *clean, blue, true,* and *shout* after he has sounded out the vowel combination.

3. In the upper section of the chart, the student can more easily remember the sounds for the vowel combinations if he marks the first vowel long.

Words for Study

Because of the number of words in the chart, do not spend any time having the student sound out words in this section unless he is progressing extremely well.

Exercise 1: Context Clues

Review the pronunciation of the words at the left. Tell the student he is to use these words to complete this little story. Have him complete the first sentence. Make sure he checks off the words at the left as he uses them. Note that, in the third paragraph, it doesn't make any difference whether the student responds *soap* and *water* or *water* and *soap*.

Exercise 2: Word Sounds

None of the words are new. Because of the length and complexity of the exercise, make sure the student knows the pronunciation of all the words at the left. If necessary, have him mark the vowels to help him remember the pronunciation.

Exercise 3: Writing Sentences

Use the same procedure as in Exercise 4 of Lesson 8. The student's finished product should look something like this: "I like it better when the sun is out." Or "I like it better when the moon is out." Some students begin to strike out on their own at this point. For example, one student wrote, "I never really look up at the sky." Anything is acceptable as long as it addresses the question and the necessary corrections are made.

Lesson 13
r-Controlled Vowel Combinations

Primary emphasis

- *r*-controlled vowel combinations *air, ear, oar, oor, our*
- Review of sounds
- Oral reading

Secondary emphasis

- Story comprehension (oral discussion)
- Using context clues
- Word associations (choosing the unrelated word)

Chart

1. Cue words are necessary only for the sounds for *ear* and the sounds for *our*. Recommended cue words are *ear, bear, hour,* and *four*.

2. In the review of sounds, vowels followed by the letter *w* have not been formally studied. However, the student has studied *saw* and *now*, and the words listed under these key words should give him no special difficulty.

3. Keep in mind that even though the sounds are being reviewed, many words in the review of sounds are new.

4. Because the student has not yet studied *sm* and *sch,* tell him the pronunciations of *smart* and *school* after he has sounded out the rest of the word. Most students can read *school*.

Words for Study

Help the student to sound out *paint, Joan,* and *forget*. With *forget,* cover the second syllable. After he pronounces *for,* uncover it. After he says *get,* have him put the two syllables together.

Exercise 1: Word Sounds

Review the pronunciation of the words in the boxes. Explain that each set of words is to be used for the sentences directly to the right. Have the student complete the first set during the preview.

Exercise 2: Words That End in *-er*

Have the student pronounce the words at the left. Make sure the student knows the definitions of these words. Many students think that a diner is solely a place to eat. Make sure that the student knows *diner* can also refer to a person.

Exercise 3: Word Study

Use the same procedure that you did for Exercise 3 in Lesson 10.

Exercise 4: Marking the Vowels

The student has not completed an exercise on marking vowel sounds for awhile. He should have no difficulty, but if he has forgotten the procedure, have him complete the third and fourth items during the preview.

Lesson 14
Vowels Followed by the Letter *l*

Primary emphasis

- Vowels followed by the letter *l*
- The endings *-ful* and *-less*
- Oral reading

Secondary emphasis

- Story comprehension (oral discussion)
- Using context clues
- Synonyms and antonyms
- Common expressions

Chart

1. The student can remember the sound for *ild* better if he marks the *i* long.
2. The *ul* words in particular often give the student trouble. Spend some extra time reviewing their pronunciation.

Exercise 1: The Ending *-ful*

Use the following guidelines for your preview:

- Point to *-ful* in the directions and tell the student how it is pronounced. Have the student repeat it.
- Have the student pronounce the words at the left. Include the ending *-ful* in the pronunciation.
- Have the student read the example sentence.
- Ask the student if he understands what he is to do in this exercise. Most students have become so familiar with the exercise format by now that they do not need to complete an item. If the student is confused, have him complete an item on his own.

Exercise 2: The Ending *-less*

Use the same guidelines for this exercise. After the student has read the example sentence, ask him what the difference is between *harmless* and *harmful*. After he has demonstrated that he understands the difference, ask him the difference between *careful* and *careless*. After he has correctly responded to this, ask him the difference between *helpful* and *helpless*. These three examples usually prove sufficient in teaching the difference between *-ful* and *-less*.

Exercise 3: Words That Mean the Same

Review the pronunciations of the words. Remind the student to work by process of elimination. Although the student knows how to complete these exercises by now, have him do one item.

Exercise 4: Word Opposites

Use the same procedure as you did for Exercise 3.

Exercise 5: Sayings

Review the pronunciations of the words at the left. Tell the student that all these words are used in common expressions. Have him read the example and complete one item. Remind him to work by process of elimination.

Lesson 15
Digraphs and Consonant Blends

Primary emphasis

- Digraphs and consonant blends: *ch, sh, st,* and *sk*
- The endings *-est* and *-iest*
- Oral reading

Secondary emphasis

- Story comprehension (oral discussion)
- Using context clues
- Matching synonyms

Chart

Make sure the student can pronounce the digraph or consonant blend before he begins to sound out the words.

Words for Study

1. With your assistance, the student should be able to sound out *couldn't, holding, pointed, anything,* and *fainted.*
2. *couldn't* and *I'll*: Teach these contractions as you have the others.

Exercise 1: The Ending *-est*

Teach the *-est* spellings in the same way that you presented the *-er* spellings in Lesson 11.

Exercise 2: Changing *y* to *i* and Adding *-est*

Teach the *-iest* spellings in the same way that you presented the *-ier* spellings in Lesson 11.

Exercise 3: Word Sounds

Some of the words are new to the student. Review the pronunciations of the words he is to use to fill in the blanks. Have the student complete the first item.

Exercise 4: Words That Mean the Same

Have the student complete one item after he has reviewed the pronunciation of the words.

Lesson 16
Consonant Blends

Primary emphasis

- Consonant blends: *bl, cl, fl, gl, pl, sl*
- Compound words
- Oral reading

Secondary emphasis

- Story comprehension (oral discussion)
- Using context clues
- Forming compound words
- Writing sentences

Chart

Make sure the student can pronounce the consonant blends before he begins to sound out the words.

Words for Study

1. *Dr.*: Draw the student's attention to the spelling of this word.
2. *haven't*: Teach this contraction as you have the others.
3. Have the student sound out *such, spite, nurse, rest,* and *before.*

Exercise 1: Word Sounds

Make sure the student can pronounce the words in the boxes. Use the same procedure that you did for Exercise 1 in Lesson 13.

Exercise 2: Compound Words

The student is introduced to the concept of compound words. Use the following guidelines for your preview work.

- Have the student pronounce the words in Lists **A** and **B**.
- Tell him that he is going to use a word from **A** and add a word from **B** to it to form what's called a compound word.
- Explain that a compound word is made up of two smaller words. Tell the student he has already been working with compound words. To illustrate this point, write *girlfriend* on paper. Have the student read it and identify the two smaller words.
- If you think it's necessary, use additional examples such as *birthday, herself, payday,* and *something.*
- Have the student read the example sentence and note that *down* and *town* are joined.
- Have the student complete items 2 and 3 to make sure he understands how to do this exercise. Be sure that he doesn't write the answers as two separate words.
- Remind him to check off the words in the columns as he uses them.
- Review the definition of a compound word.

Lesson 17
More Consonant Blends

Primary emphasis

- Consonant blends: *br, cr, dr, fr, gr, pr, tr, str*
- Classifying words
- Oral reading

Secondary emphasis

- Story comprehension (oral discussion)
- Using context clues

Chart

Make sure the student can pronounce the consonant blends before he begins to sound out the words.

Words for Study

1. *hadn't*: Teach this contraction as you have the others.
2. Have the student sound out *upset, decide, shirt, slacks, cleaner, anywhere,* and *check.*
3. Many students find the word *calm* particularly troublesome. Spend some extra time with the definition, pronunciation, and use of this word.

Exercise 1: Word Sounds

Make sure the student can pronounce the words in the boxes.

Exercise 2: Putting Words in Classes

The student is introduced to classifying words. Use the following guidelines for your preview work.

- Have the student pronounce the words in the left column.
- Have the student read the headings for the three categories.
- Explain that he is to decide under which heading each word in the column fits best. Whether you actually use the word *category* in your explanation depends on your assessment of the student's ability to understand this word.
- Point out that *barn* is listed under **Farm** and have him explain why.
- Have the student read the second item in the column. After he reads *bus stops,* he will probably say, "That could go under **Town** or **School**." Tell him that he's right and should therefore skip it for now and go on to the next item.
- Students have no difficulty perceiving that *churches* should be listed under **Town** and understand what they are to do with the words. If not, have your student complete a few more items and remind him to work by process of elimination.

Exercise 3: Best and Least

After you explain to the student that he is to write what he likes best to the left and what he likes least to the right, have the student complete the first two items. These examples help him to remember what he is to do later during his homework time. Remind him that this exercise calls for his own opinions. There are no "right" answers; it's just another way to review words.

Lesson 18
More Digraphs and Consonant Blends

Primary emphasis

- Digraphs and consonant blends: *wh, th, thr, tw, sm, sn, sp, sw*
- Reading the words for numbers 1-20
- Oral reading

Secondary emphasis

- Story comprehension (oral discussion)
- Using context clues
- Forming compound words

Chart

1. Make sure the student can pronounce the digraphs and consonant blends before he begins to sound out the words.
2. Some students pronounce the *wh* digraph as *w*; others pronounce it as *hw*. Either way is acceptable. If you find that your own pronunciation of *wh* differs from the student's, try to pronounce the sound his way during the work on the word chart. This courtesy enables the student to sound out the *wh* words more efficiently. Also, adapt yourself to the student's pronunciation whenever he has difficulty with *wh* words in subsequent stories or exercises. In all other situations, however, pronounce *wh* words as you normally would.

Words for Study

1. *I've*: Teach this contraction as you have the others.
2. Have the student sound out *Billy, afternoon,* and *grade.*

Exercise 1: Word Sounds

Make sure the student can pronounce the words in the boxes.

Exercise 2: Numbers

Spend some time with the pronunciation of the words for the numbers 1-20. Consider using these words as the basis for future spelling practices. Make sure the student is writing the word for each answer. He is not to write the number.

Exercise 3: Compound Words

Use the same procedure that you did for the exercise on compound words in Lesson 16.

Lesson 19
Still More Consonant Blends

Primary emphasis

- consonant blends: *sc, scr, shr, spl, spr, squ, str, chr*
- The prefixes *un-* and *re-*
- Oral reading

Secondary emphasis

- Story comprehension (oral discussion)
- Using context clues
- Word associations (choosing the unrelated word)

Chart

These consonant blends are usually troublesome for the student. Do not worry if the student seems almost as confused at the end of the chart work as he did at the beginning. These consonant blends are not used as frequently as the others he has studied, but the student becomes increasingly familiar with these sounds with practice.

Words for Study

1. Because of the difficulty posed by the chart, have the student sound out words only if he found the chart work fairly easy.
2. *we're*: Teach this contraction as you have the others.

Story

Before the student reads the story orally, review the chart words as they appear in the story. For example, have the student pronounce *scrubbing, screeching, screen, strike,* and *screams* in the first paragraph. This review of the chart words helps the student with both his reading and comprehension.

Exercise 1: Word Sounds

Review the words at the left.

Exercise 2: Colors

After the student has read the words in the left column, have him complete the first item.

Exercise 3: Which Word Does Not Fit?

Explain that this is another exercise in which he is to choose the word that doesn't fit with the rest. Have him complete the first item during the preview.

Exercises 4 and 5: Words That Begin with *un-* and *re-*

Use the procedure outlined for teaching the ending *-ful* in Lesson 14, Exercise 1. Because *un-* and *re-* are being studied as sounds rather than prefixes, mention neither the term *prefix* nor definitions for *un-* and *re-* at this time.

Lesson 20
Sounds for *c* and *g*

Primary emphasis

- The sounds of hard and soft *c*
- The sounds of hard and soft *g*
- The sound for *dge*
- Oral reading

Secondary emphasis

- Story comprehension (oral discussion)
- Using context clues
- Classifying words
- Answering general information questions
- Writing sentences

Chart

Students often experience difficulty with this word chart. Encourage the student by reminding him that he has almost completed the reading book and that he's doing just fine.

Words for Study

1. Have the student sound out *tonight, paycheck, groaned, silly, anybody,* and *snacks.*
2. Most students can easily sound out *I'd* and *shouldn't* at this point. Explain the contractions according to procedure.

Exercise 1: Word Sounds

Make sure that the student understands that *or* indicates he is to use only one choice and the *and* indicates he is to use all the choices. Have the student complete the first two items to make sure he can distinguish between *and* and *or*. Additionally, the student is to review all the words at the left.

Exercise 2: Putting Words in Classes

Have the student review the words and read the headings. Most students understand exactly what they are to do. If not, have the student complete one or two items with your assistance.

Exercise 3: Twelve Questions

In your preview, explain that the student is to answer *true* or *false* for the twelve questions. Point to the words as they appear in the directions so that he sees the spelling. Explain that, even if he does not know an answer, he is to make an intelligent guess. After all, he has a 50-50 chance of accuracy. The exercise is designed primarily for word review and exposure to this type of question.

Have the student complete the first item during the preview. If his answer is incorrect, inform him, "No, it's true. Cape Cod is on the East Coast." Have the student correct his answer, but emphasize his reading accuracy rather than his incorrect response.

When you and the student discuss this exercise during the homework review, take some time to elaborate on items missed by the student. Keep the tone of these elaborations light; somber and exhaustive explanations dampen curiosity.

Note: Cats do not have fangs. Either *true* or *false* is correct for #4. According to some sources, both deer and bears can run at a speed of 30 miles per hour. Other sources claim that deer can run 40 miles per hour.

First Review and Second Review

These reviews give the student an opportunity to work with many of the words and concepts he has studied in this book one more time before he begins Book 2. As was the case in the lessons, the student is not expected to read the directions for each section. Additionally, he is not expected to be able to sight read all these words. In many instances, the student still needs your help in sounding out words although, generally speaking, his decoding skills should be vastly improved.

Use the following suggestions to prepare for this review work:

- The reviews can either be completed in class or assigned as homework. Some students could really use a break at this point. For these students, working on the reviews during class time is recommended.

- Preview the exercises just as you have been doing for the lesson work. For the sake of variety and the student's enjoyment, three new types of exercises appear in the reviews—multiple choice questions, analogies and word pairs. Preview these exercises just as you have other new types of exercises.

- If you think your student still needs too much assistance in sounding out the words, keep in mind that Book 2 in this series reinforces the words and concepts introduced in Book 1.

- After the student has corrected his last mistake in the second review and read his last sentence, some sort of celebration is in order. If providing an actual treat is not possible, at least take some time for discussion so that the student has an opportunity to acknowledge his accomplishment. He's earned it, and so have you.

1. Introduction to Book 2

Because Book 2 builds on the concepts and skills introduced in Book 1, it is important to take some time to familiarize yourself with the material which precedes the lesson notes for Book 1. This material gives a detailed description of guidelines and techniques that the remedial reading teacher may find quite helpful.

Book 2 is generally used by students who have completed Book 1 in this series. Book 2 is also an appropriate starting place for the student who can read at 2.0-3.0 grade level and needs the type of work in phonics and comprehension skills that this book provides.

The primary purpose of Book 2 is to reinforce phonics skills, vocabulary, and reasoning skills introduced in Book 1. Very few new words are presented in Book 2 in order to give the student an opportunity to review thoroughly what he has learned so far.

Book 2 differs from Book 1 in several respects. In Book 1, the student reads short stories. All first readings are oral in order to help the student develop accurate and expressive reading habits. Also, story comprehension is developed through oral discussion work. Oral discussion helps the student to become more comfortable with both the demands of reading and the teacher.

In Book 2, the student reads brief, nonfiction passages about a wide variety of subjects. Unless the student demonstrates a need for intensive oral reading work, all first readings are silent in order to help the student develop reading independence. Comprehension questions for the student to answer in writing appear after each reading passage.

For the first time, the student is required to answer interpretive questions based on the reading passages. To answer these questions, the student must make inferences and draw conclusions based on the reading selections.

In Book 2, review exercises appear after every five lessons. These exercises provide the student with additional opportunities to review words and concepts. Also, they introduce him to the practice of referring to previous lessons to answer some questions.

Scheduling Considerations

The recommended length of time for each lesson and review is one hour. This gives the student ample time to go over all the material, do some oral reading and discussion work, complete appropriate reinforcement activities, and preview the next lesson which he will complete as a homework assignment.

Book 2 works well in three types of instructional settings. All types have both advantages and disadvantages that you should consider in preparing the lessons.

Tutorial Setting

The advantage of working with only one student is that you can offer him your undivided attention. The student usually progresses rapidly because you can pace the work and plan reinforcement activities exclusively tailored to meet his needs.

The disadvantage is that the student is deprived of the kind of support and stimulation that can be best provided by other students. For example, many students find the brief discussions about the reading passages more interesting when other students participate.

Classroom Setting with 3 to 5 Students

The advantage of this setting is that students do receive the support and stimulation from one another that makes learning a more enjoyable activity. Also, the more advanced students can assume much of the responsibility for giving explanations and leading reinforcement activities. This, in turn, reinforces their own reading skills. Experience indicates that less advanced students usually benefit from peer instruction when the teacher is available for any clarifications that need to be made.

The disadvantage is that the teacher cannot usually be so thorough in addressing each student's needs in this situation. Additionally, the teacher may sometimes need to address behavioral issues that can impede students' overall reading progress.

Tutorial Setting with 3 to 5 Students

In this situation, each student works at his own pace. Often, students can team up, or the more advanced students can help those having trouble with the lesson material. This type of learning environment works very well for students who either won't or don't know how to work well with others on a consistent basis.

One disadvantage of this setting is that some students begin to perceive the lessons more as a competition than as an opportunity to improve reading. You may find yourself saying, "It's more important that you know what you're doing than how fast you're doing it," more often than you'd like to.

A second disadvantage is that this type of learning situation makes incredible demands on the teacher. Not only must you be familiar with many lessons simultaneously, but also you must be able to sustain a high level of concentration and stamina in order to work with this many students on a tutorial basis.

Lesson Considerations

Again, it is important for you to take some time to familiarize yourself with the material preceding the lesson notes for Book 1. Although the following considerations pertain to Book 2, they all build upon explanations and procedures discussed earlier.

Words for Study

This section, which precedes the reading passage in each lesson, lists new words that appear in the reading passage and exercises. As was the case in Book 1, words appear in the same form in which they initially appear in the reading passage or exercises. This gives the student additional practice in pronouncing word endings accurately.

Many students, especially those who start their reading program in Book 2, can sight read most of the words. Have the student sound out the words he doesn't know with as little help from you as possible. This not only gives him the opportunity to practice sounding out words, but also helps him to recall them better if he has done most of the work.

Use the following suggestions to help the student sound out unfamiliar words.

- Have the student sound out one-syllable words according to the method he used in Book 1. For the student starting this series in Book 2, teach the sounds found in the unfamiliar word if he does not know them. If necessary, allot time during the reinforcement activities for a review of sounds.

- Students working in Book 2 often have difficulty sounding out words of more than one syllable. Have the student sound out such words as *recorded,* which appears in Lesson 1, by telling him to cover every letter except *re.* After you have helped him sound out this syllable, have him uncover and sound out the second syllable, pronounce the two syllables in order, and then go to work on the third syllable in the same manner. After the student can pronounce all the syllables in the word, have him respond to the direction, "Say it fast," if he has not yet pronounced the word as it is normally spoken.

- Cue words and vowel markings also help the student sound out unfamiliar words. Again, the examples are drawn from words appearing in Lesson 1. If the student is working on the word *Clark* and has forgotten the sound for *ar,* he quickly recalls it if you write *car* in the margin and underline *ar.* Also, most students have no difficulty sounding out *touch* if you draw a line through the *o* to indicate that it is silent. Students who completed Book 1 are familiar with cue words and vowel markings. You need to take a few minutes to explain their helpfulness to a student starting this series in Book 2.

- Combining phonics methods with verbal clues helps students remember many words introduced in Book 2. For example, after the student has sounded out *Pin* in *Pinocchio* (Lesson 1), ask, "Do you remember the story of the little boy whose nose grew every time he told a lie?" Most students are familiar with this story and respond, "Pinocchio." If the student doesn't know the answer, tell him and briefly summarize the story of Pinocchio. When students cannot respond accurately to a clue for any given word, they usually enjoy hearing more about the word than just how to pronounce it.

After the student has pronounced all the words in Words for Study, do a brief random review. Suggestions for random reviews appear in Chapter 3. If the student can pronounce three-fourths of the words correctly without too much assistance from you, he is ready to read the passage.

It is important to remind the student that if he encounters any word in either the Words for Study or the other parts of the lesson that he doesn't understand, he is to tell you. Most students readily comply with this request. If a student doesn't, explain that if he tells you when he doesn't know the meaning of a word, he will save himself time and be able to do the exercises with greater accuracy.

Reading Passages

It is important to explain to the student that the passages in Book 2 are not stories; they are brief articles about a variety of subjects. Many students who work in Book 2 hope eventually to pass the High School Equivalency Examination. They find extra incentive to do well if you explain that they will have to read brief passages on different subjects on that test.

Keep the following four factors in mind as you plan your work for these passages.

- Throughout his work in Book 2, the student often needs to be reminded that he is not obligated to agree with the point of view presented in any article. His skill as a reader is based on how well he understands what he reads—not on whether or not he agrees with the author. Many beginning readers do not initially understand this point.

  Students also need to be reminded that, although they are reading material adapted from reputable sources, authors themselves do not always agree. One example of this appears in Lesson 17, which is about Black Bart. The source from which this reading passage was adapted claims that Black Bart was a schoolteacher. In another historical source, however, Black Bart is described as a chronic ne'er-do-well.

  Students logically ask, "Why should I waste my time reading something I disagree with or something that we don't even know is true?" A helpful analogy is to compare reading with talking and listening. Most students readily agree that although many disagreements arise in conversation, talking is not a useless activity.

  Of course, if either a student or you finds a particular reading passage too objectionable, just skip it and concentrate on the other segments of that lesson.

- The first reading passage should be read aloud by the student in class so that he has a chance to become more comfortable with this type of reading while you are present to offer any necessary assistance. Unless the student demonstrates a need for intensive oral reading practice, all subsequent first readings are to be done for homework, so the student can develop silent reading skills.

You cannot assume, however, that the student is always reading the passage in its entirety. Some students become quite adept at skimming the reading passage for the correct answers to the comprehension questions. Skimming does not contribute to the student's development as an accurate decoder. And as the reading passages become increasingly complex, the skimmer is often at a loss when it comes to questions involving inference, tone, and general interpretation of the passage.

One way to correct this tendency to skim is to remind the student as often as necessary that he will make greater reading progress in the long run if he takes the time to read the passage before he begins to work on the questions. He can refer to the passage for answers whenever he needs to, which gives him practice in skimming in the form most helpful to the beginning reader.

The best way to counteract the student's tendency to skim is to allot time for the student to read the passage orally during the homework review. During this oral reading period, the student should be expected to strive for accuracy. Give him as much assistance as he needs to read the passage correctly. Keep in mind that good reading patterns can only be developed if there is a consistent and supportive emphasis on accuracy.

- Students working in Book 2 are not expected to sight read all the words in the reading passages or the exercises. Encourage the student to sound out rather than skip words that give him difficulty during his silent reading of the passage. Note the difficulties he has sounding out words during the oral reading and plan appropriate reinforcement activities to help him in these areas.

- Brief discussions of the reading passages help the student to understand and enjoy reading. For suggestions on conducting these brief discussions, please refer to Chapter 4.

Exercises

In Book 2, the student assumes responsibility for reading the directions to the many types of exercises that appear in each lesson. You will note that sometimes the wording of the directions for the same type of exercise changes. This practice is both a response to the student's growing vocabulary and a gentle reminder to the student that he shouldn't assume that he knows the words in the directions prior to reading them.

A few deliberately difficult items have been included in most of the exercises in order to challenge the student's reasoning abilities. Keep the following points in mind as you work with the student on these exercises.

- The first exercise always pertains to comprehending the reading passage. Encourage the student to refer to the reading passage when necessary and to spell his answers accurately and legibly. When a long line appears beneath the question, he is to write his answer in the form of a complete sentence. Any necessary corrections can be made by the student during the homework review.

- The student is not to skip items he does not know. Explain that he is to make "intelligent guesses." Any necessary corrections can be made during the homework review.

Students often need to be reminded that mistakes are an inevitable and constructive part of the learning process. Because many beginning reading students regard even one mistake in an exercise as a sign of total failure, remind them of the value of mistakes as often as necessary. Meanwhile, make a mental note of recurring mistakes so that you can include the appropriate words and concepts in the reinforcement activities.

- As often as necessary, remind the student to use context clues and process of elimination to figure out answers. Students quickly understand the concept *process of elimination*. Because the term *context clues* is usually too complex for Book 2 students, simply remind them to read the entire sentence before answering the question.

- All exercises are to be corrected during the homework review. Students who are in a learning environment in which formal grades are issued breathe a deep sigh of relief if you tell them their grades are based on their corrected work rather than on their mistakes. This practice does not encourage hasty or sloppy work. Rather, experience indicates that most students strive to answer questions correctly because this is easier than making corrections.

- The teacher should be aware that common American expressions and cliches appear in many exercises, particularly the word sound exercises. Students enjoy seeing connections made between spoken and written English. Also, they often appreciate learning more about these expressions, so spend a few moments whenever the situation calls for it to explain them more fully. For example, the expression "Don't count your chickens before they are hatched" is referred to in the word sound exercise for Lesson 8. After a brief discussion about this expression, one student exclaimed, "I always wanted to know what people meant when they said this, but I was too afraid to ask."

Occasionally, a student grumbles, "I never heard anybody use this expression before, so why do I have to know it?" It's helpful to remind the student that all learning involves expanding one's personal knowledge. Keep in mind that most beginning reading students don't really understand this because they haven't given the nature of learning much thought. Generally speaking, when a student complains about anything in the lesson, his objection comes from this lack of awareness rather than arrogance, regardless of the tone of his complaint. Keeping this in mind will help you foster a patient attitude.

- Do not worry too much if the student does not completely grasp the words and concepts emphasized in any particular exercise. He has many opportunities to review words and concepts in subsequent exercises. It is this repetition that helps him become a more proficient reader.

- Specific suggestions for the exercises are given in the lesson notes for Book 2, the next chapter of this manual.

Reinforcement Activities

Suggestions and procedures for reinforcement activities dealing with those words and concepts that give the student difficulty are discussed in detail in Chapter 6. Additionally, appropriate word charts and exercises from Book 1 can be used to help the student master specific difficulties.

Student Writing

Student writing is discussed in Chapter 7. Use these suggestions in planning writing assignments for the student. It is recommended that the student working in Book 2 complete weekly writing assignments in addition to the writing he does in each lesson.

Some students benefit most from the type of sentence writing suggested for students working in Book 1. These students put so much effort and time into completing the lessons that they should not be taxed with the additional task of demanding writing assignments.

Other students, however, are ready to develop further their writing skills. Personal letters and short paragraphs of 70-90 words about discussion topics that interest the student are appropriate writing assignments. For example, after having completed Lesson 4, many students enjoy writing about their opinion of the legal drinking age. Also, if the student has acquired the necessary skills, writing a letter to Santa Claus is a popular assignment— even with adults.

Draw from the brief discussions about the lesson, student comments and interests, and current issues to help you select appropriate writing assignments. Most students enjoy offering ideas for writing assignments, but they expect you to assume overall responsibility for both the topics and suggestions for developing the topics.

As was the case for students working in Book 1, all writing should be corrected and revised. Refer to Chapter 7 for suggestions about revision.

The Lesson Format

After the first class in which Lesson 1 is completed and Lesson 2 is previewed for homework, the procedure for each lesson should be as consistent as possible. Experience indicates that the following procedure works very well with Book 2 students.

1. **Writing assignment.** If the student has been given a writing assignment, have him read his work and make any necessary corrections with your assistance.

2. **Oral reading.** Have the student read aloud as much of the reading passage he has studied for homework as time permits. Help him make any necessary corrections in pronunciation and oral expression. The Words for Study should be reviewed only if you think it is necessary.

3. **Homework review.** Have the student go over the exercises he has done for homework and make any necessary corrections.

4. **Reinforcement activity.** Have the student complete one or more reinforcement activities which concentrate on words and sounds that continue to give him difficulty.

5. **Homework preview.** Have the student preview the next lesson, which he will complete for homework. Have him pronounce the Words for Study and read the title of the passage so he has a general sense of the topic. Also have him read the directions for each exercise and complete an item for exercises that initially seem confusing.

Individual Lesson Notes

The individual lesson notes, which appear in the next chapter, contain suggestions and procedures for specific items in the Book 2 lessons. Unless you are working with a small group in which each student works at his own pace, you do not need to familiarize yourself with more than one set of lesson notes at a time.

2. Lesson Notes for Book 2

Lesson 1

Sneezing

Primary emphasis

- Comprehension (written questions and answers)
- Using context clues
- Silent *e* rule

Secondary emphasis

- Oral reading
- Review of word sounds
- Review/learn the five senses
- Words that sound the same

Words for Study

1. Use the procedure outlined in the preceding chapter to help the student sound out unfamiliar words.
2. Ask the student if he knows why *January* and *Pinocchio* are capitalized. If he doesn't know, give him a brief explanation for each word.

Reading passage

1. For this lesson, have the student do the first reading orally. This helps the student to become more comfortable with the type of readings in Book 2 and gives you an opportunity to assess the student's strengths and weaknesses.
2. For this and all subsequent reading passages, make sure the student gets into the habit of reading the title. Explain that the title helps him to focus on the reading.
3. In the second paragraph, the phrase *seventeen-year-old* appears. In Book 2, many numbers appear in word form to give the student additional practice in reading.
4. Briefly discuss the passage before proceeding to the comprehension questions. Usually, students enjoy discussing June Clark's sneezing fit.

Exercise 1: About the Reading

Because this is the first lesson, have the student complete these questions in class so that good working patterns can be established.

1. After the student has read the directions and the first question, indicate the length of the line beneath the question. Explain that when the line is this long, he is to answer the question in a complete sentence. (Students who have worked in Book 1 are able to answer questions in complete sentences.) Have the student write complete sentence answers for the first and second questions so that he has a general idea what is expected of him. Assist the student in making any

necessary corrections. Remember that you are setting good writing patterns, so accuracy is important.

2. If necessary, remind the student that he can refer to the reading passage for either the answers to questions or accurate spelling. He is not expected to remember all the details in the reading.
3. **What do you think?** Explain that the answer to this type of question is not found in the passage. He is to write his own opinion in a complete sentence.

Exercise 2: Word Sounds

1. Have the student read the directions aloud.
2. Have the student read the example (sentence 1) and ask him to explain what he is to do in this exercise. Students usually see immediately what they are supposed to do. If the student is confused, help him articulate a clear explanation.
3. Have the student complete the second sentence. If necessary, remind him that it is necessary to read the entire sentence in order to fill in the blank correctly. It is not necessary to mention the term *context clues*.
4. Tell the student to reread his sentence after he has filled in the blank to make sure the sentence makes sense.
5. After the student has written the three words in the left column, have him read them. Many of these words are new to the student who started in Book 1, but he has studied the phonics rules needed to sound out the words accurately.
6. Remind the student, if necessary, to ask for definitions of any words he does not know. Sometimes, a student asks how he is supposed to fill in the blanks in the sentences if he does not know all the words. For this type of exercise and all other exercises in Book 2, encourage the habit of "intelligent guessing." In other words, the student is *not* to develop the habit of skipping items. Students need to be taught that, even if their "intelligent guesses" are sometimes incorrect, their reasoning skills improve more rapidly if they at least make an effort. It is extremely important that you remind the student as often as necessary that mistakes are both an inevitable and constructive part of learning and that they do not signify failure.
7. Make sure all answers are accurate and legible.
8. Once the student understands the idea of how to complete this type of exercise, he often prefers to write out the three words in the left column prior to filling in the blank in the sentence. This method is perfectly acceptable.
9. Because this is the first lesson, have the student complete the entire exercise in class. This helps the student overcome any anxieties about making mistakes

and reinforces the habits of spelling accuracy and legibility.

Exercise 3: Matching

After the student has read the directions, have him complete this exercise in class and read his answers orally. Again, make sure his answers are legible and spelled correctly.

Exercise 4: Marking the *e*'s

After the student has read the directions, review the long *e*, the short *e*, and the silent *e*. Have the student complete this exercise in class.

Exercise 5: Words That Sound the Same

1. Have the student read the directions aloud.

2. After he has read the two words to be used in the first sentence, have him read the sentence. Students find it helpful to read sentences of this type in this way: *Blank* can't see as well when my right *blank* is covered.

3. Point out to the student that, as was the case in the Word Sounds exercise, reading the entire sentence will help him figure out the correct answers.

4. If necessary, remind the student that all answers which appear as the first word in the sentence need to be capitalized.

5. It is not necessary to introduce the word *homonym* at this point.

Notes

1. For any exercise in Book 2, consider two or fewer mistakes an *excellent* score. The exercises in Book 2 are not to be viewed as easy work. The exercises are designed to challenge the student's reading and reasoning abilities and encourage the practice of learning from mistakes.

   Also, keep in mind that words and concepts are repeated frequently in Book 2 and that this repetition both improves the student's accuracy rate and increases his sight reading vocabulary.

2. You should make a mental note of the troublesome words and concepts and incorporate these in reinforcement activities.

3. At the end of the lesson, give the student an opportunity to ask questions or make comments about what he has just accomplished. If he seems overwhelmed by the work, point out the strengths he has shown in completing the work. Remind him that this is only the first lesson and that he'll get used to the work more quickly than he thinks is possible.

Lesson 2
Cats

Primary emphasis

- Silent reading comprehension (written questions and answers)
- Using context clues
- Classifying information

Secondary emphasis

- Oral reading
- Review of word sounds
- Words that sound the same

Words for Study

1. Use the procedure outlined in the preceding chapter to help the student sound out unfamiliar words.

2. Make sure the student knows why *United States* is capitalized.

3. The student does not need to be able to distinguish between *it's* and *its* at this point. Offer this information only if he requests it.

Reading passage

It is assumed that the student has completed the entire lesson for homework. Nevertheless, have the student read the passage orally. If he wants to know why he has to reread something he has already read, tell him that you need to know what difficulties, if any, he is having so that you know how you can best help him improve his reading. Most students quickly develop an enjoyment for oral reading. If you are working with a group of students rather than in a tutorial setting, have each student read as often as possible.

Exercise 1: About the Reading

1. Make sure all answers are corrected if the student has made any mistakes. Also, check for spelling accuracy and legibility.

2. Most students enjoy discussing the passage briefly after they have corrected this section. Two favorite topics are their attitudes about pets and the plans they would make if someone were to leave them $415,000.

Exercise 2: Word Sounds

Use the procedure outlined for **Word Sounds** in Lesson 1. The student is to read his work orally and make any necessary corrections. Again, check for spelling accuracy and legibility. Briefly discuss the definitions of any words that are unfamiliar to the student.

Exercise 3: Putting Words in Classes

Most students have no difficulty with this exercise. If necessary, remind the student that he should use process of elimination to complete this type of exercise and check off the choices as he eliminates them. The student does not have to list the characteristics in the order in which they appear at the beginning of the exercise.

Exercise 4: Words That Sound the Same

Use the procedure outlined for this type of exercise in Lesson 1. Again, check for spelling accuracy and legibility.

Note

The teacher may assume for all subsequent lessons that the primary objective pertaining to comprehension entails silent reading. In a few instances, the student may need to do first readings orally rather than silently in order to gain confidence. As long as you prepare him for the fact that he is to eventually do all first readings without your assistance, it is perfectly acceptable to have the student do the first two or three initial readings in class. Students who also wish to complete the exercises with your assistance are not ready for Book 2 and should be started in Book 1.

By the fourth or fifth lesson, all students should do first readings for homework. In most instances, students are ready for this procedure by the second lesson.

Lesson 3
The Number Seven

Primary emphasis

- Comprehension (written questions and answers)
- Using context clues
- Number words

Secondary emphasis

- Oral reading
- Review of word sounds

Words for Study

1. Students often need definitions for *Rome, sin, renewed, tailor,* and *scroll.* Take some time to discuss these and any other words with which the student is unfamiliar. A globe or map is extremely helpful for all geographical words.

2. Draw the student's attention to the capitalization of *Rome* and *Bible.*

Reading passage

Many students benefit from discussing the passage as they read it orally rather than waiting until they have corrected the comprehension questions, which is the usual procedure.

Exercise 1: About the Reading

The correct answer to question 6 for the student who does not smoke is, "I do not smoke." Many students enjoy elaborating on this fact. For questions of this nature, remind the student that he is to write a sentence response even if the question does not apply to him personally.

Exercise 2: Word Sounds

Use the procedure outlined for this type of exercise in Lesson 1.

Exercise 3: Word Sounds (sounds for *ow*)

If necessary, remind the student to use process of elimination for this type of exercise; he does not have to record the words in the order in which they are listed in the left column.

Exercise 4: Number Words

This is the student's first exposure to **Do you know?** questions. Encourage the student to try to find out the correct answer if he does not already know it. If he is unable to find anyone to give him the correct information, he is to make an "intelligent guess." Students usually enjoy seeing if their "intelligent guesses" come close to the correct answers. As in all other exercises, make sure all necessary corrections are made and check for legibility and spelling accuracy.

Lesson 4
A Few Facts about Beer

Primary emphasis

- Comprehension (written questions and answers)
- Using context clues
- Determining relative size
- Word opposites

Secondary emphasis

- Oral reading
- Review of word sounds

Words for Study

1. Students often need definitions for *term, pubs, Egypt,* and *Mayflower.* Additionally, many students are confused about the difference between *English* and *England.* A globe or map is helpful for *Egypt* and *England.*

2. Draw the student's attention to the capitalized words in this section.

Reading passage

Have the student read the passage orally. You may need to mention during the oral reading work the difference between *God* and *god* in paragraph 2. Other discussion work about the passage can take place after the student has reviewed the comprehension questions.

Exercise 1: About the Reading

1. Continue to use the procedure outlined earlier for these exercises. Most students enjoy hearing additional information about the *Mayflower* if this word is new to them. If possible, bring in a picture (most encyclopedias have one) and spend some time discussing this event.

2. **Do you know?** The answers to questions in Book 2 that appear under this heading are factual answers that have not been included in the reading passages. Encourage students to ask a friend or take a guess at the correct answer for this type of question. Unless the student clearly demonstrates that he is ready for dictionary or encyclopedia work, do not suggest this as a means of finding answers unless someone is available for assistance.

Exercise 2: Word Sounds

Use the procedure outlined earlier for this type of exercise.

Exercise 3: Word Sounds

Remind the student to read each sentence completely before filling in the blanks. For example, the second sentence should be read, "Dave was so *blank* of the *blank* he drew in art class that he said in a *blank* voice, 'Hey everybody, look at my picture!'" Remind the student to use process of elimination to complete this exercise if any of the sentences give him trouble.

Some numbers are written as Arabic numerals while others appear in word form to give students practice reading numbers both ways.

Exercise 4: Smallest and Biggest

The main purpose of this exercise is to give the student an opportunity to review words in a different context. Most students have little difficulty answering the questions.

Exercise 5: Word Opposites

Remind the student to use process of elimination to complete this exercise and to check off the words in the left column as he uses them. It is not necessary that the student complete the items in the order in which they appear.

Lesson 5
Love Letters

Primary emphasis

- Comprehension (written questions and answers)
- Using context clues
- Reviewing occupation words

Secondary emphasis

- Oral reading
- Review of word sounds
- Marking vowels

Words for Study

Students do not usually know what a *scribe* is. Instead of giving them a definition, have them learn about this word from the reading passage. Additional information about scribes can be presented while the student is correcting the comprehension questions. For example, most students do not realize that, in former times, very few people knew how to read and write.

Reading passage

If the student has difficulty reading the number 1,875,000, allot some time during the reinforcement activity for work on reading numbers comprised of many digits.

Exercise 1: About the Reading

Use the procedure outlined for this type of exercise in earlier lessons.

Exercise 2: Word Sounds

Use the procedure outlined for this type of exercise in earlier lessons.

Exercise 3: Who Does What?

The main purpose of this exercise is to give the student an opportunity to review words in a different context. Most students have little difficulty answering these questions. If necessary, remind the student to work by process of elimination, write legibly and spell his answers accurately.

Exercise 4: Words That Sound the Same

Use the procedure outlined for this type of exercise in Lesson 1.

Exercise 5: Marking Vowels

The student who started this reading series in Book 1 should have no difficulty with this exercise. Take some time to review vowel sounds and markings only if the student demonstrates the need for such a review.

Review: Lessons 1-5

Explain to the student that reviews appear after every five lessons. Unlike the lessons, these reviews contain no reading passages. The major purpose of the reviews is to review words and concepts which have been emphasized in the previous lessons.

The reviews are to be assigned as homework. Preview each section of the review just as you preview the lesson. Use the following suggestions to help you plan this work.

Word Chart

Many students neglect the word chart review that introduces this work. Be sure to allot time for the oral pronunciation of these words because they reinforce many of the phonics principles with which the student has been working. Do not expect the student to be able to sight read all these words. Occasionally, he will need your assistance in order to sound them out. When necessary, review the meanings of these words.

Exercise 1: Choosing the Answer

This is the student's first introduction to multiple choice questions in Book 2. Have the student complete the first two items during the preview so that he fully understands what he is supposed to do. Remind the student of the art of "intelligent guessing" if necessary.

Exercise 2: Number Words

Make sure the student understands that he is to write the number word, not the number, for each answer. Encourage him to take seriously the advice in the directions about getting outside help. Most students readily follow this advice.

Exercise 3: Facts

If the student does not recall this information, tell him to refer to the lesson in which he worked on an exercise about the five senses.

Word Index

Mention to the student that this list includes all the words in Lessons 1-5 that had not been studied in Book 1. The index can be used as the basis for word reviews, spelling checks, and sentence writing. In the manual for Book 1, the section on reinforcement activities discusses how the teacher can use the word index as an instructional tool.

Lesson 6
Wigs

Primary emphasis

- Comprehension (written questions and answers)
- Using context clues
- Word associations (choosing the unrelated word)

Secondary emphasis

- Oral reading
- Review of word sounds
- Review of the sounds for *ea*
- Divide compound words

Words for Study

1. Most students need an explanation for *B.C.* It is helpful if you mention the concept *A.D.* in your explanation.

2. Use a globe or map to indicate the location of France. At this point, begin to review some of the other places the student has studied, such as Rome and Egypt.

3. Students usually need definitions for *lice* and *compound*. Save your explanation of compound for the preview of Exercise 5, which pertains to compound words.

Reading passage

Have the student read the passage orally. During the reading of the first paragraph, the student finds it helpful to review the meaning of B.C. Many students enjoy figuring out exactly how many years have passed since 4000 B.C.

Exercise 2: Word Sounds

Use the procedure outlined for previous exercises of this type.

Exercise 3: Which Word Does Not Fit?

This is the student's first introduction to this type of exercise in Book 2. During the preview, have the student complete the second item after he has read the directions and studied the example. Make sure he can offer a sound reason for his answer. Also, have the student give reasons for his answers during the homework review. This practice is one way in which you can help the student develop the habit of thinking about what he does.

Exercise 4: Vowel Sounds

If necessary, remind the student to use process of elimination to complete this type of exercise and to check off the words as he uses them. He does not have to record the words in the order in which they appear in the left column.

Exercise 5: Compound Words

Students who started this series in Book 1 have worked with compound words, but they have not formally studied this term. Make sure they read and understand the directions in which compound words are explained. Most students have no trouble with this type of exercise.

Lesson 7
Skunks

Primary emphasis

- Comprehension (written questions and answers)
- Using context clues
- Synonyms
- Antonyms

Secondary emphasis

- Oral reading
- Divide compound words

Words for Study

1. Students usually need definitions for *pouches* and *forest*.
2. Make sure the student understands that *he's* is the contraction for *he is*. If necessary, review the word *apostrophe*. Students who completed Book 1 are already familiar with this word.

Reading passage

Have the student read the passage orally during the homework review. Students often enjoy relating their experiences with skunks after they have corrected any mistakes in their answers to the comprehension questions.

Exercises 2 and 3: Words That Mean the Same and Word Opposites

After the student has read the directions and studied the examples, have him complete one item in each exercise during the preview. Remind him, if necessary, to use process of elimination in completing these exercises.

Exercise 4: Compound Words

Have the student review the definition of a compound word.

Exercise 5: Silly Verses

After the student has read the directions, have him complete the first line of the first verse during the preview. During the homework review, encourage the student to read these verses with appropriate expression. Most students need to be taught to follow the punctuation signals; they tend to let their voices drop at the end of each line rather than heeding the punctuation.

Lesson 8
Eggs

Primary emphasis

- Comprehension (written questions and answers)
- Using context clues
- Word analogies

Secondary emphasis

- Oral reading
- Review of word sounds
- Form compound words

Words for Study

1. Avoid giving a definition for the word *clutch*. Tell the student he will be working with this word in both the reading passage and comprehension exercise and that the word will be discussed during the homework review.
2. Make sure the student understands why *Easter* is capitalized.

Reading passage

Have the student read the passage orally during the homework review. Students often enjoy giving their opinions about the chicken-egg argument after they have corrected any mistakes in their answers to the comprehension questions.

Exercise 2: Word Sounds

Use the procedure outlined in earlier exercises.

Exercise 3: Which Word Fits Best?

1. Have the student read the directions and the example. Have him explain why *glass* is the correct answer. Give him any necessary assistance in forming a sound explanation.
2. Have the student complete the second item.

   - Suggest that the student do his first reading of the item in this manner: "Ship is to sea as plane is to *blank.*"
   - Ask the student to explain the relationship between *ship* and *sea.*
   - Have the student read the four choices and decide which choice best goes with *plane* in the same way that *sea* goes with *ship*. Most students have no difficulty completing the analogy.
   - After the student has written the correct answer on the line, have him read the completed analogy and explain why his answer is correct.

3. Have the student complete the third analogy during the preview only if you sense he is somewhat confused.
4. Remind the student that process of elimination is often helpful in selecting the correct answer.

5. Avoid using the term *analogy*; it tends to confuse students more than it helps them. They do, however, enjoy hearing that this type of question appears frequently on college entrance tests.

Exercise 5: Word Sounds
(the *oo* vowel combination)

If necessary, remind the student to use process of elimination for this exercise. He does not have to record the words in the order in which they appear at the left.

Lesson 9
Gold

Primary emphasis

- Comprehension (written questions and answers)
- Using context clues

Secondary emphasis

- Oral reading
- Review of word sounds
- Review of definitions
- Marking vowel sounds

Words for Study

1. Students usually need definitions for *forty-niners, El Dorado, glitters,* and *ye.*
2. Make sure the student understands why the capitalized words are capitalized.
3. Make sure the student understands that *isn't* is the contraction for *is not.* Review the word *apostrophe* if necessary.

Reading passage

After the student has read the passage orally and corrected any mistakes in his answers to the comprehension questions, he often enjoys discussing briefly the difference between "a lot of money" in 1848 and "a lot of money" now. Most adolescents enjoy hearing how much such items as movie tickets and snack foods cost when you were their age.

Exercise 2: Word Sounds

Use the usual procedure.

Exercise 3: Vowels + the Letter *l*

After the student reads the directions during the preview, have him read the words listed in the left column to make sure he can correctly pronounce them. Remind the student to use process of elimination and to check off the words as he uses them. Have him complete the first item only if you sense he is confused. Most students have no difficulty completing this exercise.

Exercise 4: Marking the Vowels

Take some time to review vowel sounds and markings only if the student demonstrates the need for such a review.

Exercise 5: Matching

After the student has read the directions, have him read the words listed in the left column to make sure he can correctly pronounce them. Have him complete the first item during the preview only if you think he is confused.

Lesson 10
Mother Goose

Primary emphasis

- Comprehension (written questions and answers)
- Using context clues
- Word associations (choosing the unrelated word)

Secondary emphasis

- Oral reading
- Review of word sounds
- Silent letters

Words for Study

1. Students usually need definitions for *claim* and *rhymes.*
2. Use a globe or a map to indicate the location of Boston.

Reading passage

Students often enjoy hearing how the nobility of ages past had to worry about being poisoned by their enemies. Mention to the student that the "Spoon's" job in this reading passage was not atypical.

Exercise 2: Word Sounds

Use the usual procedure.

Exercise 3: Which Word Does Not Fit?

If necessary, refer to the procedure outlined in Lesson 6 for this type of exercise.

For item 11, the student may need to be taught that women are referred to as *cowgirls,* not *cowboys.*

Exercise 4: Silent Letters

After the student has read the directions and studied the first item, have him complete the second to make sure he understands what to do. If necessary, have him read the twelve words during the homework preview to make sure he can decode them.

Exercise 5: Words That Sound the Same

If necessary, refer to the procedure outlined in Lesson 1 for this exercise. Again, it is not necessary to mention the term *homonym.*

Review: Lessons 1-10

Use the general procedure from the previous review for this work. No new type of exercise appears in this review.

Lesson 11
Sleeping

Primary emphasis

- Comprehension (written questions and answers)
- The sound for *aw*
- Reordering words into meaningful sentences

Secondary emphasis

- Oral reading
- Using context clues
- Review of long and short vowels

Words for Study

Students often need definitions for *mow* and *pawns.* Additionally, some students confuse *dawn* with *dusk.* This is an appropriate time to clarify the meanings of these two times of day.

Reading passage

During the oral reading, mention that REM stands for Rapid Eye Movement and that this measurement has provided scientists with much of the information available about sleeping patterns. Students invariably enjoy discussing their own sleep habits and dreams.

Exercise 2: Word Sounds

In going over this exercise during the homework review, teach the student to read these sentence pairs with the appropriate inflection if his initial reading indicates he needs assistance. Not only is the student more receptive to this type of exercise when he knows how to read it well, but also he tends to recall the words more easily.

Exercise 3: Long and Short Vowels

Because these word pairs are difficult for most students, make sure they pronounce the words in the column at the left during the preview. Review the silent *e* rule.

Exercise 4: Putting Words in Order

During the preview of this exercise, remind the student to capitalize the first word of each sentence. If he seems unclear about what he is to do, have him complete the first sentence during the preview.

Lesson 12
Honeybees

Primary emphasis

- Comprehension (written questions and answers)
- Using context clues

Secondary emphasis

- Oral reading
- Review of initial consonants and consonant blends
- The ending *-ly*
- Spelling (adding *-y* to words)
- Common sayings

Words for Study

At this point, the student should be expected to discern the meanings of some words from the reading passage itself. Thus, if the student is unfamiliar with the meaning of *drone* or *unmated,* tell him that he will have a better understanding of these words after he has read the passage. Remind him that being able to figure out the meaning of a word from context clues clearly indicates reading progress. If necessary, spend a few moments discussing the meanings for *nectar* and *sly,* which appear in the exercises.

Reading passage

Students often enjoy briefly discussing the fate of the drone.

Exercise 2: Word Sounds

Use the procedure outlined previously.

Exercise 3: Words That End in *-y*

After the student has completed an example for each column during the homework preview, have him summarize the three spelling rules.

Exercise 4: Words That End in *-ly*

After the student has read the directions, have him read the words listed in the left column. Remind him to work by process of elimination when completing this exercise for homework.

Exercise 5: Common Sayings

Students often report that they have never heard some of these sayings. Remind them to use process of elimination and the art of intelligent guessing to complete this exercise. The average score on this exercise is 80%, which is a good score. The initially pessimistic student who has achieved this score should be reminded that he has demonstrated an ability to do well in spite of his fears. Even if the student has not scored 80%, he should be complimented for doing as well as he did and reminded that, as long as he made a genuine effort, learning is taking place.

Lesson 13
Handwriting

Primary emphasis

- Comprehension (written questions and answers)
- Interpreting and applying information from the reading passage

Secondary emphasis

- Oral reading
- Review of synonyms
- Review of antonyms
- Review of r-controlled vowel sounds

Reading passage

This passage represents neither a comprehensive nor a definitive statement on the study of graphology. During the preview, teachers should encourage students to see this reading as a very brief sketch about what *some* people have found to be true about handwriting. The student need not agree with these findings. During the discussion period following the oral reading, students particularly enjoy sharing their reactions to the first sentence of the reading: "Everything we do tells other people something about who we are."

Exercise 1: About the Reading

The Just for Fun section of this exercise is truly just for fun. Many students, particularly adults, enjoy hearing that brief self-analysis quizzes of this nature are common features in many magazines. If possible, bring in a few sample of these quizzes, help the student complete them, and briefly discuss them. This type of reinforcement activity helps the student to feel that he is a typical reader and usually boosts his confidence and enthusiasm in his own reading progress.

Exercises 2 and 3: Words That Mean the Same and Word Opposites

In addition to reading the directions during the homework preview, have the student pronounce the words at the left. If necessary, remind him to work by process of elimination.

Exercise 4: Vowel Sounds

After the student has read the directions and the words at the left, have him complete the first item for both the second and third columns and review all guide words and examples. Remind the student to take his time with this exercise and to work by process of elimination.

Lesson 14
To Be a Slave

Primary emphasis

- Comprehension (written questions and answers)
- Determining categories
- Sequencing events accurately

Secondary emphasis

- Oral reading
- Words that end in -er
- Spelling (adding -er to words)

Words for Study

Briefly mention the meaning of the prefix *ex*, which appears in *ex-slave* and means *former*.

Reading passage

Many students are not familiar with the Civil War. Briefly discuss this period of American history and mention that the passage has been taken from a book in which the thoughts and feelings of many ex-slaves are recorded.

During the discussion period, some students are interested in learning more about the Civil War. Others are more interested in exploring the concept of freedom. Adult students living in institutions who have completed this exercise frequently comment that their experience of "freedom" is quite similar to that of the ex-slave whose story is told in this passage. The following applied level questions might be helpful in a brief discussion about freedom. (Applied level questions are discussed in Chapter 4 of this manual.)
1. What does it mean to be free?
2. What does it mean to feel free?
3. What, if anything, is necessary before a person can either be free or feel free?
4. Is freedom something that we genuinely desire?

Encourage students to perceive brief discussions of this nature as opportunities to reflect on issues that confront us rather than as verbal battlefields. In other words, "I'm right-and-you're-wrong" points of view should be discouraged.

Exercise 2: Choosing the Right Heading

During the preview, have the student complete one item to make sure he understands how to do this exercise.

Exercise 3: Words That End in er

During the preview, have the student summarize the spelling rule illustrated in each of the three examples. He should be able to complete the entire exercise for homework with no difficulty.

Exercise 4: More Words That End in -er

If necessary, remind the student to use process of elimination to complete this exercise.

Exercise 5: Putting Sentences in Order

During the preview, mention that these sentences have been taken from the same book as the reading passage. When placed in the correct order, the sentences are the account of another ex-slave who is recalling an incident from his days of slavery. Students greatly appreciate it if you have them number the five sentences in correct order as a first step. Then, after you have checked their numbering during the homework review and helped them with any necessary corrections, they should write out the sentences in correct order to improve their accuracy in copying and spelling.

Lesson 15
A Very Strange Hobby

Primary emphasis

- Comprehension (written questions and answers)
- Review of words that rhyme

Secondary emphasis

- Oral reading
- Sequencing events accurately
- Using context clues
- Collective nouns

Words for Study

Students usually need definitions for *brink, swizzle,* and *strand.*

Reading passage

For many students, the idea of having any type of hobby seems strange. They often enjoy spending a few moments discussing why people would choose to spend their leisure time and money on hobbies. If students do have hobbies, spend a few moments discussing these activities.

Exercise 1: About the Reading

For item 4, have the student number the sentences in correct order for homework. He can write out the sentences after any necessary corrections have been made.

Exercise 2: Working with Words That Rhyme

Use the procedure for previous Word Sounds exercises.

Exercise 3: How Do You Say It?

After the student has read the directions during the preview, have him read the words at the left and complete one or two items. If necessary, remind him to use process of elimination.

Review: Lessons 1-15

The only exercise that you want to give special emphasis to during the preview is Exercise 4, which generally gives students difficulty. After the student has read the directions and studied the example, have him complete the next two items in class so that he is certain how he is to proceed with this exercise.

The other exercises in this review should give the student no difficulty. As you have done with the previous reviews, be sure to have the student pronounce the words listed on the chart at the beginning of the review when you go over the completed work with the student.

Lesson 16
Whales

Primary emphasis

- Comprehension (written questions and answers)
- Using context clues
- Analogies

Secondary emphasis

- Oral reading
- Spelling (changing *y* to *i*)

Words for Study

Students usually need definitions for *hind, limb, gills,* and *mammals.* If students do not know the meanings of *cold-blooded* and *warm-blooded,* tell them that these terms are explained in the passage.

Reading passage

Students often benefit from a brief discussion about the thought presented in the last paragraph of the passage. They are somewhat familiar with the fact that many species are endangered and are often curious to understand more precisely what this means.

Exercise 2: Changing the *y* to *i*

After having read the directions and studied the examples, the student should have no difficulty with this exercise.

Exercise 3: More Work with Changing the *y* to *i*

Have the student pronounce the words in the left column during the preview of the homework.

Exercise 4: Silly Little Stories

Have the student pronounce the words in the left column during the preview. If necessary, remind the student to use process of elimination to complete this exercise.

Exercise 5: Which Word Fits Best?

After the student has read the directions, have him complete at least one item during the preview so he understands what he is to do. Use the term *analogy* with discretion. Some students are terrified by such a "fancy" word. Others, however, especially when they learn that this type of question appears on college entrance examinations, are motivated.

Lesson 17
Black Bart

Primary emphasis

- Comprehension (written questions and answers)
- Review of synonyms
- Review of antonyms

Secondary emphasis

- Oral reading
- Using context clues
- The ending -*ful*

Words for Study

1. Make sure that the student understands that *he'd* is the contraction for *he would*. Review the term *apostrophe*.
2. Remind the student that the hyphen is considered part of the correct spelling in such words as *high-class* and *middle-aged*. Students often benefit from completing a brief spelling quiz comprised of hyphenated words during the reinforcement segment of the lesson. Use the final word index in Book 2 to make up your list of spelling words.

Reading passage

For the teacher's information, Black Bart's real name was either Charles E. Boles or Charles Bolton, depending upon which historical source one reads. Also, some sources do not describe Black Bart as a former schoolteacher; they report that he was a chronic ne'er-do-well. Whether or not students enjoy hearing these historical discrepancies can be determined by the frequency with which the student makes personal responses which are directly related to the passages. Experience indicates that there is no correlation between curiosity and reading proficiency. In other words, avoid making the assumption that many teachers unconsciously make—that only the "good" students want more information than what has been presented in the reading passage.

Exercises 2 and 3: Words Than Mean the Same and Word Opposites

In addition to reading the directions during the homework preview, have the student pronounce the words in the left columns. If necessary, remind him to work by process of elimination.

Exercise 4: The Ending -*ful*

Preview this section as you did the exercises on synonyms and antonyms.

Exercise 5: A Verse from Black Bart

In going over this exercise during the homework review, help the student to read this verse correctly. Many students enjoy spending a few moments speculating on why Black Bart bothered to leave such verses at the scenes of his robberies. It is thought that the PO8 with which Black Bart signed these verses is his spelling of *poet*. Ask the students for their interpretations of the PO8 signature.

Lesson 18
One Idea about How the Earth Was Formed

Primary emphasis

- Comprehension (written questions and answers)
- Review of word sounds
- Using context clues

Secondary emphasis

- Oral reading
- Sequencing events accurately
- The ending -*less*
- Review of the concepts *same* and *opposite*
- Spelling (scrambled words)

Reading passage

Many students are fascinated to hear you read the account of the earth's beginning in Genesis. Not only do they enjoy listening to you read, but also they enjoy comparing and contrasting these two descriptions of the earth's birth.

Exercise 1: About the Reading

For item 5, have the student number the seven sentences in proper order for homework. After you have helped him to make any necessary corrections, he is then to write out the sentences in order.

Exercise 2: Word Sounds

The consonant blends emphasized in this exercise tend to give some students difficulty. If necessary, allot a few extra moments to review them.

Exercise 3: The Ending *-less*

After the student has gone over this exercise during the homework review and made any necessary corrections, spend a few moments discussing the meanings of the *-less* and *-ful* suffixes. (The student worked with the *-ful* suffix in Lesson 17.) It is not necessary to use the term *suffix* in your explanation; *ending* is easier for the student to understand.

Exercise 4: Same or Opposite?

Students either have no difficulty with this exercise, or they experience a great deal of difficulty. For those students who have trouble grasping the difference between the concepts of *same* and *opposite*, use an appropriate variation of the following procedure. *Fresh* and *stale* have been selected because students who have trouble with this type of exercise often miss this item.

1. Have the student say, "People like to go to Jimmy's Bakery because his bread is always so fresh."
2. Have the student briefly explain this sentence.
3. Indicate the word *stale* and have the student read it.
4. Ask the student how Jimmy's customers would respond if his bread were stale.
5. Have the student determine whether *fresh* and *stale* mean the same or opposite in light of what he has just said.

As students develop the practice of thinking of words in concrete situations, they become better at determining whether word pairs of this nature are similar or opposite in meaning.

Exercise 5: Spelling Check

Students who dislike spelling respond particularly well to this exercise if it is presented as a game or puzzle rather than just another exercise. Remind students to cross out letters as they use them. This practice usually boosts their accuracy rate.

Lesson 19
Jails on the High Seas

Primary emphasis

- Comprehension (written questions and answers)
- Words that begin with *un-*
- Word associations (choosing the unrelated word)

Secondary emphasis

- Oral reading
- Words that sound the same
- Common sayings (using context clues)

Words for Study

If necessary, help the student understand the meanings of *inland* and *port*. Have him figure out the meaning of *galley* from the reading passage.

Reading passage

Many students enjoy briefly discussing whether people are treated better today than they were in former times.

Exercise 2: Words That Sound the Same

It is unnecessary to introduce the term *homonym* at this point. Students usually have little difficulty completing this exercise with at least 80% accuracy.

Exercise 3: Which Word Does Not Fit?

If you think it necessary, have the student complete the first item after he has read the directions during the preview.

Exercise 4: Words That Begin with *un-*

After the student has completed this exercise during the homework review and made any necessary corrections, ask him what he thinks *un-* means in the words he has just worked with. It is not necessary to introduce the term *prefix* at this point.

Exercise 5: Common Sayings

These sayings provide excellent topics for student compositions. Two sayings that students particularly enjoy relating to their own experiences are "Don't count your chickens until they are hatched" and "Don't wear your heart on your sleeve."

Lesson 20
The Father of Our Country

Primary emphasis

- Comprehension (written questions and answers)
- Review of vowel sounds
- Compound words

Secondary emphasis

- Oral reading
- Review of the ending -ly
- Using context clues
- More common sayings

Words for Study

Students usually need help with the meaning of the word *vice*. Take some time to help them distinguish between *vice* as in vice-president and *vice* as it is used in this passage.

Reading passage

For the teacher's information, one result of the British Parliament's replacing the Julian calendar with the Gregorian calendar was that the vernal equinox occurred 11 calendar days too late. To correct this, 11 days were omitted from September 1752 and added later to compensate.

Exercise 1: About the Reading

The **Do you know?** questions provide a source for brief discussions on any or all of the following topics:

- The terms of a senator and representative and the respective roles of each in Congress.
- The qualifications and responsibilities of a voter.
- A brief outline of the presidents of the United States and the years of their terms of office that correspond with the life spans of the students.
- A brief sketch of the people who appear on other denominations of currency. Some students enjoy learning this information in the form of a mini-research project in which they ask around for this data and then bring their findings to class.

Exercise 2: Vowel Sounds

Because this exercise reviews many of the sounds with which the student should be familiar, the words in the left column can be used as the basis for a spelling quiz.

Exercise 3: More Work with the Ending -ly

If necessary, review the definition of the word *swiftly* and remind the student to work by process of elimination.

Exercise 4: Compound Words

After the student has gone over this work during the homework review, have him give the definition for *compound word*.

Exercise 5: More Common Sayings

Again, these sayings provide excellent topics for student compositions. If the student has just completed a short composition for one of the sayings in Lesson 19, keep the sayings in this exercise in mind for future use.

Review: Lessons 1-20

Encourage the student to refer to previous lessons for any of the items in Twenty Questions that he cannot figure out by using process of elimination. The remaining exercises in this review should give the student no difficulty. If the student completes this review with a score of 75% or more, he is definitely ready to proceed to Book 3.

It is not necessary for the student to be able to read every word listed in the word index. However, keep in mind that the word index can be a helpful review for the student working in Book 3. For example, if the student demonstrates difficulty with the pronunciation of certain consonant blends presented in Book 3, have him review the pronunciation of the words in the word index at the end of Book 2 which contain these sounds.

1. Introduction to Book 3

The format of Book 3 corresponds to that of Book 1. Each lesson begins with a word chart in which a specific phonics principle is emphasized. The readings are short fictional pieces. These stories provide the student with a different type of reading experience than that offered by the non-fiction pieces in Books 2 and 4.

The student who has completed Books 1 and/or 2 should be able to sound out or sight read the words on the chart without much assistance from you. At this point in his reading development, the student can do the initial story reading and answer the comprehension questions by himself. However, he should read all or most of the stories aloud when he subsequently goes over his work during the homework review. Oral reading not only reinforces accuracy, but also helps to bolster the student's confidence.

The practice of previewing the exercises that appear in each lesson should be continued according to procedures you established for Books 1 and 2. During these previews, the student should be strongly encouraged to develop the habit of reading directions.

These exercises provide the student an opportunity to see words in various contexts, to develop vocabulary, and to improve reasoning skills. Most exercises follow formats introduced in the earlier books of this reading series. The student is formally introduced to two new concepts in Book 3. In Lesson 13, *consonant* is introduced; in Lesson 15, *syllable* is introduced.

For some students, Book 3 is an appropriate starting place. If a student can complete the final review in Book 2 with an accuracy rate of 80% or better, he is ready for Book 3. When this review is used as a diagnostic tool, the first exercise is optional. The exercise, entitled Twenty Questions, covers factual material introduced in the Book 2 lessons. Keep in mind, however, that much can be learned about the student's general knowledge, working style, and attitude toward new material by having him complete this exercise. Generally speaking, the student for whom Book 3 is an appropriate starting point is able to complete the first exercise and still maintain an overall accuracy rate of 80% or better.

Another useful diagnostic tool is the Peabody Individual Achievement Test (PIAT). If a student scores in the 3.0-4.5 range on the three reading sections of the PIAT, Book 3 is usually the best starting point.

The student starting in Book 3 does *not* need the intensive phonics work that all students who began in Book 1 and most students who started in Book 2 need. The Book 3 beginner's difficulty is not so much a lack of basic reading skills as it is careless work habits.

For example, when a student who started in Book 1 misses a word, he is usually able to pronounce it correctly by using the phonics rules he has learned. When a student who starts in Book 3 misses a word, he can usually make the proper correction upon hearing you say, "Look at it again." It is accuracy rather than phonics rules that needs to be emphasized with the student who starts in Book 3. For this student, you should consider the word chart a helpful warm-up activity and an orderly way to present new material.

Scheduling Considerations

The recommended class time for each lesson and review is one hour. This gives the student sufficient time to go over all the material, do some oral reading and discussion work, complete an appropriate reinforcement activity, and preview the next lesson which the student completes as a homework assignment.

Book 3 works well in two types of instructional settings. Each type has both advantages and disadvantages that you should consider in preparing for the lessons.

Classroom setting with 3 to 5 students

The advantage of working in this type of setting is that the students receive the support and stimulation from one another that makes learning a more enjoyable activity. Also, the more advanced students can assume much of the responsibility for giving explanations and leading reinforcement activities, which, in turn, reinforces their own reading skills. Experience indicates that the less advanced students usually benefit from peer instruction when you are available for any clarifications that need to be made.

The disadvantage is that the teacher cannot usually be as thorough in addressing each student's needs in this situation. Additionally, the teacher may sometimes need to address behavioral issues that can impede students' overall progress.

Tutorial Setting with 3 to 5 Students

In this situation, each student works at his own pace. This type of learning environment works very well for students who either won't or don't know how to work well with others on a consistent basis. If students do work well together, they can team up, or the more advanced students can help those who are having more trouble with the lesson material. Adolescents, in particular, benefit from this type of instructional setting.

One disadvantage is that some students begin to perceive the lessons more as a competition than as an opportunity to improve reading. You may find yourself saying, "It's more important that you know what you're doing than how fast you're doing it," more often than you'd like.

A second disadvantage is that this type of learning situation makes incredible demands on the teacher. Not only must he be familiar with many lessons simultaneously, but also he must be able to sustain a high level of concentration and stamina in order to work with this many students on a tutorial basis.

Lesson Considerations

It is extremely important that the teacher who is starting with this book take some time to familiarize himself with the manual for Book 1. There are two reasons for this. First, Book 3 continues to build on learning practices and procedures which are discussed in detail in the manual for Book 1. Second, and more important, the manual for Book 1 suggests approaches and attitudes that the teacher should consider in working with students. Keeping in mind that people considerations are as important as lesson considerations, here are some lesson considerations which pertain to Book 3.

Word Chart

Like Book 1, Book 3 uses common phonics principles to organize the introduction of new words. Words presented in this manner help the student to better understand the many logical patterns in English. This awareness, in turn, contributes to the student's reading development. How much emphasis you give to the phonics principles depends upon the needs of the student.

- For students who started in Book 1 and those students who started in Book 2 who demonstrate a need for phonics work, the words on the word chart should be sounded out according to methods they have used to sound out new words in the earlier books. This work can be done either during the preview or at the beginning of the homework review.

- The students who start with Book 3 do not usually benefit from a step-by-step approach to sounding out unfamiliar words. Because these students usually demonstrate good sight reading ability, it is often appropriate to simply tell them the pronunciation of an unfamiliar word. Then, briefly mention how that word follows a particular phonics principle. Plan to incorporate any troublesome words into future reinforcement activities. Also, keep in mind that troublesome words appear frequently in the exercises and that the student has many opportunities to master these words.

Students can pronounce the words on the word chart during the preview or at the beginning of the homework review. When appropriate, briefly mention phonics principles that are applicable. For example, most students appreciate being reminded that, in Lesson 1, the silent e's indicate that the preceding vowel is long. These brief explanations help the student understand the fact that logical patterns do exist in our language

which, in turn, makes the task of reading development seem much more manageable.

- Make sure that all students have a general idea of the meanings of the words included in each word chart. If the student shows signs of alarm upon being confronted with many unfamiliar words, reassure him that these strange words appear so frequently in reinforcement activities and subsequent lessons that he will be familiar with them in no time.

The main reason that students complain about learning the meaning of new words is that they usually have no idea that this activity is part and parcel of reading development. Take some time to explain this to them. Some students may grumble; but, generally speaking, they develop the habit of taking vocabulary work more seriously because they have a better understanding of its importance. Definitions of troublesome words should be discussed at the same time the student is pronouncing the words.

- By paying attention to the student's energy level and skills, you will know whether word chart work should be done during the preview or the homework review. A student who responds well to context clues and is adept at using process of elimination usually prefers saving the word chart work for the homework review, even though many of the word chart words appear in both the story and the exercises.

On the other hand, some students have good skills, but need to feel as prepared as possible before they tackle the lesson. These students should do word chart work during the preview.

In terms of energy level, the student who has difficulty settling into work should do the word chart work as the first activity during the homework review. This practice helps the student to settle down and focus on the work.

Words for Study

This section, which precedes the story in each lesson, lists words that appear in the story and exercises. These words are making their first appearance in this reading series.

As was the case in the earlier books, words appear in the same form in which they initially appear in the lesson. This gives the student additional practice in accurately pronouncing word endings.

Story

It is important for the student to understand that the readings in Book 3 are stories rather than articles about different subjects such as those that appeared in Book 2. The terms *fiction* and *nonfiction* can be introduced. The student who enjoys non-fiction appreciates hearing that he'll be reading this type of material in Book 4. Remind him that good readers are able to comprehend both types of writing. Brief explanations of this nature help the student who prefers nonfiction develop a more responsive attitude toward the lessons. In working with the story component of each lesson, please keep the following points in mind.

- It is helpful for the student to remember information about the characters from preceding stories in order to better understand the story he is currently reading. Whenever necessary, you should assume responsibility for reminding the student of information if he cannot immediately recall it.

- Oral reading is listed as a secondary objective for each lesson. If it is not always expedient to have the student read the story aloud during the homework review, try to have him read either the story or exercises aloud as often as possible. Not only is oral reading a skill that requires practice, but also students generally enjoy it and become increasingly confident in their abilities through this activity. The stories in Book 3 lend themselves to oral reading practice because most of them are written in dialogue.

- All students working in Book 3 should be able to handle the initial story reading as a silent reading activity.

Exercises

Please take a few moments to skim the suggestions for working with the exercises in the introduction to Book 2. The same procedures are recommended for all work in Book 3. In evaluating the student's work, the following points are to be kept in mind:

- Consider an overall average of 80% or better an *excellent* score. When the student occasionally has great difficulty with one exercise, help him to pinpoint exactly what went wrong. Quite often, the problem is simply that the student didn't bother to follow the directions. Remind the student of the importance of directions and also draw his attention to the fact that he did quite well on other exercises in the lesson.

- Because a fundamental premise of this reading series is that mistakes can be a valuable source of learning, it is strongly recommended that students attending a school in which grades are given be evaluated in terms of corrected work. This practice, which does *not* foster careless work habits, does encourage the student to learn from his mistakes.

- Keep in mind that words and concepts are repeated frequently in Book 3 and that this repetition improves both the student's accuracy rate and sight reading ability. Thus, if a student doesn't immediately recall certain words or concepts the second time he sees them, don't worry because he will see them again.

Reinforcement Activities

Suggestions and procedures for reinforcement activities for those words and concepts that give the student diffi-

culty are discussed in detail in Chapter 6 of the Book 1 manual. The only significant difference in implementing these reinforcement activities is that, for the Book 3 student, the emphasis should be placed more on vocabulary than on phonics principles. As often as necessary, remind the student that there is a strong relationship between size of vocabulary and skill in reading.

Student Writing

Student writing is discussed in Chapter 7 of the Book 1 manual. Use these suggestions to help you plan writing assignments for the student. It is recommended that the student working in Book 3 complete weekly writing assignments in addition to the sentence writing he does in each lesson.

Short paragraphs (70-90 words) about discussion topics that interest the student and personal and/or business letters are appropriate writing assignments. Many students are ready to further develop their writing skills through writing compositions of 150-200 words. As was the case with students working in earlier books, most students enjoy offering ideas for writing assignments. However, they usually expect you to assume overall responsibility for both suggesting topics and providing ideas for developing them.

The Lesson Format

After the first class in which Lesson 1 is completed and Lesson 2 is previewed for homework, the procedure for each lesson should be as consistent as possible.

1. **Writing assignment.** If the student has been given a writing assignment, have him read his work and make any necessary corrections with your assistance.

2. **Oral reading.** The student reads as much of the reading passage he has studied for homework as time permits. Help him to make any necessary corrections in pronunciation and oral expression. The Words for Study should be reviewed only if you think it is necessary.

3. **Homework review.** The student goes over the exercises and makes any necessary corrections.

4. **Reinforcement activity.** The student does one or more reinforcement activities which emphasize words that continue to give him difficulty. As was mentioned previously, vocabulary should be emphasized.

5. **Homework preview.** The student notes what is to be done in the next lesson, which he is to complete for homework. He pronounces the words listed on the word chart and learns the meanings of those words which are unfamiliar to him. (As was previously noted, some students benefit more from this activity if it is completed during the homework review.) He then pronounces the Words for Study and reads the title of the story so he has a general sense of its focus. Finally, he reads the directions for each exercise and completes

an item for those exercises that initially seem confusing. Whether or not the student reads the directions silently or aloud depends upon your assessment of which is more beneficial.

Individual Lesson Notes

These lesson notes which follow pertain to suggestions and procedures for specific items in the Book 3 lessons. Unless you are working with a small group in a tutorial manner, you do not need to familiarize yourself with more than one set of lesson notes at a time.

2. Lesson Notes for Book 3

Lesson 1

Review of Long and Short Vowels

Primary emphasis

- Silent reading comprehension (written questions and answers)
- Review of long and short vowels
- Using context clues

Secondary emphasis

- Oral reading
- Divide compound words
- Spelling (adding -*ing* to words)

Word Chart

1. Students who started with Book 1 and some students who started with Book 2 should sound out the words according to procedures suggested in the Book 1 manual. Students who started with Book 2 benefit from this discipline only if they demonstrate minimal sight reading ability. As was stated in the introduction to Book 3, this work can be done either during the preview or the homework review.

2. Students who start with Book 3 need not use a step-by-step method to sound out unfamiliar words. Simply tell them any unfamiliar words and briefly mention the phonics principle or principles involved. Upon hearing your brief explanation, most students recall having learned the principle and are able to apply it to subsequent words which follow the same principle. Troublesome words appear frequently in the exercises and should apppear in reinforcement activities. This work can be done either during the preview or homework review.

3. Give more emphasis to the phonics principles being reviewed with the Book 1 and/or 2 students than with students who start this series in Book 3.

4. Be sure all students have a general idea of the definitions for the word chart words. For example, in the word chart for Lesson 1, words that often confuse the student include *gale, gaze, pact, eve, dense, kin, cove* and *cud*. It is not necessary to dwell on definitions because students encounter troublesome words in later lessons and reinforcement activities. It is this repetition that ultimately results in word mastery.

Story

The student whose starting point is Book 3 should be told that the Words for Study are words that have not appeared earlier in this reading series. If necessary, remind students who began their work in earlier books of this fact.

Spend some time discussing the meanings of the contractions which appear in this lesson's Words for Study. A beneficial reinforcement activity for this lesson is a short spelling quiz on contractions, including the two which appear on the word chart and a few chosen from the index at the end of Book 2.

Mention to all students that the reading passages in Book 3 are comprised of fictional pieces in which many of the same characters reappear. As many students have described them, the Book 3 readings are like a soap opera. Students are ready for an introduction to the concepts of *fiction* and *nonfiction*.

Because this is the first lesson, consider having the student read the story orally and allow ample time for discussion. If necessary, help the student to read the dialogue with appropriate inflection. Many students really enjoy hamming up these stories, which is fine as long as their histrionics do not interfere with a smooth reading pace.

Exercise 1: About the Story

During the preview, tell the students they are to answer the questions in complete sentences. Have them complete the first question in class and make any necessary corrections so they understand what is expected. Some students may protest, of course, but a reminder that good writing skills are considered a vital part of literacy usually suffices. Additionally, many students are heartened by the reminder that the more one writes, the easier it becomes.

As was the case with the two previous books, make sure that all necessary corrections are made during the homework review. Remind the student that all your evaluations of his writing are based on progress and finished products. Students working in educational environments in which grades are given especially appreciate this and—more often than not—consider this method of evaluation as an incentive to improve their writing.

Exercise 2: The Ending -*ing*

After the student has read the directions and studied the three examples during the preview, have him state the spelling rule for each example. The exercise is to be completed for homework.

Exercise 3: How Do These People Earn a Living?

Make sure that all students know how to work by process of elimination. Most students who start this series in Book 3 are unfamiliar with this term.

Exercise 4: Compound Words

Make sure that all students know what a compound word is. Mention to them that they need to be familiar with this term because many exercises in this book focus on compound words.

Notes

1. In Lesson 1, silent reading comprehension refers to both the story and all the exercises, which the student is to complete for homework. Again, it is suggested that the initial story reading for this lesson be done orally. However, the student is to complete all subsequent stories as a silent reading activity in order to improve this skill.

2. After the student has gone over the exercises and made any necessary corrections during the homework review, give him an opportunity to ask questions or make comments about what he has just accomplished. If he seems overwhelmed by the work, point out the strengths he has shown in completing the work and assure him that mistakes are an inevitable and valuable part of the learning process. Additionally, remind him that this is only the first lesson and that he'll get used to the work more quickly than he thinks is possible.

Lesson 2
Review of Consonant Blends and Digraphs: Part 1

Primary emphasis

- Comprehension (written questions and answers)
- Review of consonant blends (*ch, sh, st*)
- Using context clues

Secondary emphasis

- Oral reading
- Divide compound words
- Spelling (adding -*est* to words)

Word Chart

Use the procedure suggested for Lesson 1.

Story

1. **Words for Study:** Students usually need help in understanding the words *yoga* and *splurge.*
2. Many students enjoy discussing how they respond to being laughed at or laughing at others, which is mentioned in the last paragraph of the story.

Exercise 1: About the Story

If necessary, during the preview remind the student to answer all questions in complete sentences. During the homework review, the student is to correct his writing so that his sentences are accurate and clear statements.

Exercise 2: Adding -*est* to Words

After the student has read the directions and studied the three examples during the preview, have him state the spelling rule for each example.

Exercise 3: How Do These People Earn a Living?

Review the concept *process of elimination* and remind the student he is to make intelligent guesses when he is unsure of the answer. (The student starting in Book 3 is sometimes unfamiliar with the words *scribe* and *tailor*.)

Exercise 4: Compound Words

If necessary, review the definition for *compound word.*

Note

Oral reading is listed as a secondary objective in this and all subsequent lessons. If it is not always expedient to have the student read the story aloud during the homework review, try to have him read either the story or exercises aloud as often as possible. Oral reading is a skill that requires practice, and students generally enjoy it and become increasingly confident in their abilities through this activity.

Lesson 3
Review of Consonant Blends: Part 2

Primary emphasis

- Comprehension (written questions and answers)
- Review of consonant blends (*bl, br, cl, cr, fl, fr*)
- Using context clues

Secondary emphasis

- Oral reading
- Divide compound words
- Spelling (adding -*y* to words)

Word Chart

Use the procedure suggested for Lesson 1.

Story

1. **Words for Study:** Students usually need help in understanding the words *yogurt* and *reform.* Tell them that they are to try to figure out the meaning of *vowed* from reading the story.
2. Many students enjoy briefly discussing their own experiences in a library or offering explanations about why they have never been in one.

Exercise 1: About the Story

At this point, you may notice that some students are developing the habit of giving incorrect responses. In these instances, remind the students that they are to refer to the passage for any answers they cannot recall from their initial reading. Occasionally, a student remarks that he feels that he is cheating if he does this. Gently inform him that he's not cheating and that skimming a story for an answer is an undeniable reading skill.

Exercise 2: Adding -y to Words

After the student has read the directions and studied the three examples during the preview, have him state the spelling rule for each example.

Exercise 3: Who Uses What?

At this point, students are familiar with this type of exercise and have no difficulty completing it correctly.

Exercise 4: Compound Words

A brief spelling quiz containing some of the compound words studied so far is a helpful reinforcement activity.

Lesson 4
Review of Consonant Blends: Part 3

Primary emphasis

- Comprehension (written questions and answers)
- Review of consonant blends (*gl, gr, pl, pr, sl, str*)
- Using context clues

Secondary emphasis

- Oral reading
- Divide compound words
- Spelling (the ending -*y*)

Word Chart

Use the procedure suggested for Lesson 1.

Story

1. **Words for Study**: Students usually need help in understanding the words *nonsense, throbbing,* and *highness*.
2. Many students enjoy briefly sharing their impressions of Ginger and Jerome's relationship.

Exercise 1: About the Story

Use the procedure suggested in the previous lesson.

Exercise 2: Changing the y to i

After the student has read the directions and studied the two examples during the preview, have him state the spelling rule for each example. Because some students have particular difficulty pronouncing the -*er* and -*est* endings, be sure to have them say the words correctly during the homework review.

Exercise 3: More Work with the Ending -y

After the student has read the directions and studied the examples during the preview, suggest that he write out

the words in the left column prior to placing them correctly in the sentences.

Exercise 4: Who Uses What?

Students should have no difficulty completing this exercise correctly.

Exercise 5: Compound Words

Again, a brief spelling quiz incorporating some of the compound words studied so far is a helpful reinforcement activity. An enjoyable variation is to dictate twenty words that are parts of ten compound words and then have the students match them correctly.

Lesson 5
Review of Consonant Blends: Part 4

Primary emphasis

- Comprehension (written questions and answers)
- Review of consonant blends (*dr, tr, thr, sc, sk, sw*)
- Using context clues
- Vocabulary review (synonyms)

Secondary emphasis

- Oral reading
- The ending -*ly*
- Divide compound words

Word Chart

Use the procedure suggested for Lesson 1.

Story

1. **Words for Study**: Make sure the student knows the meaning and correct pronunciation for *etc.* If necessary, review the term *abbreviation*. Students enjoy learning that this abbreviation comes from Latin and that many words in English have come to us from other languages.
2. Needless to say, a favorite topic with students is being rich!

Exercise 1: About the Story

Remind students that, for **What do you think?** questions, they are to respond with their own opinions in good sentence form. There is no one right answer. However, students are to base their opinions on information they have about Jerome so far. Students usually need to be taught that there is such a thing as an intelligently-formed opinion.

Exercise 2: The Ending -ly

After the student has read the directions and studied the examples during the preview, remind him to write out the words in the left column prior to placing them in the sentences.

Exercise 3: Words That Mean the Same

Remind the student to work by process of elimination. There is no need to introduce the term *synonym* at this point.

Exercise 4: Compound Words

Spend a few moments discussing the meaning of *Thanksgiving*. Many students neither recognize that this word has a specific meaning nor know much about the reason for this holiday.

Lesson 6
Review of Consonant Blends and Digraphs: Part 5

Primary emphasis

- Comprehension (written questions and answers)
- Review of consonant blends (*sm, sn, sp, scr, th,* and *wh*)
- Using context clues
- Vocabulary review (antonyms)

Secondary emphasis

- Oral reading
- The ending -*ly*
- Divide compound words

Word Chart

Some students pronounce the *wh* sounds as *hw*; others pronounce it *w*. Either pronunciation is acceptable. When working with the student specifically on this sound, adapt your own pronunciation to his so that unnecessary confusion is avoided.

Story

1. **Words for Study**: Students usually need definitions for *fate* and *oozing*.
2. During the discussion of the story, ask the student why he thinks the story has been titled "A Strange Twist of Fate."

Exercise 2: More Work with the Ending -*ly*

Although students usually put *squarely* and *mildly* in the correct blanks, they sometimes are still uncertain about the meanings of these words. A concrete demonstration is helpful. For example, ask the student to look you squarely in the eye based on what he thinks this expression means and help him, if necessary, to do this correctly.

Exercise 3: Word Opposites

Remind the student to work by process of elimination. There is no need to introduce the term *antonym* at this point.

Exercise 4: Compound Words

Students usually need help in understanding the meaning of *tailspin*.

Lesson 7
Review of Silent Letters

Primary emphasis

- Comprehension (written questions and answers)
- Review of silent letters (*kn, wr, gn, tch, dge, gh,* and *ght*)
- Vocabulary review (synonyms and antonyms)

Secondary emphasis

- Oral reading
- The endings -*ful* and -*less*
- Divide compound words

Word Chart

Emphasize the phonics rules used to sound out these words with both the student who has worked in the earlier books and the student who has begun this series in Book 3. This emphasis helps to develop more accurate spelling.

Story

1. Make sure the student knows the definitions for *you've* and *restless*.
2. A brief discussion about eating habits is a good follow-up topic for this story.

Exercise 2: The Endings -*ful* and -*less*

After the student has made any necessary corrections during the homework review, have him explain what -*ful* and -*less* mean. It is not necessary to introduce the term *suffix* at this point.

Exercise 3: Same or Opposite?

As was the case with students working in Book 2, students either have no difficulty with this exercise, or they experience a great deal of difficulty. For those students who have trouble grasping the difference between the concepts of *same* and *opposite* when they appear in the same exercise, use an appropriate variation of the following procedure. Gloom and joy have been selected because students who have trouble with this type of exercise often miss this item.

1. Have the student say, "Most people are filled with gloom when they have to visit the dentist."
2. Have the student briefly interpret this sentence.
3. Ask the student how people would apppear as they sat in the waiting room of the dentist's office if they were filled with joy.

4. Have the student determine whether *gloom* and *joy* mean the same or opposite in light of what he has just said.

As students develop the practice of thinking of words in concrete situations, they become better at determining whether word pairs of this nature are similar or opposite in meaning.

Exercise 4: Compound Words

Some students need help in understanding the meanings of *lighthouse* and *comeback*.

Lesson 8
Review of Vowel Combinations: Part 1

Primary emphasis

- Comprehension (written questions and answers)
- Review of vowel combinations (*ai, ēe, ĕa, ea,* and *ui*)
- Using context clues
- Vocabulary review (synonyms and antonyms)

Secondary emphasis

- Oral reading
- The endings *-ful* and *-less*
- Form compound words

Word Chart

Use the same procedure suggested for Lesson 1.

Exercise 1: About the Story

After the student has made any necessary corrections, spend some time briefly discussing Gail's relationship with her father as it is described in this story and parent-children relationships in general.

Exercise 2: More Work with the Endings *-ful* and *-less*

Students usually have no difficulty completing this exercise. If necessary, have the student review the meanings of *-ful* and *-less*.

Exercise 3: Same or Opposite?

If necessary, use the procedure suggested for this type of exercise in Lesson 7.

Exercise 4: Compound Words

After the student has read the directions and studied the example during the preview, have him complete the second item so that he is certain how to complete this exercise. Remind the student to use process of elimination to find all the answers.

Lesson 9
Review of Vowel Combinations: Part 2

Primary emphasis

- Comprehension (written questions and answers)
- Review of vowel combinations (*oa, oo, ou, oi,* and *oy*)
- Using context clues
- Vocabulary review (choosing the unrelated word)

Secondary emphasis

- Oral reading
- The ending *-en*

Word Chart

Use the procedure suggested for Lesson 1.

Story

1. Students often need definitions for *you'll* and *pleasant*.
2. This story lends itself to oral reading practice. If you are working with a group of three students, consider having one student act as a narrator and the other two take the parts of Steven and Jerome.

Exercise 1: About the Story

After the student has made any necessary corrections, spend some time briefly discussing his answer to the last question and the nature of friendships in general.

Exercise 2: The Ending *-en*

Some students have trouble pronouncing this ending. In these instances, have the student pronounce the words in the left column during the preview.

Exercise 3: Which Word Does Not Fit?

After the student has read the directions, have him complete the first item during the preview so that he understands what he is to do. Some students wonder why they simply cannot circle the correct answer. Your response? "Writing out the answers is good spelling practice."

Lesson 10
The Sound for *au*

Primary emphasis

- Comprehension (written questions and answers)
- The sound for *au*
- Using context clues
- Vocabulary review (choosing the unrelated word)

Secondary emphasis

- Oral reading
- The ending -en
- Spelling (scrambled words)

Word Chart

The student who began his reading studies in Book 1 has not formally studied the sound for *au*. Be patient. This is often a difficult word chart for him.

Story

Students also enjoy reading this story as if it were a play. For many adults, a brief discussion of the trials and tribulations of life at the laundromat is an enjoyable topic. Experience indicates that many adolescent males are fairly convinced that washing clothes is a woman's job.

Exercise 2: More Work with the Ending -en

Those students who have difficulty with the pronunciation of this ending should pronounce the words in the left column during the preview.

Exercise 3: Which Word Does Not Fit?

Have the student complete one item during the preview only if he experienced difficulty with this type of exercise in the previous lesson.

Exercise 4: Spelling Check

After the student has read the directions during the preview, have him complete the first item in class so that he understands what he is to do. Suggest to him that he cross out the letters as he uses them in order to insure greater spelling accuracy. Students respond to this type of exercise better if you present it as a puzzle or game.

Lesson 11
Review of the *r*-Controlled Vowel

Primary emphasis

- Comprehension (written questions and answers)
- Review of the *r*-controlled vowel
- Using context clues
- Vocabulary review (synonyms)

Secondary emphasis

- Oral reading
- Words that begin with *re*-
- Classifying words

Word Chart

Use the procedure suggested for Lesson 1.

Story

1. **Words for Study**: Students often need help in understanding the meaning of the word *breed*. Additionally,

spend a few moments discussing the difference between *remain* and *remains*.

2. Students usually enjoy discussing city vs. country living.

Exercise 2: Words That Begin with *re*-

After the student has read the directions, have him read the words in the left column. Unless more than three words confuse him, encourage him to try to complete the exercise using process of elimination and tell him that the words will be discussed more fully during the homework review. Most students average at least 80% correct responses on this exercise.

Keep in mind that the sound for *re* is being emphasized in this exercise. There should be no mention of *re*- as a prefix. This only confuses the student.

Exercise 3: Words That Mean the Same

It helps some students if they pronounce the words in the left column during the preview. Base all decisions regarding the extent of the preview activities on your observation of the students' strengths and weaknesses.

Exercise 4 and 5: What Is Where?

If necessary, remind the student to work by process of elimination to complete these two exercises.

Lesson 12
Review of Vowels Followed by the Letter *l*

Primary emphasis

- Comprehension (written questions and answers)
- Review of vowels followed by the letter *l*
- Using context clues
- Vocabulary review (antonyms)

Secondary emphasis

- Oral reading
- Words that begin with *re*-
- Form compound words

Word Chart

Use the procedure suggested for Lesson 1.

Story

1. **Words for Study**: Students often need definitions for *ulcer, spangled,* and *banner.*
2. Some students are unfamiliar with "The Star-Spangled Banner." Give them a brief history of this anthem and, if necessary, tell them that it is often sung or played just before sports events.

Exercise 2: More Work with Words That Begin with *re-*

Use the procedure suggested for this type of exercise in Lesson 11.

Exercise 3: Word Opposites

Again, it helps some students if they pronounce the words in the left column during the preview.

Exercise 4: Compound Words

Have the student complete one item during the preview only if you think it is necessary.

Lesson 13
Review of the Hard and Soft *c* and *g*

Primary emphasis

- Comprehension (written questions and answers)
- Review of the hard and soft *c* and *g*

Secondary emphasis

- Oral reading
- Words that begin with *in-*
- Syllabication (divide between double consonants)

Word Chart

Use the procedure suggested for Lesson 1.

Story

1. **Words for Study:** Many students need definitions for *scheme, halt, pane,* and *keg.* After the student has read the story, ask him why he thinks it is titled "Jerome's Scheme."
2. Many students, particularly adults, enjoy relating their own versions of Jerome's situation in this story.

Exercise 2: Words That Begin with *in-*

Use the procedure suggested for the exercise dealing with words that begin with *re-* in Lesson 11. Again, keep in mind that the sound for *in-* is being emphasized. There should be no mention of *in-* used as a prefix. This only confuses the student.

Exercise 3: Which Word Fits Best?

After the student has read the directions during the preview, have him complete the first item in class so he has a good understanding of how to complete this exercise. Many students are impressed upon being informed that this type of question appears on college entrance examinations.

Encourage the student to use process of elimination to complete this exercise.

Exercise 4: Consonants

After the student has read the directions and studied the example during the preview, have him complete one item and explain the meaning of *consonant.*

Review the definition of *consonant* after the student has gone over this exercise during the homework review.

Lesson 14
The *gh* and *ght* Words

Primary emphasis

- Comprehension (written questions and answers)
- *gh* and *ght* words
- Vocabulary review (synonyms and antonyms)
- Using context clues

Secondary emphasis

- Oral reading
- Syllabication (divide between double consonants)

Word Chart

Use the procedure suggested for Lesson 1.

Exercise 1: About the Story

After the student has made any necessary corrections in his writing, allot time for a brief discussion about neighbors. Many students also enjoy speculating about just what Mrs. Darkpill has to do with the fact that Tony and Ginger missed Jerome's party.

Exercise 2: The *gh* and *ght* Words

Many students may need to review the words in the left column during the homework preview. If necessary, remind the student to use process of elimination to complete this exercise. In going over this work during the homework review, help the student read these couplets with appropriate rhythm if necessary.

Exercise 3: Same or Opposite?

Use the procedure suggested for this type of exercise in Lesson 7.

Exercise 4: More Work with Double Consonants

Students usually understand what they are to do. Have the student complete one item during the homework preview only if you think this is necessary.

Lesson 15

Review of *r*-Controlled Vowel Combinations

Primary emphasis

- Comprehension (written questions and answers)
- *r*-controlled vowel combinations (*air, ear, eer, oar, oor,* and *our*)
- Using context clues
- Syllabication (divide words into syllables)

Secondary emphasis

- Oral reading
- General information (working with units)

Word Chart

Use the procedure suggested for Lesson 1.

Story

Students usually enjoy reading this story orally as if it were a play.

Exercise 2: The *ea* and *ear* Words

Students may need to review the words in the left column during the homework preview. If necessary, remind the student to use process of elimination to complete this exercise. In going over this work during the homework review, help the student read these verses with appropriate rhythm if necessary.

Exercise 3: Syllables

After the student has read the directions, have him complete one or two items during the preview so he understands what he is to do in this exercise. Review the definition of the word *syllable* during the homework review.

Exercise 4: More Work with Units

If necessary, remind the student to use process of elimination to complete this exercise.

Lesson 16

Common Word Beginnings: Part 1

Primary emphasis

- Comprehension (written questions and answers)
- Common word beginnings (*de-, ex-, mis-, com-, con-*)
- Using context clues

Secondary emphasis

- Oral reading
- The sounds for *ow*

- Syllabication (combine syllables to form words)
- General information (questions about nutrition)

Word Chart

Again, it is the sounds which are being emphasized. Mentioning the term *prefix* only confuses the student.

Exercise 1: About the Story

Students usually enjoy elaborating on the answer they wrote for Question 8. Some students benefit from developing their answers into short compositions in addition to discussing this topic in class.

Exercise 2: Sounds for *ow*

Some students need to review the words in the left column during the homework preview.

Exercise 3: More Work with Syllables

After the student has read the directions and studied the example during the preview, have him complete one item in class. If necessary, remind him to cross out the syllables listed in the box as he uses them.

Exercise 4: Brain Benders

During the preview, emphasize that the student is to make a good guess even if he does not know the answer. Grade-conscious students often need to be reminded that evaluations are based on the completed work.

By informing the student that this brief survey of knowledge about nutrition is similar to surveys found in many magazines, you can usually arouse the student's interest in this type of activity.

Lesson 17

Common Word Beginnings: Part 2

Primary emphasis

- Comprehension (written questions and answers)
- Common word beginnings (*de-, ex-, com-, con-,* and *un-*)
- Vocabulary (choosing the unrelated word)

Secondary emphasis

- Oral reading
- The sounds for *ow*
- Divide compound words
- Syllabication (divide words into syllables)

Word Chart

Use the procedure suggested for Lesson 1. Again, avoid using the word *prefix.*

Exercise 1: About the Story

An appropriate composition exercise for this lesson is "The Ideal Boss." Adults particularly enjoy writing about this topic.

Exercise 2: More Work with the Sounds for *ow*

Most students are familiar with this type of exercise by now. However, you may need to review the pronunciations of the words in List A and List B.

Exercise 3: Which Word Does Not Fit?

This exercise is difficult for some students. Remind students to take their time and work by process of elimination. A score of nine or more correct responses is excellent.

Exercise 4: More Work with Syllables

Review the definition for *syllable* after the student has made any necessary corrections during the homework review.

Lesson 18
Common Word Beginnings: Part 3

Primary emphasis

- Comprehension (written questions and answers)
- Common word beginnings (*ex-*, *dis-*, *un-*, *im-*, and *in-*)
- Using context clues

Secondary emphasis

- Oral reading
- Classifying words
- Spelling (scrambled words)

Word Chart

Use the procedure for the previous charts on common word beginnings.

Story

This story also lends itself to oral reading practice.

Exercise 1: About the Story

Many students enjoy briefly discussing Jerome and Steven's points of view in this story.

Exercise 2: Short Stories

Some students need to review both the pronunciation and meaning of many of the words in the left column during the homework preview.

Exercise 3: Who Uses What?

Usually, students have no difficulty with this exercise, and there is no need to have the student complete any of the items during the homework preview. Simply have the student read the directions and note the categories.

Exercise 4: Spelling Check

Again, remind the student to cross out the letters as he uses them.

Lesson 19
Up-, Down-, Out-, Over-, and Under-

Primary emphasis

- Comprehension (written questions and answers)
- Common word beginnings (*up-*, *down-*, *out-*, *over-*, and *under-*)

Secondary emphasis

- Oral reading
- General information (the calendar)
- Word associations

Word Chart

Use the procedure suggested for previous charts on common word beginnings.

Exercise 2: The Months of the Year

Have the student read the verse during the preview. Help him to read the verse with appropriate stress if necessary. Many students do not know the answers to some of the questions. Encourage them to make an intelligent guess and plan to spend class time discussing troublesome items.

For questions 9-12, the student is to use calendar dates rather than weather patterns as the basis for his answer. This is an appropriate time to briefly introduce and explain the concepts of *solstice* and *equinox*.

Consider using the months as a basis for a spelling quiz. Students can also be introduced to the abbreviations for the months at this time.

Exercise 3: The Four Seasons

This exercise, also, is difficult for many students. Again, encourage them to make an intelligent guess and plan to spend class time discussing troublesome items. Adults especially respond with curiosity to this discussion topic: With all the talk we hear each day about the weather, why do you think we pay so little attention to the events and changes that characterize each season? More often than not, students are fascinated upon realizing how little they know about growing crops, the habits of animals, and other phenomena that are clearly associated with the cycle of seasons.

Exercise 4: Twelve Questions

Students are encountering some of the italicized words in these questions for the first time. Generally, however, they have no difficulty completing this exercise with an 80% accuracy rate.

Lesson 20
More Work with Compound Words

Primary emphasis

- Comprehension (written questions and answers)
- Using context clues

Secondary emphasis

- Oral reading
- Compound words
- Vocabulary review (synonyms and antonyms)

Word Chart

Use the procedure suggested for Lesson 1.

Story

Because this is the last story in Book 3, consider having the student read it orally during the homework review. Allot time for summarizing and responding to the main characters and their activities.

Exercise 2: More Work with Compound Words

Some of the words presented in the multiple choices are new to the student. Remind him to work by process of elimination and to make an intelligent guess for any item that confuses him. Generally, students complete this exercise with a far greater accuracy rate than they thought possible—which is your cue to remind the student that process of elimination and intelligent guessing really do have merit.

Exercises 3 and 4: Words That Mean the Same and Word Opposites

Students can be expected to score 80% or better on each exercise.

Exercise 5: Feelings

After the student has read the directions, have him complete the first item in class so that he fully understands what is expected of him. Make sure that he understands that his choice is to be an appropriate response to the situation and that his sentence explanation must be an appropriate response to his choice. What is being reviewed in this exercise is the concept of intelligently formed opinions.

Review: Lessons 1-20

The purpose of this review is to give the student one more opportunity to work with many of the words and concepts emphasized in Book 3 before he begins working in Book 4. This review should *not* be perceived as a test, although it can be used as a diagnostic tool for any student you are considering starting in Book 4.

Preview each exercise with the student just as you would preview a lesson. If you think it necessary, have the student complete an item for each exercise during the preview.

In this reading series, reviews are to be perceived like weddings: something old and something new. New material is a gentle way of reminding the student that there is always something more to learn. The student may have finished a reading book, but he has not finished learning more about reading.

Keep in mind that the following include new material for the student and may require a bit of extra time during the preview.

Exercise 1: Word Study

Although no new words are introduced in this exercise, the student has not been exposed to this format for reviewing vocabulary in any other Book 3 exercises.

Exercise 5: Word Sounds

This exercise reviews some of the basic phonics principles emphasized in the word charts. Students tend to do either quite well on this exercise or quite poorly. If the student has difficulty with this exercise, plan to incorporate this type of work in future reinforcement activities. Generally speaking, there is a correlation between the ability to complete this type of work accurately and good spelling.

Exercise 6: Spelling Check

Although students are familiar with scrambled words, they have not yet used the initial letter of each answer to respond correctly to a question. During the preview, make sure the student understands how he is to fill in the blanks to discover the name of the dessert.

After the student has made any necessary corrections during the homework review, spend a few moments reviewing and evaluating the student's reading progress. Many students enjoy perusing the word index because it represents a concrete symbol of accomplishment. The word index should be kept in mind for planning reinforcement activities as the student works in Book 4.

1. Introduction to Book 4

The format of Book 4 corresponds to the one used in Book 2. Book 4 primarily reinforces vocabulary, reasoning skills, and phonics principles introduced in earlier books and develops reading comprehension.

Relatively few new words are introduced in Book 4 in order to give the student an opportunity to review thoroughly what he has learned so far. The introduction of the terms *singular* and *plural* represents the only new word analysis skill presented in this book.

In Book 4, the student reads brief, nonfiction passages which contain information on a wide variety of subjects. Written comprehension questions appear after each reading passage for the student to answer. Most students respond with enthusiasm to these passages when they learn that the high school equivalency examination includes brief readings in science and history. In working with the passages in Book 4, students often demonstrate increased confidence and ability to achieve this long-range educational goal.

A review appears after every five lessons. These reviews provide the student with additional opportunities to review words and concepts. Also, they help the student to develop the habit of referring to previous lessons for correct answers to some of the questions. The word indexes listed at the end of each review are a source for reinforcement activities.

Book 4 is generally used by students who have completed Book 3 in this series. Book 4 is also an appropriate starting place for the student who can read at 4.0-5.0 grade level. The three reading tests included in the Peabody Individual Achievement Test provide helpful diagnostic information about placement.

Book 4 builds upon procedures and practices emphasized in the earlier books in this series. Thus, you will find it worthwhile to look through the manual notes for the previous books. The Book 1 manual is especially helpful because it contains many suggestions and considerations which should be taken into account when working with older adolescent and adult reading students. It is not necessary to review the sections of the manual notes that pertain to specific lessons.

Scheduling Considerations

As was the case with the earlier books, the recommended class time for each lesson and review is one hour. This gives the student sufficient time to go over all the material, do some oral reading and discussion work, complete an appropriate reinforcement activity, and preview the next lesson.

Book 4 works well in three types of instructional situations. The first is a tutorial setting. The second is a classroom setting in which three to eight students are working together. The third is a classroom setting in which three to eight students are working independently.

If you have worked with the earlier books in this series, you may wonder why the recommended class size has increased. Because students working in Book 4 are becoming more proficient readers, you usually do not need to focus so intensively on skill development. Additionally, Book 4 students are able to assist each other with less need for your supervision. Thus, the classes can have more students without hindering reading development.

For a more detailed description of the recommended classroom settings for Book 4 students, please refer to the introduction to the Book 3 manual.

Lesson Considerations

Again, please take some time to familiarize yourself with the manual notes for the earlier books in which the principles and procedures that provide the foundation for this reading series are described in detail.

The following notes outline lesson considerations that pertain to Book 4.

Words for Study

This section, which precedes each reading passage, lists words that appear in the passage and exercises. These words are making their first appearance in this reading series.

As was the case in the earlier books, words appear in the same form in which they initially appear in the lesson. This gives students additional practice in pronouncing word endings accurately.

When previewing the Words for Study with the student, emphasize only the correct pronunciation. In Book 4, the student is to learn the meanings of unfamiliar words from the lesson itself. The individual lesson notes indicate those instances when this procedure is not advisable and definitions should be discussed during the preview. In most instances, troublesome words should be discussed during the homework review.

Reading passage

It is important for the student to understand that the readings in Book 4 are nonfiction rather than the fictional pieces which appeared in Book 3. The terms *fiction* and *nonfiction* should be introduced or reviewed. With the exception of the first lesson in which the student becomes familiar with the Book 4 format, the initial reading of all passages and exercises should be considered silent reading activities.

But oral reading, which appears as receiving secondary emphasis in the notes for each lesson, should not be neglected. Try to have the student read either the passage or the exercises aloud as often as possible during the homework review. This practice helps you assess the student's strengths and weaknesses and helps the student develop greater confidence and enjoyment in his reading.

Exercises

A wide variety of exercises helps the student develop his recall and reasoning abilities. As often as it seems appropriate, draw the student's attention to the fact that reasoning is an essential part of reading. Help the student develop patterns such as reasoning out answers to inferential and applied reading comprehension questions, using process of elimination, making intelligent guesses, and referring to previous lessons. Such practices not only contribute to overall progress, but also they help the student develop a healthy self-image. As one man remarked, "You know, I really feel like a student."

Consider an overall average of 80% or better an excellent score for the lessons in Book 4. When the student occasionally has great difficulty with an exercise, help him pinpoint exactly what went wrong. The student should be encouraged to learn from his mistakes rather than feel like a failure because he has made errors.

Because the student is encouraged to learn from his mistakes, he should not be penalized for making them. If you work in a school which gives report cards, it is strongly recommended that evaluations be based on corrected work and overall progress rather than the student's initial effort. In no way does this practice encourage the typical reading student to be careless in completing his homework. Rather, the student usually becomes more interested in reading than report cards, is more relaxed and patient with himself in completing assignments, and develops a more realistic definition of academic progress.

Reinforcement Activities

Suggestions and procedures for reinforcement activities incorporating those words and concepts that give the student difficulty are discussed in detail in Chapter 6 of the Book 1 manual. As was the case with students working in Book 3, emphasis should be placed on vocabulary rather than on phonics principles. As often as necessary, remind the student of the strong relationship between knowledge of vocabulary and skill in reading.

Student Writing

Student writing is discussed in Chapter 7 of the Book 1 manual. Use these suggestions to help you plan writing assignments. It is recommended that the student working in Book 4 complete weekly writing assignments in addition to the sentence writing he does in each lesson.

Paragraphs or brief essays about discussion topics that interest the student and personal and/or business letters are appropriate writing assignments. The recommended minimum length for writing assignments is 85-100 words. Many students are capable and eager to write longer compositions.

Most students enjoy offering ideas for writing assignments. They usually, however, expect you to assume the overall responsibility for both topics and suggestions for developing topics.

The Lesson Format

After the first class in which Lesson 1 is completed and Lesson 2 is previewed for homework, the procedure for each lesson should be as consistent as possible.

1. **Writing assignment.** If the student has been given a writing assignment, have him read his work and make any necessary revisions and corrections with your assistance.

2. **Oral reading.** The student reads as much of the reading passage he has studied for homework as time permits. Help him when necessary with pronunciation and oral expression. The new words should be reviewed only if you think it is necessary.

3. **Homework review.** The student goes over the exercises and makes any necessary corrections.

4. **Reinforcement activity.** The student completes one or more reinforcement activities which emphasize words that continue to give him difficulty. As mentioned earlier, vocabulary should be stressed.

5. **Homework preview.** The student notes what to do in the next lesson, which he is to complete for homework. He pronounces the Words for Study and reads the title of the passage so he has a general sense of the topic.

He then reads the directions for each exercise. It is recommended that he read the directions silently and ask for clarification when necessary. The Book 4 student is ready to assume this responsibility but may need your help in doing so. For example, when it becomes clear that a student is making many mistakes because he has difficulty understanding directions, gently remind him to ask for clarification whenever he feels the least bit unsure about what the directions are telling him to do. Since most students prefer getting their work right the first time, sooner or later these reminders definitely sink in. When appropriate, the student can complete an item or two for those exercises that seem initially confusing.

Individual Lesson Notes

The lesson notes which follow pertain to suggestions and procedures for specific items in the Book 4 lessons. Unless you are working with a small group in a tutorial manner, you do not need to familiarize yourself with more than one set of lesson notes at a time.

2. Lesson Notes for Book 4

Lesson 1
The Heart

Primary emphasis

- Comprehension (written questions and answers)
- General information (parts of the body)
- Working with common expressions

Secondary emphasis

- Syllabication (divide words into syllables)
- Spelling (the ending -er)
- Oral reading

Words for Study

Mention to the student that these words are listed because they appear in either the reading passage or exercises and have not been previously studied by students who are using this reading series. Make sure that the student knows how to pronounce the words, but have him learn the meanings of any unfamiliar words from the lesson itself. Use any words that continue to give students difficulty in reinforcement activities.

Keep in mind that these words appear frequently in subsequent lessons, and this repetition helps the student to improve his vocabulary. Thus, it is not necessary for the student to master the words in any given lesson prior to going on to the next lesson.

Reading Passage

Mention that the reading passages in Book 4 are non-fiction. Explain briefly the difference between *fiction* and *nonfiction*. You may want to tell students that high school equivalency examinations include many brief nonfiction passages followed by comprehension questions.

Because this is the first lesson, have the student or students read the story aloud and allow ample time for discussion. If you have time, try to supplement the information presented in this and all subsequent passages with data or visual aids that you have gathered. Usually, any extra information you can provide not only gives the student a better understanding of the topics of these lessons, but also motivates him to broaden his general knowledge.

Exercise 1: About the Reading

1. **True or False?** If the student has made three or more errors in this section, he has probably not referred to the passage for the necessary information. Students often need to be reminded that they should not rely exclusively on their memory for the answers and that skimming through a passage for specific information is definitely a reading skill. (Some students believe that they are cheating if they do this.)

   A helpful practice for students who have trouble with this section is to have them underline the part of the passage that provides the answer for a missed question and write the letter of the question in the margin. Thus, if a student has missed the first item, the student underlines the appropriate part of the first sentence in the fourth paragraph and writes *a* in the margin.

2. Tell the student that all questions requiring lengthy responses are to be written in complete sentences. If necessary, remind him that good writing skills are considered an important part of literacy.

3. **What do you think?** Mention to the student that questions of this nature call for a reasoned opinion written in good sentence form. The answers to this type of question cannot be found in the passage. Many of these questions lend themselves to more fully-developed compositions.

Exercise 2: The Human Body

Encourage the student to refer to the passage, use process of elimination, and rely upon his common sense to complete this exercise.

Exercise 3: The Ending -er

During the preview, have the student verbalize the spelling principle for each of the examples. Unless the student seems confused, there is no need for him to complete any items during the preview.

Exercise 4: Syllables

The student who has completed Book 3, in which the concept of syllables is introduced, has no difficulty with this exercise. Some students who are beginning this series in Book 4 are not familiar with syllabication. In these instances, have the student complete one or two items during the preview.

Students who began their reading work in Book 1 benefit from the long and short vowel review because they are still sounding out many of the words they encounter in the reading passage and/or exercises. With all other students, have them mark the vowels in addition to dividing the words into syllables only if you think they will benefit from this practice.

Exercise 5: Brain Benders

1. If the student declares that he's never heard of these expressions, tell him to make an intelligent guess anyway. Remind him that his grades (if grades are given) are based on corrected work and overall progress and

that he will often find himself working with new material in Book 4. Point out that new material helps to sharpen his mind and increase his confidence.

2. Some students want to know why they can't simply put the letter of the answer on the line. Gently remind them that they are usually required to write out the answers because this contributes to spelling improvement.

3. During the homework review, allot time for discussing some of the expressions included in this exercise. Adults, particularly, state a desire for more work with common expressions. It is not unusual to hear an adult student comment, "I hear people saying that all the time, and I always wondered what it meant."

Note

After the student has gone over the exercises and made any necessary corrections during the homework review, give him an opportunity to ask questions or make comments. This activity is especially recommended for the student who starts with Book 4 because it contributes to the development of a good working relationship.

Lesson 2
Babe Ruth

Primary emphasis

- Comprehension (written questions and answers)
- Vocabulary review (synonyms and antonyms)
- General information (games and sports)

Secondary emphasis

- Syllabication (dividing words into syllables)
- Spelling (the ending -er)
- Oral reading

Words for Study

Use the procedure suggested for Lesson 1.

Reading Passage

During the homework review, make sure the student understands that the dates in parentheses indicate the dates of Babe Ruth's birth and death.

Exercise 1: About the Reading

A brief discussion or composition assignment about heroes is appropriate for this lesson. However, brace yourself for some rather astonishing responses if you are of the "older generation." Quite often, students—particularly adolescents—select themselves when asked to name favorite heroes.

Exercise 2: Games and Sports

During the preview, encourage the student to take the last sentence in the directions seriously. Experience indicates that students tend to learn better and with more enthusiasm when they involve others in their learning. Generally speaking, the possibility of the student's leaning too heavily on others for answers is *not* an issue. Most students working in this series acknowledge that their reading needs improvement and assume responsibility for completing the work in a mature manner.

Exercises 3 and 4: Words That Mean the Same and Word Opposites

If necessary, remind the student to use process of elimination to complete these two vocabulary reviews. Students working in Book 4 are ready to use the dictionary and should be encouraged to do so when words give them difficulty. Allot some time for making sure that the student understands how to use the dictionary efficiently.

Exercise 5: More Work with the Ending -er

Use the procedure suggested for this type of exercise in Lesson 1.

Exercise 6: Syllables

Review the definition of *syllable* with all students during the homework review.

Lesson 3
Time

Primary emphasis

- Comprehension (written questions and answers)
- Sequencing (words pertaining to time)
- Using context clues

Secondary emphasis

- Syllabication (dividing words into syllables)
- Spelling (the ending -y)
- Oral reading

Words for Study

Use the procedure suggested for Lesson 1.

Reading Passage

It has not occurred to many students that cultural differences exist. If you are unable to bring in information about foreign cultures, a brief discussion about differences among cultures in the United States is recommended. This does not need to be an in-depth discussion.

Exercise 1: About the Reading

1. Make sure the student understands the meaning of *concept*.
2. Question 9 can serve as the basis for a discussion topic or short composition assignment.

Exercise 2: Time

Students, particularly adolescents, often have difficulty with this exercise. It may be necessary to complete it in class rather than assigning it as part of the homework.

Exercise 3: More About Time

Remind students to use process of elimination and context clues to complete this exercise.

Exercise 4: The Ending -y

Use the procedure suggested for this type of exercise in Lesson 1.

Exercise 5: Syllables

Mention briefly that *Southwest* is capitalized only when it refers to a section of the country. If necessary, have the student refer to the reading passage to note the context in which *Southwest* appears.

Lesson 4
Insects

Primary emphasis

- Comprehension (written questions and answers)
- Using context clues
- General information (insects and bugs)
- Analogies

Secondary emphasis

- Syllabication (dividing words into syllables)
- Spelling (the ending -*y*)
- Oral reading

Words for Study

Use the procedure suggested for Lesson 1.

Exercise 2: Name That Insect or Bug

Some students prefer using the dictionary for this exercise rather than relying solely on context clues. This is perfectly alright.

Exercise 3: Which Word Fits Best?

Students who have worked in the earlier books of this reading series are quite familiar with analogies. Have the student who is starting this series in Book 4 complete the first item during the preview to make sure he understands what is expected of him. As was mentioned in earlier lesson notes, many students enjoy hearing that this type of question appears on college entrance examination tests.

Exercise 4: More Work with the Ending -y

Use the procedure suggested for this type of exercise in Lesson 1.

Exercise 5: Syllables

At this point, students should have no difficulty completing this type of exercise.

Lesson 5
The Brain Sees All

Primary emphasis

- Comprehension (written questions and answers)
- Sequencing events
- Categorizing
- Using context clues

Secondary emphasis

- Syllabication (dividing words into syllables)
- Oral reading

Words for Study

Use the procedure suggested for Lesson 1.

Exercise 1: About the Reading

Both **What do you think?** questions are sources for good discussions. If time permits, bring in some ads clipped from magazines and have the students comment on their appeal to potential consumers.

Exercise 2: Putting Sentences in Order

Students appreciate it if you allow them to number the sentences and then write them out after any necessary corrections have been made during the homework review. The only guideline is that the sequence must make sense. For example, whether the set is turned on before or after Mrs. Woods has checked the *TV Guide* is up to the student.

Exercise 3: Syllables

Students should have no difficulty completing this exercise.

Exercise 4: Working with Headings

After the student has read the directions during the preview, have him note the capitalization of the main words in the headings. Mention that he is to adhere to this capitalization when he places the headings on the correct lines.

Exercise 5: Words That End in -y

Keep in mind that it is the sound for -*y* that is being emphasized in this exercise. Because some students still need practice with this sound, this exercise has been included at this point.

Review: Lessons 1-5

It should be emphasized that this is a review, not a test. Tell the student that he may refer to previous lessons or the dictionary as often as he needs to.

The word index at the end of this and subsequent reviews can be used as the basis for pronunciation reviews, spelling tests, sentence writing, or other appropriate reinforcement activities.

Lesson 6
The Sun

Primary emphasis

- Comprehension (written questions and answers)
- Classifying
- Compound words

Secondary emphasis

- Spelling (the ending -*ing*)
- Review of confusing word pairs
- Oral reading

Words for Study

Use the procedure suggested for Lesson 1.

Exercise 1: About the Reading

For students who make three or more errors on these true/false statements, use the procedure suggested for this type of comprehension exercise in Lesson 1.

Exercise 2: Working with Headings

During the preview of this exercise, make sure the student understands that solids, liquids, and gases comprise the three forms of matter.

If necessary, remind the student to use process of elimination to complete this exercise.

Exercise 3: Compound Words

During the homework review, have the student orally identify the components of each compound word listed in the left column.

Exercise 4: The Ending -*ing*

Use the procedure for this type of exercise suggested in Lesson 1.

Exercise 5: Some Confusing -*ing* Words

During the preview, many students may need to pronounce the words they are to use for the blanks. Students find it helpful if you remind them that doubling the consonant keeps the preceding vowel short (items 3, 4, and 5).

Lesson 7
Thomas Edison

Primary emphasis

- Comprehension (written questions and answers)
- Using context clues
- Analogies

Secondary emphasis

- Form compound words
- Syllabication (divide words into syllables)
- Oral reading

Words for Study

Use the procedure suggested for Lesson 1.

Exercise 2: More Work with Compound Words

Students who have worked in the earlier books in this reading series are familiar with this type of exercise. Have the student who has started in Book 4 complete at least one item in addition to reading the directions and studying the example during the preview.

A composition topic that many students enjoy is: "If you could have invented one of the many inventions already invented, what would it be and why?"

Exercise 3: Which Word Fits Best?

If students experienced difficulty completing the previous exercise of this nature, they should be reminded to take their time, work by process of elimination, and THINK.

Exercise 4: Syllables

An appropriate reinforcement activity for this exercise is to say ten words and have the student tell you or write down how many syllables are in each word.

Lesson 8
Knives, Forks, and Spoons

Primary emphasis

- Comprehension (written questions and answers)
- General information (facts about food)
- Singular and plural words

Secondary emphasis

- Using context clues
- Spelling (changing the *f* to *v*)
- Oral reading

Words for Study

Use the procedure suggested for Lesson 1.

Exercise 1: About the Reading

During the preview, spend a few moments discussing how question 5 is to be answered. Make sure the student understands the meaning of *key* as it is used in this context.

During the discussion, students often enjoy elaborating on their answers to the last question.

Exercise 2: The Last Word on Knives

If necessary, help the student read the verse about the Johnson boys with appropriate rhythm.

Exercise 4: Singular and Plural Words

This exercise marks the first time the concepts *singular* and *plural* appear in this reading series. Be sure to preview this exercise thoroughly. Additionally, make sure that the student knows how to pronounce *singular* and *plural* correctly.

Exercise 5: One Knife/Two Knives

Plan to spend more time than usual on the preview of this exercise. If necessary, remind the student to complete the plural forms prior to filling in the blanks of the sentences with the correct choices. During the homework review, make sure that the student is pronouncing the plural forms of the words in the left column correctly.

absence of manners as a basic sickness in our society. Ironically enough, experience indicates that the basic task of the teacher in moderating such a discussion is to encourage each person to present his views on this controversial topic in a mannerly way.

Exercise 2: Which Word Does Not Fit?

After the student has read the directions and studied the example, have him complete the second item during the preview so that he fully understands what he is to do.

Exercise 3: Recipes

Again, allow the student to number the sentences in proper order and make any necessary corrections prior to writing out the sentences on the lines.

Exercise 4: Singular and Plural Words

Students generally have no difficulty completing this section. During the homework review, review the definitions for *singular* and *plural*.

Exercise 5: More about Manners

During the preview, mention that this exercise is similar to the brief information quizzes that appear in many magazines and is to be completed just for enjoyment.

Lesson 9
Manners

Primary emphasis

- Comprehension (written questions and answers)
- Vocabulary review (choosing the unrelated word)
- Sequencing

Secondary emphasis

- Oral reading
- General information (manners)
- Singular and plural words

Words for Study

Use the procedure suggested for Lesson 1.

Reading Passage

This passage lends itself to oral reading practice. Students enjoy reading this as if they were actually teaching a class on manners.

Exercise 1: What Do You Think?

The issue of manners is an excellent topic for both oral discussion work and brief composition assignments. Whereas some students perceive the presence of manners as a sign of a phony, manipulative person, others see the

Lesson 10
Flying Saucers

Primary emphasis

- Comprehension (written questions and answers)
- Using context clues
- Vocabulary review

Secondary emphasis

- Multiple meanings and pronunciations
- Oral reading

Words for Study

Use the procedure suggested for Lesson 1.

Reading Passage

Some students are more familiar with the term *UFO's* than they are with *flying saucers*. Others have heard of UFO's but do not know what the letters stand for. Ask the students why they think *UFO* has replaced *flying saucer* in the vocabularies of so many people. This is an appropriate time to mention to the students that language is always undergoing change. Any examples you can give of this fact are helpful. For example, students usually enjoy hearing that *ain't* used to be considered an acceptable word in American English.

Exercise 1: About the Reading

Both questions 7 and 8 can be considered as sources for good discussion topics or brief composition assignments.

Exercise 2: More About Meteors

If necessary, remind the student to use process of elimination to complete this exercise.

Exercise 3: Choosing the Right Word

During the homework review, have the student tell you whether the correct answer is an example of the first word or means the same thing as the first word. Some students confuse examples with synonyms, and this exercise provides an excellent opportunity to help the student clear up this confusion.

Exercise 4: Word Study

After the student has read the directions during the preview, have him focus on the the pronunciations of the words in the left column so that he has a clearer understanding of how to complete this exercise.

Review: Lessons 1-10

Again, remind the student that this is not a test, but rather an opportunity to review many of the words and concepts he has studied before he moves ahead in the reading book.

Have the student skim the directions for each section during the preview and remind him, if necessary, to refer to previous lessons or the dictionary for any relevant information.

Lesson 11
Accepting Who You Are

Primary emphasis

- Comprehension (written questions and answers)
- Using context clues

Secondary emphasis

- Silent letters
- Word endings
- Spelling (changing *y* to *i* and double crostic)
- Oral reading

Words for Study

Use the procedure suggested for Lesson 1.

Exercise 1: About the Reading

1. For students who continue to demonstrate difficulty with true/false questions, use the procedure suggested for this type of question in Lesson 1.

2. Students, particularly adolescents, often need suggestions for answering question 2. For example, one student who was confused by this question was asked to name one thing that he did one year ago at this time which he no longer does. (His response was that he used to skip school but now attends regularly.) The student was then told that this was clearly an example of a change he had made and was asked if he considered this change as something that made his life happier or worse. At this point, the student understood how to approach this question and was able to respond to it clearly. (P.S. He did not write about school.)

Many students need help for this question because they are not accustomed to perceiving themselves as consciously making changes in their lives. Consider this question as an introduction to this concept. Belaboring the point often results in more confusion than clarity for the student who does not think in terms of making conscious changes.

Exercise 2: Changing the *y* to *i*

After the student has read the directions and studied the examples during the preview, he should have no difficulty with this exercise. Have him complete the second item during the preview only if you think it is necessary.

Exercise 3: Word Endings

During the homework review, emphasize the sounds of these endings and consider a brief spelling quiz which emphasizes common endings. The student finds that an awareness of these endings helps his spelling improve considerably.

Exercise 4: Silent Letters

After the student has read the directions and studied the example, have him complete the second item during the preview so that he has a better understanding of how to complete this exercise correctly.

Exercise 5: Happiness

Thoroughly preview this exercise. Remind the student to work back and forth between the quote and the questions to find all the answers. Most students really enjoy this type of exercise.

Lesson 12
Anne Frank: Part I

Primary emphasis

- Comprehension (written questions and answers)
- Vocabulary review (synonyms and antonyms)
- Using context clues

Secondary emphasis

- Word beginnings
- Hard and soft *g*
- Oral reading

Words for Study

Use these words as a point of departure for presenting general background information on World War II. Any pictures that you can bring in help the student prepare himself for this reading passage, which is continued in Lesson 13.

Also, make sure the students understand where Germany and Holland are and know what a diary is.

Reading Passage

This passage lends itself to oral reading practice.

Exercise 1: About the Reading

Question 12 provides a good source for class discussion and/or a brief composition assignment.

Exercise 2: Word Beginnings

Remind the student to recall information he has learned from the diary excerpts and your brief sketch of World War II to answer these questions. Process of elimination and context clues are also helpful resources.

Exercises 3 and 4: Words That Mean the Same and Word Opposites

Generally, these exercises give the student no trouble. Occasionally, a student asks if he can use the dictionary which, of course, is perfectly acceptable.

Lesson 13
Anne Frank: Part II

Primary emphasis

- Comprehension (written questions and answers)
- Using context clues
- Classifying

Secondary emphasis

- Word endings
- Oral reading

Words for Study

Use the procedure suggested for Lesson 1.

Reading Passage

This passage also lends itself to oral reading practice. During the homework review, review Anne Frank's life and her fate and basic data pertaining to World War II.

Exercise 1: About the Reading

Question 7, in particular, is a good source for a brief composition assignment.

Exercise 2: World War II

By using process of elimination, students should have no difficulty with this exercise.

Exercise 3: Cities, States, and Countries

Although students generally seem to enjoy using a globe or map to complete this activity, they can also use the dictionary. During the homework review, have the student identify the countries in which the listed cities are located. Make sure all items are capitalized.

Exercise 4: More Work with Word Endings

Use the procedure suggested for this type of exercise in Lesson 11.

Lesson 14
The Ship of the Desert

Primary emphasis

- Comprehension (written questions and answers)
- Review of compound words
- Using context clues

Secondary emphasis

- Word endings
- Syllabication (dividing words into syllables)
- Oral reading

Words for Study

Use the procedure suggested for Lesson 1.

Exercise 1: About the Reading

Adolescent students, in particular, enjoy writing compositions about pets they have either had or would like to have.

Exercise 2: Compound Words

If necessary, remind the student to use process of elimination to complete this exercise. Many students enjoy using the dictionary to complete this work.

Exercise 3: More Work with Word Endings

Use the procedure suggested for this type of exercise in Lesson 11.

Exercise 4: Syllables

Students generally have no difficulty with this exercise. As was recommended previously, marking the vowels can be omitted if you think this work is of no special benefit to the student.

Lesson 15

Some Facts about Southpaws

Primary emphasis

- Comprehension (written questions and answers)
- Common expressions
- Vocabulary

Secondary emphasis

- Singular and plural words
- Oral reading

Words for Study

For this lesson, discuss the meanings of *southpaw* and *culture* prior to the student's reading the passage for homework.

Exercise 1: About the Reading

For students who have difficulty with the true/false questions, use the procedure suggested in Lesson 1.

Exercise 2: "Handy" Sayings

Remind the student to make an intelligent guess for any items that are completely unfamiliar to him. Discuss troublesome expressions in greater detail during the homework review.

Exercise 3: "Handy" Words

Students generally have no difficulty either sounding out the new words or answering the questions correctly in this exercise.

Exercise 4: Singular and Plural Words

After the student has read the directions and studied the examples during the preview, have him complete one or two items if you think this is necessary.

Review: Lessons 1-15

Use the same procedure for this review as you did for the two previous reviews.

Lesson 16

Some Thoughts about Dying

Primary emphasis

- Comprehension (written questions and answers)
- Sequencing events
- Using context clues

Secondary emphasis

- The ending -*ly*
- Compound words
- Oral reading

Words for Study

Use the procedure suggested for Lesson 1.

Reading Passage

Because the tone and subject matter of this passage are considerably different, some students may have difficulty following the author's train of thought. If you think your students will find this passage confusing, plan the initial reading as a class activity and allow ample time for discussion. Students are to complete all exercises for homework.

This procedure can also be used in a classroom setting in which students work independently. When a student is ready for Lesson 16, simply have all students stop what they are doing and have one of them begin the oral reading. Students who are quite a bit behind the others appreciate this experience because their ability to read the passage and participate in the discussion increases their confidence. Allow all students to complete the exercises for this lesson at this point. Students can help each other do this and make any necessary corrections in a group homework review.

Exercise 2: About the Reading

Have the student number the sentences in correct sequence and make any necessary changes before they write out the sentences.

Exercise 3: The Ending -*ly*

Encourage the student to add -*ly* to each word listed at the beginning of the exercise prior to filling in the blanks correctly.

Exercise 4: More Work with the Ending -*ly*

After the student has read the directions and studied the example during the preview, he should have no difficulty with this exercise.

Exercise 5: More Work with Compound Words

During the homework review, briefly discuss the meanings of all choices for each sentence. The student can either define the words, use them in sentences, or guess the meaning from hearing you or another student use them in sentences.

Lesson 17

The Number One Eater in America

Primary emphasis

- Comprehension (written questions and answers)
- Using context clues
- Common expressions

Secondary emphasis

- The ending -*ful*
- Syllabication
- Oral reading

Words for Study

Use the procedure suggested for Lesson 1.

Reading Passage

Students enjoy reading this passage aloud. A brief discussion in which contemporary eating habits are compared and contrasted with those of Diamond Jim Brady is often a good follow-up activity.

Exercise 1: About the Reading

Adult students particularly enjoy either discussing or writing a composition about Question 9.

Exercise 2: Food for Thought

Remind the student to make an intelligent guess for any item that gives him difficulty. These expressions can be discussed more fully during the homework review.

Exercise 3: The Ending -*ful*

Encourage the student to add -*ful* to each word listed at the beginning of the exercise prior to filling in the blanks correctly.

Exercise 4: Working with Syllables

If necessary, remind the student to cross out the syllables in the box as he uses them.

Lesson 18

The Great Hunger

Primary emphasis

- Comprehension (written questions and answers)
- Using context clues
- Vocabulary review

Secondary emphasis

- The ending -*less*
- Oral reading

Words for Study

Use the procedure suggested for Lesson 1.

Reading Passage

During the homework review, it is often productive to contrast the famine of this passage with the feasts in the preceding lesson. Adult students, particularly, find this type of discussion helpful.

Exercise 1: About the Reading

Students who continue to experience difficulty with true/false questions are to use the procedure suggested in Lesson 1.

Exercise 2: More About Potatoes

As long as students take their time, work by process of elimination and use context clues, they should have no difficulty with this exercise.

Exercise 3: Where Would You Find It?

After the student has read the directions and studied the example during the preview, have him complete the second item if you think he is still somewhat confused.

Exercise 4: The Ending -*less*

Again, encourage the student to add -*less* to each word listed at the beginning of the exercise prior to filling in the blanks correctly. During the homework review, review the meanings of -*ful* and -*less* as word endings. It is not necessary to introduce the term *suffix*.

Lesson 19

Digestion

Primary emphasis

- Comprehension (written questions and answers)
- Cause and effect relationships
- General information (the human body)

Secondary emphasis

- Word endings
- Oral reading

Words for Study

Use the procedure suggested for Lesson 1.

Exercise 2: More About Digestion

After the student has previewed the directions, have him verbalize what he is to do, so that you know he understands the proper way to complete this section. The student does *not* need to write his description of how each part aids in digestion in sentence form.

Exercise 3: Cause and Effect

Some students need a more detailed explanation for the word *effect*. Explaining that an effect is a result helps them to better understand this word. Allow the student to number the effects correctly and make any necessary changes during the preview prior to writing the effects on the lines provided.

Exercise 4: The Human Body

Remind the student to use information he has gained from the reading passage and process of elimination to complete this exercise.

Exercise 5: Word Endings

Use the procedure suggested for this type of exercise in Lesson 11.

Lesson 20
Nail Soup

Primary emphasis

- Comprehension (written questions and answers)
- Reading a menu
- Vocabulary review (synonyms and antonyms)

Secondary emphasis

- Using context clues
- Word endings
- Oral reading

Words for Study

Use the procedure suggested for Lesson 1.

Reading Passage

"Nail Soup" is adapted from an old Russian folk tale. It is also commonly known as "Stone Soup." Students particularly enjoy reading this as if it were a play during the homework review.

Exercise 1: About the Reading

For the sake of a logical progression of thought, no distinction has been made between comprehension questions and **What Do You Think?** questions in this exercise. Because the student is used to seeing these two types of questions separated, you may need to point out to him that some of the questions require him to give information from the story whereas others call for an intelligently-formed opinion.

Exercise 2: May I Take Your Order?

There is no one right answer for questions 3, 4, and 5. However, student answers should reflect intelligent reasoning.

Exercise 3: Same or Opposite?

Encourage all students to use a dictionary for those items that give them difficulty. Generally, all students can work with the concepts of *same* and *opposite* in the same exercise at this point.

Exercise 4: More Work with Word Endings

Use the procedure suggested for this type of exercise in Lesson 11.

Review: Lessons 1-20

The purpose of this review is to give the student one more opportunity to work with many of the words and concepts emphasized in Book 4. As was recommended in the notes for previous reviews, this review should not be perceived as a test, although sections of it are appropriate for use as a diagnostic tool for any student you are considering starting in Book 5.

After any necessary corrections have been made by the student during the homework review, spend a few moments reviewing and evaluating the student's reading progress. Many students enjoy perusing the word index because it represents a concrete symbol of accomplishment. The word index should be kept in mind for planning reinforcement activities for the student as he works in Book 5.

Answer Key for Book 1

Lesson 1

1 Copying Sentences
See student text.

2 Word Sounds
1. Tim, time
2. tube, tub
3. not, note
4. can, cane
5. quit, quite

Lesson 2

1 Copying Sentences
See student text.

2 Word Sounds
1. huge
2. cut
3. met
4. us
5. cope
6. rode
7. hopes
8. at

Lesson 3

1 Word Sounds
1. mad, mud, made
2. hot, hates, hat
3. six, sit, sip
4. cop, cope, cup
5. man, men, mine
6. us, fuse, used
7. at, as, am
8. late, dates, Kate
9. pet, pep, pen

2 Marking the Vowels
1. fīr¢
2. sĭp
3. cān¢
4. nīc¢
5. wōk¢
6. sŭn
7. hōl¢
8. bĕd
9. āt¢
10. ūs¢
11. mē
12. lĭd
13. jăb
14. cūt¢
15. kēep
16. rūl¢

Lesson 4

1 Word Sounds
1. cute
2. tub
3. rod
4. Cape
5. ripe
6. rid
7. wine
8. fad
9. hope
10. fuss
11. let
12. feel
13. hot
14. ham
15. feed

2 Yes or No
Answers will vary.

Lesson 5

1 Adding -ed
1. looked
2. lasted
3. talked
4. asked
5. messed
6. relaxed

1. faced
2. saved
3. joked
4. hired
5. lined
6. refused

1. hopped
2. sipped
3. patted
4. gunned
5. popped
6. sobbed

2 Word Sounds
1. phone
2. bus
3. sale
4. bed
5. pan
6. red
7. cane
8. hut
9. bone
10. hugs
11. horn
12. name
13. park
14. lap

Lesson 6

1 Adding -ed
1. called
2. hunted
3. landed
4. walked
5. dumped
6. mended

1. baked
2. named
3. liked
4. dated
5. tired
6. hoped

1. robbed
2. kidded
3. ripped
4. netted
5. topped
6. rammed

2 Word Sounds
1. sick
2. sent
3. hunt
4. damp
5. ducked
6. hand
7. kick
8. pond
9. sent
10. neck
11. end

Lesson 7

1 Adding -ing
1. going
2. fixing
3. singing
4. looking
5. missing

1. taking
2. having
3. baking
4. joking
5. hoping

1. running
2. sipping
3. patting
4. jabbing
5. hopping

Lesson (2)

2 Word Sounds
1. sat
2. hen
3. pig
4. zone
5. rat
6. side
7. dot
8. nuts
9. pale
10. dump
11. file
12. pick
13. lump
14. fond
15. band

Lesson 8

1 Word Sounds
1. code
2. fox
3. dam
4. pad
5. dive
6. tame
7. rate
8. dined

2 Using a and an
1. an
2. a
3. a
4. an
5. an
6. a
7. a
8. a
9. an
10. an

3 Marking the Vowels
1. fūm¢
2. lĕss
3. nĕck
4. rōb¢
5. tĭck
6. hănd
7. sŏck
8. sāf¢
9. quĭck
10. cĕnt
11. mīnd
12. rēfūs¢
13. ŭs
14. bēef
15. fēmāl¢

4 Words That Mean the Same
1. huge
2. keep
3. seek
4. honk
5. six
6. jab
7. fix
8. fun
9. weep
10. females

5 Writing Sentences
Answers will vary.

Lesson 9

1 Adding -y to Words
1. messy
2. fussy
3. bumpy
4. needy
5. robbery

1. icy
2. nosy
3. lacy
4. bony
5. wiry

1. funny
2. sunny
3. Mommy
4. Daddy
5. nutty

2 Words That End in -ly

1. quickly   4. friendly
2. lovely   5. weekly
3. safely

3 Words That End in -y

1. baby   6. Andy
2. candy   7. muddy
3. sixty   8. handy
4. lobby   9. forty
5. ninety   10. Bucky

4 Words That Mean the Same

1. hide   7. joke
2. behind   8. refuse
3. ten cents   9. funny
4. male   10. jack
5. not happy   11. Sunday
6. mock   12. Saturday

Lesson 10

1 Word Sounds

1. gas, pass
2. fact, acts
3. None, one, done
4. knew, few, new
5. right, lights, night
6. see, fee, knee
7. wrote, note, vote
8. heck, neck, wreck
9. dock, locked, knock
10. lay, way, day

2 Word Opposites

1. night   6. huge
2. last   7. wrong
3. back   8. play
4. bad   9. there
5. sad   10. same

3 Word Study

1. yesterday   6. females
2. friend   7. wine
3. foot   8. numb
4. ant   9. cot
5. sun   10. fit

Lesson 11

1 Adding -er to Words

1. quicker   1. finer   1. bigger
2. tighter   2. ruder   2. fatter
3. fewer   3. cuter   3. hotter
4. boxer   4. baker   4. winter
5. hunter   5. later   5. hitter
6. burner   6. diner   6. mugger

2 Words that End in -er

1. bumper   5. pepper
2. hammer   6. ruler
3. Copper   7. worker
4. summer   8. better, better

3 Changing y to i and Adding -er

handier   1. luckier
happier   2. happier
luckier   3. lovelier
lovelier   4. fussier
fussier   5. bumpier
bumpier   6. handier

4 Who Does What?

1. a hunter   5. a banker
2. a writer   6. a fighter
3. a singer   7. a player
4. a joker   8. a thinker

Lesson 12

1 Context Clues

five, work, house
eat, meat, boiled, tea, mug, fork
soap, water, night (water, soap, night)

2 Word Sounds

1. deer   8. peas   15. mouse
2. road   9. soak   16. coals
3. due   10. moon   17. main
4. far   11. pain   18. dirt
5. barn   12. foot   19. bored
6. ails   13. maid   20. hard
7. load   14. real

3 Writing Sentences

Answers will vary.

Lesson 13

1 Word Sounds

1. moon   11. meal   21. lean
2. noon   12. mean   22. lead
3. soon   13. code   23. leaf
4. mail   14. cope   24. worn
5. main   15. cone   25. horn
6. maid   16. tore   26. corn
7. carve   17. sore   27. torn
8. cart   18. wore   28. born
9. card   19. more
10. meat   20. leak

2 Words That End in -er

1. painter   4. boarder   7. helper
2. keeper   5. voter   8. teacher
3. catcher   6. diner

3 Word Study

1. head   6. air
2. year   7. food
3. pear   8. tea
4. dice   9. fake
5. oven   10. wages

4 Marking the Vowels

1. ădd   9. fūmȼ
2. bītȼ   10. rēēl
3. gātȼ   11. hīkȼ
4. dămp   12. hŭnt
5. sĕnd   13. dōzȼ
6. clŏck   14. dŭnk
7. pŏp   15. zōnȼ
8. sāmȼ   16. dĕck

Lesson 14

1 The Ending -ful

handful   1. useful
harmful   2. handful
helpful   3. helpful
careful   4. harmful
useful   5. careful
thankful   6. thankful

2 The Ending -less

harmless   1. jobless
helpless   2. careless
hopeless   3. homeless
homeless   4. harmless
careless   5. hopeless
jobless   6. helpless

3 Words That Mean the Same

1. carve   6. shout
2. ill   7. hurt
3. handy   8. bare
4. film   9. poor
5. soaked   10. dead

4 Word Opposites

1. cold   6. messy
2. start   7. others
3. day   8. false
4. worse   9. dumb
5. take   10. harmless

5 Sayings

1. told   6. hills
2. call   7. ball
3. cold   8. will
4. bell   9. fall
5. milk   10. fill

Lesson 15

1 The Ending -est

1. nearest	1. finest	1. biggest
2. cheapest	2. safest	2. hottest
3. richest	3. rudest	3. fattest
4. smartest	4. ripest	4. maddest
5. loudest	5. latest	5. reddest

2 Changing y to i and Adding -est

funniest	1. loveliest
happiest	2. fussiest
luckiest	3. luckiest
fussiest	4. happiest
loveliest	5. funniest

3 Word Sounds

1. chess	5. wall	9. Last
2. odd	6. loaf	10. well
3. sharp	7. case	
4. talked	8. vote	

4 Words That Mean the Same

1. wish	5. queer	9. two
2. drop	6. faint	10. must
3. torn	7. chair	
4. tug	8. boring	

Lesson 16

1 Word Sounds

1. mouse, house	17. bleached, beach
2. blouse	18. rage
3. coast	19. stage
4. toast	20. page
5. roast	21. plain, pain
6. flew	22. stains
7. new	23. shame, lame
8. blew	24. blamed, same
9. pale	25. rush, slush
10. stale	26. blush
11. tales	27. platter, shattered
12. slip	28. matter
13. dip	29. map
14. ship	30. clapped
15. each	31. nap, slap
16. reach	

2 Compound Words

1. downtown	6. lifeboat
2. baseball	7. weekend
3. football	8. homework
4. cupcakes	9. household
5. cookbook	10. sunshine

3 Writing Sentences

Answers will vary.

Lesson 17

1 Word Sounds

1. blow	9. chest, vests	17. clay, may
2. flow	10. pests	18. prayed, hay
3. slow, row	11. clown, gown, brown	19. drops, stopped
4. price	12. trunk	20. crops
5. pride, prizes	13. truck	21. gum, plums
6. toast	14. trust	22. drum
7. taste, tested	15. harming	
8. best	16. farm, charming	

2 Putting Words into Classes

Town	School	Farm
bus stops	classes	barn
churches	courses	cows
parks	homework	crops
stores	reading	hay
street lights	teachers	hens

3 Best and Least

Answers will vary.

Lesson 18

1 Word Sounds

1. lift	9. grilled	17. lit
2. left	10. chill	18. fibs
3. gift	11. dare	19. bib, crib
4. shift	12. fare	20. ribs
5. math, bath	13. spare	21. coach
6. path	14. flares	22. coast
7. hill	15. spit	23. coals
8. spilled	16. pit	

2 Numbers

1. eighteen	11. seven
2. twenty	12. twelve
3. fifteen	13. Answers may vary.
4. fifteen	14. four (or five counting the spare)
5. sixteen	15. Answers will vary.
6. eleven	16. Answers will vary.
7. fifteen	17. Answers will vary.
8. seven	18. Answers will vary.
9. four	19. Answers will vary.
10. thirteen	20. nine

3 Compound Words

1. armchair	6. bedroom
2. sunburn	7. checkbook
3. bathroom	8. shortstop
4. notebook	9. pancakes
5. popcorn	10. downstairs

Lesson 19

1 Word Sounds

1. list	4. math	7. spilled	10. threw
2. flops	5. egg	8. fork	11. cream
3. boss	6. other	9. wipe	12. snow

2 Colors

1. white	3. red	5. black	7. blue
2. Pink	4. green	6. brown	8. gold

3 Which Word Does Not Fit?

1. drive	4. body	7. shrimp	10. yard
2. bedroom	5. raw	8. Christmas	11. slacks
3. neck	6. whale	9. number	12. dune

4 Words That Begin with *un-*

unsafe	1. unhappy
unless	2. unless
unlucky	3. unlucky
unhappy	4. unsafe
unwrapped	5. unwrapped

5 Words That Begin with *re-*

refuse	1. return
remain	2. repaid
remind	3. refuse
repaid	4. remind
return	5. remain

Lesson 20

1 Word Sounds

1. found, ground	7. carve, starve
2. step	8. but, butter
3. marry	9. sweating, sweater
4. pity, city	10. crawl
5. steep	11. hard, hardly
6. Ms., Miss, Ms., Mrs.	12. stood, wood, hood

2 Putting Words into Classes

Breakfast	Dinner	Snacks
corn flakes	pork chops	candy bar
French toast	rice and beans	Coke
fried eggs	roast beef	ice cream cone
ham and eggs	spare ribs	popcorn
pancakes	stuffed peppers	pretzels

3 Twelve Questions

1. true	7. false
2. false	8. true
3. false	9. true
4. Either true or false	10. false
5. false	11. false
6. false	12. Answers will vary.

4 Writing Sentences

Answers will vary.

First Review

1 Choosing the Right Answer

1. bull	4. tall	7. heart	10. been
2. vase	5. Coast	8. ear	11. care
3. sick	6. close	9. anywhere	12. bless

2 Words That Mean the Same

1. scrub	5. cash	9. gleam
2. swift	6. crazy	10. patch
3. useful	7. strange	
4. mock	8. faint	

3 Word Opposites

1. tired	6. awake
2. fire	7. thick
3. answer	8. calm
4. waste	9. tame
5. huge	10. loaf

4 Using *a* and *an*

1. an	6. an
2. a	7. a
3. an	8. a
4. an	9. a
5. an	10. a

5 Putting Words in Classes

Land	Sky	Water
cities	fog	boats
farms	moon	fish
houses	rain	ships
weeds	snow	waves
woods	stars	whales

Second Review

1 Choosing the Right Answer

1. helpless	5. That's	9. unsafe
2. handful	6. I've	10. guilty
3. sadly	7. Didn't	
4. cellar	8. writer	

2 Numbers

1. twelve	6. seven
2. seven	7. sixteen
3. sixty	8. two
4. Answers will vary.	9. one
5. thirteen	10. millions

3 Which Word Fits Best?

1. father	3. pig	5. worst	7. ceiling
2. slacks	4. hushed	6. upset	8. snail

4 Word Pairs

1. salt and pepper	7. reading and writing
2. bride and groom	8. rod and reel
3. Saturday and Sunday	9. black and blue
4. knife and fork	10. cats and dogs
5. ham and eggs	11. snakes and snails
6. soap and water	12. thick and thin

5 Writing Sentences

Answers will vary.

Answer Key for Book 2

Lesson 1

1 About the Reading
1. People cover their noses when they sneeze so their germs won't go all over the room.
2. When somebody sneezes, people often say, "God bless you."
3. dust, cat hairs, weeds, black pepper, colds (any three)
4. 17 years old
5. 6 months
6. Answers will vary.

2 Word Sounds
1. cape   shape
   grape
   shape
2. drink   think
   stink
   think
3. change   change
   range
   strange
4. chew   grew
   grew
   knew
5. cries   tries
   dries
   tries
6. blob   snob
   job
   snob
7. blown   known
   grown
   known
8. smelling   Smelling
   spelling
   swelling
9. broke   smoke
   choke
   smoke
10. bluffed   stuffed
   puffed
   stuffed

3 Matching
1. hearing
2. seeing
3. touching
4. tasting
5. smelling

4 Marking the e's
1. thēse̸
2. ĕnd
3. alone̸
4. blēed
5. harmlĕss
6. nĕxt
7. use̸ful
8. pancake̸
9. rēmind
10. swĕat
11. close̸
12. choose̸

5 Words That Sound the Same
1. I, eye
2. hear, here
3. Two, to
4. Dear, deer
5. four, for
6. knows, nose

Lesson 2

1 About the Reading
1. United States
2. more than 28 million
3. $415,000
4. doctor
5. Cats can see better in dim light.
6. Answers will vary.

2 Word Sounds
1. brand   stand
   grand
   stand
2. creeps   creeps
   jeeps
   sleeps
3. fang   slang
   sang
   slang
4. bean   mean
   clean
   mean
5. clear   hear
   hear
   near
6. shrill   shrill
   skill
   spill
7. brown   crown
   clown
   crown
8. paw   paw
   raw
   straw
9. cow   Now
   how
   now
10. sends   spends
   spends
   tends

3 Putting Words in Classes
List A — Cats	List B — Dogs
always land on their feet	barking
climbing trees	chasing cars
nine lives	digging up bones
purring	man's best friend

4 Words That Sound the Same
1. By, buy
2. knew, new
3. ate, eight
4. Do, due
5. Our, hour

Lesson 3

1 About the Reading
1. seven years
2. Rome
3. dead
4. You will have seven years bad luck.
5. Every cell is renewed.
6. Answers will vary, depending on how heavily one smokes.

2 Word Sounds
1. blink   think
   drink
   think
2. brave   brave
   cave
   wave
3. blame   game
   game
   frame
4. blink   drink
   drink
   stink
5. dice   dice
   price
   spice
6. dated   stated
   plated
   stated
7. bone   throne
   cone
   throne
8. chart   part
   part
   start
9. cheek   week
   peek
   week
10. chins   sins
   grins
   sins

3 Word Sounds

Cow	Slow
clown	blow
crowd	grown
how	know
now	show
wow	snow

4 Number Words

1. twenty-four
2. thirty-one
3. thirty
4. fifty
5. forty
6. twenty-five
7. Answers will vary.
8. Answers will vary.
9. Answers will vary, depending on state law.
10. Answers will vary, depending on state law.

Lesson 4

1 About the Reading

1. pub
2. pint and quart
3. He gave away 30,000 gallons of beer as a gift to the gods.
4. They had run out of beer, which served as food, and they needed to find more food.
5. Beer left in sunlight turns cloudy and takes on a funny smell and taste.
6. People who really like beer say it should be served with a head on it.
7. "Minding your p's and q's" means being careful or watching your step.
8. 1620

2 Word Sounds

1. brewed   brewed
   chewed
   stewed
2. colds   holds
   folds
   holds
3. change   strange
   range
   strange
4. beans   beans
   jeans
   means
5. ate   ate
   date
   state
6. found   pound
   pound
   sound
7. dunes   prunes
   prunes
   tunes
8. cream   cream
   dream
   stream

3 Word Sounds

1. stairs, pair, chairs
2. proud, cloud, loud
3. brave, waves, cave
4. cried, tried, dried
5. hear, clear, near
6. range, change, strange
7. mean, beans, jeans
8. lunch, munched, bunch
9. trick, bricks, stick
10. shape, cape, grape

4 Smallest and Biggest

1. second — hour
2. day — month
3. city — country
4. hundred — million
5. shrimp — human being
6. ounce — quart
7. pint — gallon
8. light bulb — sun
9. bike — ship
10. shrimp — roast beef
11. chestnut — tree
12. Rome — world

5 Word Opposites

1. clear
2. ugly
3. anger
4. children
5. always
6. grew
7. sea
8. saved
9. change
10. brand-new

Lesson 5

1 About the Reading

1. 1875
2. scribe
3. 1,875,000
4. 1,984,000
5. Answers will vary.
6. Answers will vary. Acceptable answers include that people did not have telephones and that visiting people who lived some distance away was more difficult in the 1800's than it is today.

2 Word Sounds

1. telling
2. passed
3. mail
4. life
5. six
6. more
7. vowels
8. such
9. still
10. song

3 Who Does What?

1. cab driver
2. baseball player
3. teacher
4. doctor
5. cowboy
6. tailor
7. clown
8. painter
9. preacher
10. scribe

4 Words That Sound the Same

1. write, right
2. whole, hole
3. beat, beet
4. fare, fair
5. meet, meat
6. heard, herd
7. sale, sails
8. won, one

5 Marking Vowels

1. frāmє
2. brănd
3. ōwn
4. pīnt
5. cāvє
6. grĭn
7. těnd
8. măss
9. trĭck
10. spěnd
11. spīcє
12. thrōnє

Review: Lessons 1-5

1 Choosing the Answer
1. fifty
2. talk
3. sense
4. lace
5. mate
6. meant
7. blob
8. bluffing
9. renew
10. deadly

2 Number Words
1. seven
2. fifty-two
3. sixteen
4. eight
5. two
6. two
7. four
8. thirteen
9. fifty
10. seven
11. 19__-1620 = the answer.
12. One thousand

3 Facts
1. sight
2. hearing
3. taste
4. touch
5. smell

Lesson 6

1 About the Reading
1. wool, animal hair, gold
2. bee's wax
3. He began to lose his hair at an early age.
4. These wigs were huge, covering people's backs and floating down over their chests.
5. 12 years
6. Many years ago in Egypt, the bigger a person's wig was, the more important the person was.
7. Answers will vary.

2 Word Sounds
1. shave
2. bangs
3. hair
4. which
5. Feeling
6. Fighting
7. bugs
8. stand
9. scares
10. takes

3 Which Word Does Not Fit?
1. month
2. English
3. catbird
4. scribe
5. start
6. Anne
7. queen
8. wrist
9. cure
10. pound

4 Vowel Sounds

Long Sound for *ea*	Short Sound for *ea*
1. bean	1. bread
2. beat	2. breakfast
3. easy	3. dead
4. please	4. instead
5. squeak	5. sweat

5 Compound Words
1. bath + room
2. big + wig
3. break + fast
4. cat + bird
5. check + book
6. every + thing
7. ginger + bread
8. girl + friend
9. short + stop
10. sun + burn

Lesson 7

1 About the Reading
1. The liquid comes from two pouches under the skunk's tail.
2. A skunk can spray his liquid from a range of ten to twelve feet.
3. He has to wait one week before he can spray again.
4. A skunk sprays his liquid to ward off danger.
5. He faces whatever he thinks is chasing him.
   He stamps his forefeet.
   He raises all but the tip of his tail.
   He raises the tip of his tail and sprays his liquid.
6. You can bathe in tomato juice.

2 Words That Mean the Same
1. munch
2. hidden
3. creep
4. dim
5. sprint
6. touch
7. bluff
8. friendly
9. trouble
10. form

3 Word Opposites
1. a nobody
2. late
3. hard
4. nothing
5. sink
6. stand
7. find
8. forget
9. saved
10. lovely

4 Compound Words
1. bed + room
2. blood + stream
3. cow + boy
4. home + work
5. May + flower
6. note + book
7. side + ways
8. some + one
9. sun + light
10. what + ever

5 Silly Verses
1. state, straight, sky, cry, dates
2. France, pants, tried, cried, dance
3. sour, hour, life *or* wife, life *or* wife, shower

Lesson 8

1 About the Reading
1. Otherwise the older baby chicks might kill the younger ones.
2. They are timing their hatching.
3. Air must get into the eggshell.
4. Someone in the first book of the Bible thinks the chicken came first.
5. The man who wrote this story thinks the egg came first.
6. In this story, *clutch* means a brood of baby chicks or a group of eggs.
7. *Clutch* can also mean a pedal on a standard shift vehicle, a strong grasp, or to hold tightly.

2 Word Sounds

1. laying	laying	6. fail	fail
paying		mail	
saying		pail	
2. shell	shell	7. bust	just
smell		dust	
spell		just	
3. pounds	pounds	8. bends	spends
rounds		lends	
sounds		spends	
4. bite	white	9. cared	scared
kite		glared	
white		scared	
5. claw	raw	10. hatch	hatch
raw		patch	
thaw		scratch	

3 Which Word Fits Best?

1. glass
2. sky
3. pack
4. upset
5. England
6. Wednesday
7. armchair
8. foot
9. school
10. lung

4 Compound Words

1. babysit
2. copycat
3. handwriting
4. hideout
5. lifetime
6. necktie
7. nickname
8. rainbow
9. touchdown
10. wristwatch

1. touchdown
2. necktie
3. wristwatch
4. hideout
5. copycat
6. handwriting
7. babysit
8. nickname
9. rainbow
10. lifetime

5 Word Sounds

Book	School
1. foot	1. groom
2. hood	2. pool
3. took	3. shoot
4. wood	4. spoon
5. wool	5. tooth

Lesson 9

1 About the Reading

1. California
2. John Sutter
3. 1849
4. forty-niners
5. one ounce

2 Word Sounds

1. bread	spread	5. leans	means
dead		cleans	
spread		means	
2. bought	thought	6. boil	soil
fought		soil	
thought		spoil	
3. blind	find	7. beached	preached
find		preached	
mind		reached	
4. fool's	fool's	8. leaks	speaks
cool's		sneaks	
pool's		speaks	

3 Vowels + the letter *l*

1. belt
2. tall
3. roll
4. milk
5. gold
6. bulb
7. wall
8. bell
9. cold
10. bald
11. Jill, hill

4 Marking the Vowels

1. līcȼ
2. egghĕad
3. wăx
4. withĭn
5. flōat
6. rēason
7. rāisȼ
8. grāvȼ
9. knēē-dēēp
10. nĕst
11. Frăncȼ
12. brākȼ
13. betwēēn
14. jŭst
15. hătch
16. tīp
17. sīncȼ
18. wēak

5 Matching

1. coffee
2. peach
3. chocolate
4. bigwig
5. yolk
6. March
7. kneel
8. lice
9. news
10. hangover

Lesson 10

1 About the Reading

1. Boston
2. 1760
3. No
4. to carry soup
5. to taste the soup before the queen tried it
6. They ran off to get married.
7. The rhymes had been around for hundreds of years before they were called Mother Goose rhymes.
8. Answers will vary. Children like their rhymes, rhythms, and content.

2 Word Sounds

1. born corn horn	horn	6. block clock shock	clock
2. die pie tie	pie	7. door poor floor	door
3. close nose rose	nose	8. free three tree	three
4. bed fed red	bed	9. cane crane lane	lane
5. feet sheet street	street	10. drum plum slum	plum

3 Which Word Does Not Fit?

1. California	6. leaves	11. cowboys
2. snow	7. ice	12. smoker
3. spring	8. straw	13. beach
4. pound	9. air	14. punt
5. eggs	10. wool	

4 Silent Letters

1. knit	5. wrong	9. meant
2. breath	6. thumb	10. heart
3. clutch	7. wrist	11. lamb
4. crane	8. climb	12. watch

5 Words That Sound the Same

1. red, read	5. bear, bare
2. see, sea	6. way, weigh
3. weak, week	7. break, brake
4. through, threw	8. sense, cents

Review: Lessons 1-10

1 Choosing the Answer

1. soundly	6. sin
2. though	7. main
3. shame	8. spoil
4. peeped	9. guess
5. burp	10. hunch

2 Words That Mean the Same

1. shut	5. spoil	9. melt
2. glitter	6. break	10. slim
3. tease	7. dirt	11. rhyme
4. guide	8. brake	12. during

3 Word Opposites

1. death	5. thaw	9. forgot
2. cloudy	6. evening	10. crooked
3. rare	7. messy	11. weak
4. against	8. shut	12. lies

Lesson 11

1 About the Reading

1. We are trying to draw in more air.
2. a. Body heat goes down.
   b. Brain waves become more even.
3. a. The heart rate slows down.
   b. The body relaxes.
   c. Breathing becomes very even.
4. Most dreaming happens during the deepest stage of sleep called REM.
5. You would take quite a few seconds to move.
6. You would probably become quite sick.
7. Answers will vary. Everyone dreams. Dreams are often related to recent events or needs the dreamer has.
8. Answers will vary.

2 Word Sounds

1. paws, claws
2. thaws, straw
3. jaw, law
4. dawn, lawn
5. pawns, yawn
6. lawful, awful

3 Long and Short Vowels

1. breathe breath	4. scrap scrape
2. bathe bath	5. gripe grip
3. tap tape	6. twin twine

4 Putting Words in Order

1. Mr. Clark couldn't go to sleep.
2. First he tried counting sheep.
3. Then he fixed himself a cup of tea.
4. He still couldn't fall asleep.
5. The next day he was fired for sleeping on the job.

Lesson 12

1 About the Reading

1. 10,000
2. a. queen lays eggs
   b. workers build hives, get food, and care for the young
   c. drones mate with the queen
3. queen and workers
4. drone
5. worker
6. in the fall
7. Drones mate with the queen so she can produce worker eggs.
8. They starve to death.
9. It would not survive because the queen couldn't lay worker eggs.

2 Word Sounds

1. brands   glands   5. fly   fly
   glands   shy
   lands   try
2. buck   suck   6. ground   pound
   suck   pound
   tuck   round
3. dive   hive   7. honey   honey
   five   money
   hive   8. Drunks   Skunks
4. gives   gives   Punks
   lives   Skunks

3 Words That End in -y

1. sleepy	1. spicy	1. sunny
2. watery	2. shiny	2. snappy
3. sticky	3. noisy	3. piggy
4. corny	4. bouncy	4. kitty
5. creepy	5. flaky	5. buddy
6. worthy	6. wavy	6. foggy

4 Words That End in -ly

1. brotherly   6. weekly
2. calmly   7. barely
3. nearly   8. lonely
4. sharply   9. cheaply
5. bravely   10. commonly

5 Common Sayings

1. bat   6. beet
2. bee   7. snail
3. gold   8. fox
4. lark   9. sheet
5. the nose on your face   10. kite

Lesson 13

1 About the Reading

1. a. He looks at the slant.
   b. He studies the direction of the writing line.
   c. He studies the size and width of the letters.
2. a. false   d. false
   b. true   e. false
   c. true   f. true
3. a. Answers will vary.
   b. Answers will vary.
   c. Answers will vary.
   d. Answers will vary.
4. Answers will vary.
5. Answers will vary.

2 Words That Mean the Same

1. employer   6. certain
2. large   7. present
3. barely   8. double
4. allow   9. marry
5. bright   10. scream

3 Word Opposites

1. asleep   5. bright   9. yesterday
2. sunny   6. begin   10. summer
3. birth   7. won
4. uphill   8. young

4 Vowel Sounds

Star	Air	Ear
1. are	1. bear	1. beer
2. carve	2. fair	2. dear
3. hard	3. stare	3. deer
4. heart	4. their	4. here
5. march	5. wear	5. peer

Lesson 14

1 About the Reading

1. 1863
2. a. They had nowhere to go.
   b. They had nothing to live on.
   c. They had no background in looking out for themselves.
   d. They had nothing to work with.
3. The crowd wasn't prepared to handle all the rain and the ex-slaves didn't know what to do with their freedom.
4. Answers will vary.

2 Choosing the Right Heading

Farms	Baseball	Soups	War
Games	School	Lights	Christmas
Snacks	Water		

3 Words That End in -er

1. sticker	1. miner	1. trapper
2. hanger	2. diver	2. batter
3. heater	3. maker	3. dipper
4. cracker	4. dancer	4. zipper
5. mower	5. freezer	5. swimmer

4 More Words That End in -er

1. coaster   6. slippers
2. dresser   7. corner
3. folder   8. lighter
4. rubber   9. poker
5. campers   10. checkers

5 Putting Sentences in Order

1. When I was fifteen years old, I was put up on the block for sale.
2. A white man was there who was very rich and mean and owned many slaves.
3. He was so mean that many white and black people hated him.
4. When he bid for me, I talked right out on the block.
5. "If you bid for me, I will take a knife and cut myself from ear to ear before I would be owned by you."

Lesson 15

1 About the Reading

1. Hold Fast, Saw Tooth, Wrap Around, Brink Twist, Necktie (any three)
2. He gold-plated them and sold them to a big store.
3. Their main goal is to own at least one strand of every kind of barbed wire ever made.
4. a. The doctor gets into his helicopter.
   b. He flies over miles of fence looking for barbed wire.
   c. He sees something that looks good.
   d. He sets his helicopter down in a field.
   e. He takes out his wire cutters and snips off a strand.
5. the way they looked.
6. farmers
7. They used it to keep cattle away from their crops.

2 Words That Rhyme

1. cold, gold, folded, sold
2. brink, drink, sink, stink
3. tent, bent, went, rent
4. Mack, rack, lacked, sack
5. cared, share, bare, spare
6. Sutter, utter, cutters, butter
7. tucked, stuck, sucked, luck
8. king, bring, sting, sing
9. wiped, griped, swiped, ripe
10. crook, look, hook, book

3 How Do You Say It?

1. flock
2. loaf
3. deck
4. pack
5. pot
6. herd
7. school
8. batch
9. bunch
10. quart
11. pair
12. can
13. bar
14. book
15. load

Review: Lessons 1-15

1 Choosing the Answer

1. sticky
2. flaky
3. foggy
4. repaid
5. filed
6. crosses
7. nowhere
8. grouches
9. batter
10. bid
11. grape
12. drones
13. Fourth of July
14. North and South

2 Silent Letters

1. wrote
2. dumb
3. badge
4. Dutch
5. young
6. build
7. knee
8. dodge
9. batch
10. writer
11. witch
12. certain

3 Matching

1. rainbow
2. oven
3. mower
4. towel
5. fence
6. stamp
7. alphabet
8. piggy
9. wax
10. pepper

4 Word Sounds

1. whose
2. certain
3. allow
4. bath
5. soup
6. heading
7. flood
8. ginger

5 Compound Words

1. lipstick
2. babysitter
3. sunglasses
4. ashtray
5. firecrackers
6. overdone
7. stagecoach
8. cheesecake
9. underline
10. busybody

Lesson 16

1 About the Reading

1.

	Fish	Whales
a. Breathing	in the water	out of the water
b. Blood	cold-blooded	warm-blooded
c. Birth	lay eggs	young are born alive

2. Cold-blooded means the temperature of the blood changes as the temperature of the environment changes.
3. Warm-blooded means the temperature of the blood stays the same even when the temperature of the environment changes.
4. a. true
   b. true
   c. false
   d. true
   e. false
   f. false
   g. true
   h. true
   i. false
   j. true
   k. true
5. Answers will vary. Frequently such animals are declared endangered species and killing them is forbidden.

2 Changing the y to i

1. busier   busiest
2. noisier   noisiest
3. happier   happiest
4. luckier   luckiest
5. sleepier   sleepiest

3 Changing the y to i

1. happily
2. busily
3. noisily
4. sleepily
5. Luckily

4 Silly Little Stories

1. swear, sweater, sweat, swell
2. lot, lost, locked, loss
3. Dan, dam, dashed, damp
4. band, bank, bang, banker
5. crust, crushed (or crunched), crumbs, crunched (or crushed)
6. witch, without, wished, wings, winked

5 Which Word Fits Best?

1. people
2. mammal
3. find
4. horses
5. flower
6. football
7. cow
8. wood
9. tomorrow
10. hardly ever

Lesson 17

1 About the Reading

1. Charles
2. eight years
3. more than thirty
4. teaching
5. about two thousand dollars
6. He intended only to scare the driver.
7. a. He made careful plans.
   b. He always worked alone.
   c. He never held up stagecoaches near home.
   d. He never told anyone about his plans.
8. A teacher earned about one thousand dollars.
9. Answers may vary.

2 Words That Mean the Same

1. limbs
2. bold
3. earn
4. clue
5. robbery
6. alive
7. all right
8. cause
9. high-class
10. ton

3 Word Opposites

1. under
2. dozed
3. scared
4. full
5. awful
6. harmful
7. leave
8. fresh
9. froze
10. cool

4 The Ending -ful

1. successful
2. truthful
3. mouthful
4. thoughtful
5. sinful
6. cupful
7. forgetful
8. hopeful
9. wasteful
10. spiteful

5 A Verse from Black Bart

This is the way I get my money and <u>bread</u>.
  When I have a <u>chance</u>, why should I refuse it?
I'll not need either when I'm <u>dead</u>,
  And I only tax those who are <u>able</u> to lose it.

So <u>blame</u> me not for what I've done,
  I don't deserve your <u>curses</u>.
And if for some cause I must be <u>hung</u>,
  Let it be for my <u>verses</u>.

Lesson 18

1 About the Reading

1. The earth is more than two billion years old.
2. They can tell the age of the rocks that make up the earth's crust.
3. The heavy matter in the center of the earth is liquid iron.
4. Life began in the ocean.
5. a. The earth was a ball of hot whirling gases.
   b. The gases began to turn into liquid form.
   c. The outer shell of the earth changed from liquid to solid.
   d. The rains fell.
   e. Oceans and seas filled with water.
   f. One-celled forms came into being.
   g. Worms and starfish came into being.

2 Word Sounds

1. sprinted, spray, sprawled, sprained
2. stranger, strong, streets, strike
3. swung, swiftly, swimming, switch
4. scraped, screen, screamed, scrubbing
5. squirrel, squeezed, square, squirt

3 The Ending -less

1. sleeveless
2. breathless
3. sleepless
4. worthless
5. thoughtless
6. meatless
7. cloudless
8. useless
9. hairless
10. Needless

4 Same or Opposite?

1. same
2. same
3. same
4. opposite
5. opposite
6. same
7. same
8. opposite
9. opposite
10. same
11. opposite
12. same
13. opposite
14. opposite

5 Spelling Check

1. March
2. crown
3. universe
4. stork
5. January
6. nerve
7. iron
8. drone
9. rainbow
10. cheese

Lesson 19

1 About the Reading

1. a. They used galleys to guard the coast.
   b. They used galleys to remove ships wounded in battle.
2. Note: The details below may be listed in any order. Other details may be included as well.
   a. The galley was mainly an open boat for four hundred men.
   b. Convicts manned the oars that made the galley move swiftly.
   c. Each oar was manned by five convicts.
   d. Sometimes the convicts rowed for twenty-four hours without any rest.

e. Nobody ever washed.

3. a. They would work at their respective trades.
   b. They would get some food from the nearest town.
   c. They would get much needed sleep.
4. They used steam when it became available because it was faster.

2 Words That Sound the Same

1. be, bee
2. know, no
3. Ann, an
4. thrown, throne
5. cent, sent
6. cell, sell
7. hear, here
8. where, wear

3 Which Word Does Not Fit?

1. question
2. dry
3. person
4. hidden
5. soap
6. work
7. one-half
8. port
9. dirt
10. gripe
11. bumped into
12. water

4 Words That Begin with *un-*

1. unmated
2. untie
3. unmade
4. unarmed
5. unfriendly
6. unsafe
7. undress
8. unable
9. unfolded
10. unfair

5 Common Sayings

1. good
2. old
3. will
4. hatched
5. away
6. ton
7. play
8. heard
9. worth
10. thousand
11. heart
12. Home

Lesson 20

1 About the Reading

1. February 11
2. February 22
3. bodyguard
4. swearing
5. New York City
6. 2 terms
7. 1789
8. He was the first president of the United States. He commanded the Continental Army in its effort to gain independence from England. He also served as president of the convention that wrote the Constitution.
9. four years
10. the one dollar bill

2 Vowel Sounds

1. born, barn, burned
2. crook, crack, creaking
3. time, tame, team
4. slum, slim, slammed
5. truck, trick, track
6. slung, sling, slang
7. peeled, pail, pile
8. store, stared, stars
9. While, wheel, whale
10. drank, drinks, drunk

3 The Ending *-ly*

1. nearly
2. Surely
3. hardly
4. swiftly
5. lovely
6. really
7. badly
8. friendly

4 Compound Words

1. body + guard
2. country + men
3. check + book
4. every + where
5. cat + fish
6. busy + body
7. police + man
8. some + one
9. in + land
10. hide + out
11. under + line
12. star + fish

5 More Common Sayings

1. flies
2. boils
3. put, basket
4. wool
5. back
6. say
7. friend
8. hole
9. pod
10. candy, baby
11. speak
12. easy

Review: Lessons 1-20

1 Twenty Questions

1. George Washington
2. February
3. Fourth of July
4. Mayflower
5. galley
6. scribes
7. El Dorado
8. California
9. forty-niners
10. warm-blooded
11. cold-blooded
12. quarts
13. pints
14. ounces
15. alphabet
16. B.C.
17. Pinocchio
18. bigwig
19. drone
20. New Year's Day

2 Words That Mean the Same

1. nearly
2. bold
3. munch
4. deserve
5. rim
6. buddy
7. present
8. guide
9. cause
10. utter
11. slim
12. worthless

3 Word Opposites

1. simple
2. remember
3. thaw
4. shrank
5. deadly
6. spiteful
7. ugly
8. spicy
9. certain
10. overdone
11. bold
12. crooked

4 Which Word Fits Best?

1. peep
2. hour
3. chew
4. writing
5. cross
6. oars
7. gills
8. firecracker
9. March is to February
10. water is to ice

5 Words That Sound the Same

1. through
2. be
3. sent
4. weak
5. thrown
6. bored
7. cents
8. weigh
9. brake
10. know

Answer Key for Book 3

Lesson 1

1 About the Story
1. Steven drives a van for a living.
2. He has had this job for five years.
3. His sister's name is Ruth.
4. Steven sees Ruth once a week, on Thursday night.
5. a. The exercise class would help Steven feel more relaxed.
   b. The class would also give him an opportunity to meet new people.
6. At first, Steven gets angry.
7. At the end of the story, Steven decides to give the class a try.
8. A pact is an agreement or bargain.
9. Answers may vary. Ruth may be encouraging Steven to "get out more, do things and meet some new people" because she enjoys these activities. On the other hand, Steven does visit her every Thursday and she may be trying to prevent him from getting into a rut like she has.
10. Ruth tells Steven that he is still young, and he has been driving a van for five years. Therefore he is probably in his mid-twenties.

2 The Ending -ing
1. blessing	1. bathing	1. bedding
2. building	2. lining	2. clipping
3. clearing	3. paving	3. fitting
4. dressing	4. wiring	4. cutting
5. stuffing	5. coming	5. padding
6. washing	6. icing	6. wedding

3 How Do These People Earn a Living?
1. teacher	6. waiter
2. baker	7. boxer
3. farmer	8. manager
4. fiddler	9. teller
5. miner	10. lawyer

4 Compound Words
1. road + work	6. dish + pan
2. side + walk	7. pig + pen
3. tool + box	8. man + kind
4. rose + bud	9. home + made
5. back + fire	10. news + paper

Lesson 2

1 About the Story
1. Steven's best friend is Jerome.
2. Steven is taking a yoga class at the Y.M.C.A.
3. He wandered into the yoga class by mistake.
4. Jerome thinks yoga has stranger exercises.
5. Jerome didn't laugh at Steven for taking the yoga class.
6. Jerome seems to have let himself into Steven's apartment, and he helps himself to the stew Steven has made for dinner.

2 Adding -est to Words
1. finest	1. proudest	1. saddest
2. rudest	2. shortest	2. biggest
3. nicest	3. cheapest	3. thinnest
4. latest	4. greatest	4. dimmest
5. ripest	5. meanest	5. maddest
6. sorest	6. highest	6. hottest

3 How Do These People Earn a Living?
1. reporter	5. tailor	9. shortstop
2. carpenter	6. babysitter	10. fisherman
3. bodyguard	7. trainer	11. scribe
4. actor	8. clown	12. doctor

4 Compound Words
1. pay + check	7. class + room
2. tooth + paste	8. under + shirt
3. under + stand	9. flash + light
4. corn + starch	10. cook + book
5. chalk + board	11. work + shop
6. short + cake	12. hand + shake

Lesson 3

1 About the Story
1. Jerome hadn't been in a library for twelve years.
2. All Jerome ever did in the library was flirt with the girls.
3. She said she thought he belonged in a reform school.
4. He wanted to find out more about yoga because he wanted to talk Steven out of taking a yoga class.

5. At first Jerome thought yoga was yogurt.
6. The ladies are pleasant, smiling at him when he almost knocks over the flag.
7. He feels awful while in the library even though no one is giving him a hard time.
8. A vow is a promise.
9. Going to the library brings back bad memories of being kicked out of the high school library, but Jerome signs out the book on yoga without incident.

2 Adding -y to Words

1. tasty	1. grouchy	1. runny
2. shaky	2. stuffy	2. doggy
3. shady	3. bossy	3. patty
4. stony	4. rainy	4. knotty
5. edgy	5. squeaky	5. woolly

3 Who Uses What?

1. flashlight	7. notebook
2. punch	8. sponge
3. towel	9. Bible
4. ashtray	10. charm
5. folder	11. jet
6. oars	12. buggies

4 Compound Words

1. black + board	7. sun + light
2. ear + ring	8. suit + case
3. house + wife	9. eye + strain
4. fruit + cake	10. ring + side
5. over + grown	11. bob + sled
6. grown + up	12. free + way

Lesson 4

1 About the Story

1. Jerome was studying up on yoga.
2. It is a way to relax and free oneself from the phony nonsense in this world. He also tells her that some people claim it improves their sex life.
3. Jerome says he always goes to her place.
4. a. She is waiting for a call from her new manager.
   b. Jerome's place looks like a pigpen.
5. Ginger hangs up on Jerome.
6. Jerome won't stop clowning around.
7. Answers will vary.

2 Changing the y to i

1. grouchier	grouchiest
2. rainier	rainiest
3. icier	iciest
4. stuffier	stuffiest
5. bossier	bossiest
6. rosier	rosiest

3 The Ending -y

trashy	1. hairy	salty	6. brainy
bloody	2. jumpy	brainy	7. salty
hairy	3. puffy	tricky	8. bloody
jumpy	4. risky	puffy	9. tricky
risky	5. trashy	woody	10. Woody

4 Who Uses What?

1. iron	6. putty
2. leash	7. globe
3. grill	8. gloves
4. plow	9. platter
5. spices	10. sails

5 Compound Words

1. rail + road	5. dream + land
2. basket + ball	6. grand + father
3. under + ground	7. cheap + skate
4. grand + mother	8. wood + pecker

Lesson 5

1 About the Story

1. It got you thinking about what kinds of information the story might contain.
2. She sang with a band, wrote songs and gave voice lessons.
3. She had met Jerome six months ago in a hardware store.
4. Jerome worked as a clerk in the hardware store.
5. Ginger was in love with Jerome.
6. No one knows for sure how Jerome felt about Ginger.
7. Ginger's mother thought her daughter's apartment didn't look at all homey.
8. Ginger had not told her mother how wealthy she was.
9. Answers will vary.

2 The Ending -ly

lately	1. properly	wildly	6. costly
madly	2. shyly	oddly	7. lately
truthfully	3. truthfully	costly	8. lively
peacefully	4. madly	shyly	9. peacefully
properly	5. wildly	lively	10. Oddly

3 Words That Mean the Same

1. plead	5. frighten	9. beginning
2. brink	6. notice	10. dense
3. edgy	7. bright	11. pledge
4. shove	8. gaze	12. healthy

4 Compound Words

1. tooth + brush	6. bill + fold
2. Thanks + giving	7. snow + ball
3. over + board	8. snap + shot
4. gum + drop	9. high + way
5. flower + pot	10. cross + walk

Lesson 6

1 About the Story

1. This story takes place in the hardware store.
2. It is evening.
3. a. Ginger might stop being angry with him.
   b. It might encourage her to paint her apartment.
4. The lid came off, and paint spilled all over Jerome, the counter, and the floor.
5. Tony laughed very hard.
6. It took seven hours to clean up the mess.
7. Answers may vary. The first paragraph of the story suggests that Jerome wants to take the paint now and perhaps pay for it when he gets his next paycheck.
8. Answers may vary.

2 The Ending -ly

freshly
hourly
neatly
tightly
thickly

1. neatly
2. rarely
3. hourly
4. certainly
5. freshly

rarely
squarely
successfully
mildly
certainly

6. squarely
7. mildly
8. tightly
9. thickly
10. successfully

3 Word Opposites

1. hairy
2. costly
3. grownup
4. frozen
5. rarely
6. skinny
7. ugly
8. phony
9. tense
10. risky
11. loose
12. dumb

4 Compound Words

1. dish + rag
2. finger + nail
3. tail + spin
4. any + more
5. over + head
6. drug + store
7. finger + print
8. in + side

Lesson 7

1 About the Story

1. Steven had a slight cold and apparently wasn't feeling too well.
2. He was catching on to the yoga exercises quite quickly.
3. Holly asked Steven if he wanted to go out for a cup of coffee.
4. The sugar in it could make people grouchy, restless, fat, and unhealthy.
5. He apparently has decided not to order the chocolate cake when he says, "Well, so much for the chocolate cake."
6. Steven learned that yoga is a whole way of life. He also learned that in becoming involved with yoga he had a lot more to think about than he imagined he would.
7. a. Steven's apartment
   b. The Y.M.C.A.
   c. a coffee shop

2 The Endings -ful and -less

A. restless
   stressful
   sugarless
   spotless
   armful
   peaceful
   harmful
   tasteless

B. 1. stressful
   2. tasteless
   3. harmful
   4. armful
   5. peaceful
   6. restless
   7. spotless
   8. sugarless

3 Same or Opposite?

1. opposite
2. opposite
3. same
4. same
5. same
6. same
7. opposite
8. same
9. opposite
10. same
11. opposite
12. same

4 Compound Words

1. knock + out
2. ship + wreck
3. life + guard
4. match + book
5. light + house
6. door + knob
7. rest + room
8. come + back
9. eye + sight
10. knee + cap

Lesson 8

1 About the Story

1. This story takes place in Ginger's apartment.
2. It probably takes place in the morning since Ginger was fixing breakfast.
3. Gail wanted to stay at Ginger's for a day or two.
4. Gail goes to see her parents only when she wants money.
5. She had banged her head against the front door.
6. Ginger suggested that Gail ought to think about how she is treating her parents.
7. We know that Gail doesn't live with her parents because the story said she visited them only when she wanted money.
8. Probably most students will feel that Gail is not treating her parents very well and that she should be more considerate.

2 The Endings -ful and -less

A. countless
   faithful
   homeless
   joyful
   painful
   painless
   spoonful
   sunless
   watchful
   worthless

B. 1. homeless
   2. spoonful
   3. sunless
   4. faithful
   5. painful
   6. watchful
   7. joyful
   8. countless
   9. painless
   10. worthless

3 Same or Opposite?
1. opposite   5. opposite   9. same
2. same   6. opposite   10. opposite
3. same   7. same   11. opposite
4. same   8. opposite   12. same

4 Compound Words
1. coffeecake   5. scoreboard   9. crybaby
2. newsstand   6. waistline   10. kinfolks
3. washcloth   7. leapfrog   11. cheapskate
4. meatballs   8. pitchfork   12. spendthrift

Lesson 9

1 About the Story
1. Jerome was feeling lousy because he hadn't heard from Ginger in four weeks.
2. At first, Jerome thought Ginger was calling him.
3. Jerome wasn't pleased.
4. Steven spoke sharply, indicating he was angry.
5. Steven had called Jerome to invite him to Holly's party.
6. Going to Holly's party was better than sitting in a bar by himself.
7. Jerome is disappointed at first. At the end of the phone call, he is glad to be going to Holly's party rather than sitting in a bar by himself.
8. Probably the most obvious answer is that Jerome won't call a woman after they've had an argument. Instead, he waits for her to call him.
9. Answers will vary.

2 The Ending -en
1. frozen   7. weaken
2. forgiven   8. written
3. sunken   9. threaten
4. forgotten   10. loosen
5. broken   11. moisten
6. chosen   12. mistaken

3 Which Word Does Not Fit?
1. buddy   6. speak
2. ice cubes   7. worm
3. blouse   8. trip
4. chocolate cake   9. breathing
5. beef   10. play

Lesson 10

1 About the Story
1. a. Finding a parking place was difficult.
   b. The machines might not work properly.
   c. You have to be careful not to lose anything.
2. Holly was writing "Out of Order" signs for the machines that didn't work.
3. Holly had tried two washing machines.
4. a. The four quarters and two dimes ($1.20) she lost suggests she tried two machines — sixty cents in each machine.
   b. She was writing two "Out of Order" signs.
5. Since she had hung up on him, he felt she should phone him to apologize.
6. Jerome wants to see her, so he should call her.
7. Jerome wasn't taking any steps to get what he wanted.
8. Answers may vary.

2 The Ending -en
1. driven   5. bitten   9. given
2. fallen   6. eaten   10. ridden
3. shaken   7. spoken   11. Risen
4. straightened   8. beaten   12. rotten

3 Which Word Does Not Fit?
1. newspaper   5. pest   9. ivy
2. month   6. drum   10. season
3. deck   7. saucepan   11. whale
4. building   8. highway   12. Rome

4 Spelling Check
1. breakfast   6. coffee
2. alphabet   7. wedding
3. mammal   8. mirror
4. Christmas   9. Swiss
5. doctor   10. thirteen

Lesson 11

1 About the Story
1. a. Ginger had had her phone taken out.
   b. She had gone camping.
2. She was daydreaming about never having to work again.
3. a. She is going to buy a phone for every room.
   b. She is going to paint her walls.
   c. She is going to read all the newspapers she can find.
4. Life in the city looks safer than camping in the woods.
5. Ginger had gone camping to perk herself up after her trouble with Jerome. When she thought she heard a growling sound, she became scared and ran away as fast as she could.
6. Answers will vary.
7. Answers will vary.

2 Words That Begin with re-
1. react   6. recall
2. refuse   7. recover
3. remarks   8. repeat
4. respect   9. rejected, rejection
5. reveal   10. require

3 Words That Mean the Same
1. lousy
2. respond
3. boast
4. rejoice
5. nervous
6. faithful
7. juicy
8. require
9. recall
10. mistaken

4 What Is Where?

A Laundromat	A Library	A Diner
1. bleach	1. bookshelves	1. grill
2. coin machines	2. newspapers	2. oven
3. dryers	3. records	3. tips

5 What Is Where?

A Circus	A Concert	A Baseball Game
1. clowns	1. drums	1. center field
2. dancing bears	2. flutes	2. pitchers
3. side shows	3. stage	3. scoreboards

Lesson 12

1 About the Story
1. Steven's boss had given him the free passes.
2. The Colts and the Cowboys were playing.
3. a. She asked if they could sit behind the batter's box.
   b. She didn't recognize the coach.
   (Note: The story contains additional evidence that Holly doesn't know anything about football.)
4. When the man next to Steven bumped him, the popcorn spilled, landing on his coat and trousers.
5. "The Star-Spangled Banner" is played.
6. Holly probably knows a little about baseball. She knows the term *batter's box,* but doesn't seem to realize it is associated only with baseball.
7. Answers will vary.

2 Words That Begin with *re-*
1. revive
2. remove
3. report
4. repair
5. refreshed
6. reduce
7. retired
8. related
9. recovery
10. return
11. retreat
12. reply

3 Word Opposites
1. forgive
2. wilt
3. nervous
4. moldy
5. reveal
6. fallen
7. scratchy
8. listen
9. sunless
10. wasteful

4 Compound Words
1. footprint
2. quarterback
3. eggshell
4. deadline
5. homesick
6. daybreak
7. standstill
8. wastebasket
9. blacktop
10. courtroom
11. lukewarm
12. playground

Lesson 13

1 About the Story
1. Jerome thought it would be a way to see Ginger.
2. Tony was supposed to invite Ginger to the party.
3. a. He got rid of the cockroaches in the kitchen.
   b. He swept the cobwebs from his bookshelves and ceiling.
   c. He cleaned the carpet.
4. Jerome's party really started at ten o'clock.
5. It ended at four in the morning.
6. Ginger never arrived. Everyone else had a great time and didn't notice that Jerome was miserable.
7. Answers will vary.

2 Words That Begin with *in-*
1. inhale
2. invent
3. invade
4. invite
5. increase
6. instruct
7. inquire
8. infect
9. intend
10. inspire

3 Which Word Fits Best?
1. chirp
2. neck
3. Boston
4. coffeecake
5. look down upon
6. lung
7. land
8. steam
9. stale
10. present
11. roar
12. year

4 Consonants
1. gŭt • ter
2. măt • ter
3. sŭm • mer
4. hăp • pen
5. mŭg • ger
6. cŭt • ting
7. măm • mal
8. căt • ty
9. pĕp • per
10. slĭp • per

Lesson 14

1 About the Story
1. He didn't get along with her very well. He stayed in a motel during the week and came home on weekends only to see his children.
2. Mrs. Darkpill began to cut down Tony's chestnut tree. He tried without success to talk some sense into her.
3. She complained that he had whipped her daughter.
4. Her name seems most fitting. Her personality is far from cheerful.
5. Answers will vary.

2 The *gh* and *ght* Words
1. might, right
2. right
3. neighbor, sighed
4. ought, daughters
5. dough, rough, cough, tough
6. sleigh, height, eight, bright
7. enough

3 Same or Opposite
1. opposite
2. same
3. same
4. opposite
5. opposite
6. opposite
7. same
8. same
9. opposite
10. same
11. same
12. opposite

4 Double Consonants
1. stŭt • ter
2. clŭt • ter
3. bĭt • ten
4. wrăp • per
5. thĭn • ner
6. hĭt • ter
7. lŏb • by
8. shăt • ter
9. trăp • per
10. cŏm • mon

Lesson 15
1 About the Story
1. Ginger is parked in front of her driveway.
2. She accuses him of having girls in until all hours of the night.
3. coffee
4. booze
5. Ginger puts her arm around Mrs. Darkpill to lead her to the couch.
6. The neighbors, hearing the uproar, called the police.
7. Students will probably agree.
8. Answers will vary.

2 The *ea* and *ear* Words
1. beard, heart, feared, head
2. repeated, nearby, pleaded, freak
3. leather, dread, feather, mincemeat
4. mean, cheap, headed, beach
5. heard, beard, dreadful, preach
6. beat, sea, leap

3 Syllables
1. card • board
2. bright • ly
3. cheer • ful
4. sub • way
5. proud • ly
6. in • hale
7. un • clear
8. stair • way
9. cob • web
10. fair • ness
11. sad • ness
12. in • vade

4 More Work with Units
1. months
2. hours
3. seconds
4. quarts
5. ounces
6. feet
7. letters
8. rooms
9. states

Lesson 16
1 About the Story
1. a. peanut butter balls
   b. prune whip
   c. date-nut bread
2. Holly was writing a cookbook.
3. peanut butter balls
4. prune whip
5. He complains rather than taking action to make life better.
6. He is living by a set of outdated rules.
7. The bread was burned.
8. Answers may vary.
9. Answers may vary.

2 The Sounds for *ow*
1. flowerpot
2. bowling
3. bowl
4. crowbar
5. scarecrows
6. pillow
7. elbow
8. shower
9. grownups
10. towel rack
11. rowboat
12. cow

3 Syllables
1. yesterday
2. woodpecker
3. Cinderella
4. helicopter
5. laundromat
6. recipe
7. hangover
8. thrifty

4 Brain Benders
1. false
2. true
3. false
4. true
5. true
6. true
7. true
8. false
9. false
10. false

Lesson 17
1 About the Story
1. a. Tony's apartment
   b. a diner
   c. a men's clothing store
2. Mr. Dennis is Tony's boss.
3. Since Mr. Dennis answered the phone in an "extremely unfriendly voice," we can assume he was in a bad mood.
4. Tony tells Mr. Dennis that he is coming down with the flu.
5. He decides to check out the sale at a men's clothing store.
6. Mr. Dennis sees Tony at the store when he is supposed to be home sick.
7. Answers will vary.
8. Answers will vary.

2 Sounds for *ow*
1. dishtowel
2. landowner
3. blowout
4. snowplow
5. washbowl
6. townspeople
7. downpour
8. wildflowers
9. showoff
10. lowdown

3 Which Word Does Not Fit?

1. peas
2. unfriendly
3. knees
4. purse
5. weak
6. rain
7. shelter
8. relax
9. nervous
10. destroy
11. conceal
12. mute

4 Syllables

1. con • fess
2. booth
3. ex • treme
4. ex • treme • ly
5. shop • per
6. flu
7. six • teen
8. yes • ter • day
9. win • ner
10. pay • day
11. home • sick
12. rest • room
13. o • ver • board
14. un • friend • ly
15. bas • ket • ball

Lesson 18

1 About the Story

1. Steven thinks Jerome can't admit when he's made a mistake and take the initiative to straighten out things with Ginger.
2. Steven is trying to get Jerome to understand that he will have to take some action in order to get what he wants out of life.
3. Jerome thinks Ginger might have started the fight with Tony's neighbor just to get out of going to his party.
4. Jerome only complains and won't do anything to get back together with Ginger.
5. Jerome seems to decide Steven is right. Evidence of this is Jerome's deciding to call Ginger.

2 Short Stories

1. discussed, expands, disagreed, extra, convince
2. exceeding, exchanged, unfriendly, unfit, extra
3. exhausted, uncertain, unhealthy, expenses, income

3 Who Uses What?

Baker
1. cake pans
2. dough
3. oven
4. pie plates
5. rolling pin

Barber
1. chair
2. clippers
3. comb
4. mirror
5. shaving cream

Carpenter
1. boards
2. drill
3. hammer
4. nails
5. saws

Fisherman
1. bait
2. boat
3. hooks
4. net
5. rod

4 Spelling Check

1. thumb
2. August
3. wallet
4. paycheck
5. potato
6. Cinderella
7. waltz
8. cheapskate

Lesson 19

1 About the Story

1. Jerome decides to go see her rather than calling her.
2. Most of the story takes place at the nightclub where Ginger is singing.
3. Ginger is sitting next to the piano player when Jerome first sees her.
4. At first, Jerome tells Ginger he came to see her because he wanted to hear her sing "September Song."
5. Ginger threatens to have the bouncer throw Jerome out of the club.
6. Ginger touches Jerome gently on the cheek and goes to sing "September Song."

2 Months of the Year

1. January
2. December
3. December
4. November
5. February
6. Answer will vary
7. September (or August)
8. June (or May)
9. March
10. June
11. September
12. December
13. Answer will vary
14. Answer will vary

3 The Four Seasons

Spring
1. April
2. Easter
3. flowers blooming
4. spring training

Summer
1. August
2. beach
3. Fourth of July
4. the All-Star game

Autumn
1. falling leaves
2. October
3. schools open
4. Thanksgiving

Winter
1. Christmas
2. December
3. ice skating
4. snow storms

4 Twelve Questions

1. upstairs
2. indoors
3. infield
4. income
5. disposing
6. overdone
7. content
8. included
9. overlook
10. replying
11. request
12. deflate

Lesson 20

1 About the Story

1. Holly is giving a party to celebrate signing a contract for her cookbook.
2. Jerome asked Holly if he could bring anything to the party.
3. Holly is sick of all the health food she had to eat while testing recipes for her cookbook.
4. about midnight
5. She had to sing at the nightclub.
6. prune whip
7. chocolate cheesecake
8. Ginger likes the people from the yoga class.
9. Jerome is happy for a change.
10. Jerome seems to have learned that life has its ups and downs, and a person never knows what will happen next.

2 Compound Words

1. passport
2. Passover
3. homebody
4. backpack
5. backbone
6. firetrap
7. dishpan
8. drumstick
9. teaspoons
10. overalls

3 Words That Mean the Same

1. find
2. tired
3. overweight
4. hardly
5. hurled
6. rough
7. lance
8. wander
9. singe
10. pout

4 Word Opposites

1. female
2. sour
3. morning
4. heat
5. freeze
6. crawl
7. common
8. bored
9. certain
10. contract

5 Feelings

1. cheered. The fans were happy to see a member of the opposing team thrown out of the game for unsportsmanlike behavior.
2. excited. At last, Joan could apply for a job that really appealed to her.
3. angry. He had gotten nothing for his quarter.
4. overcome with feeling. Charles's emotions reflected his happiness at winning the money.
5. rejected. John felt his neighbor didn't want him at the party.
6. happy. His boss's leaving would remove that source of irritation.
7. thankful. She was very aware of how fortunate she was to have her son found unharmed.
8. Answers will vary.

Review: Lessons 1-20

1 Word Study

1. c	6. b	11. d
2. b	7. a	12. a
3. d	8. c	13. a
4. a	9. a	14. c
5. b	10. c	15. d

2 Words That Mean the Same

1. loyal
2. fussy
3. nervous
4. fib
5. poor
6. beg
7. content
8. hoist
9. grab
10. pledge

3 Word Opposites

1. straight
2. spotless
3. shrink
4. quiet
5. underneath
6. fancy
7. complex
8. loosen
9. phony
10. costly

4 Syllables

1. cloud • less
2. suc • cess • ful
3. rob • ber
4. side • ways
5. thir • teen
6. thought • ful
7. re • tire
8. hand • shake
9. sit • ter
10. peace • ful • ly

5 Word Sounds

1. walk
2. city
3. gentle
4. great
5. good
6. plow
7. could
8. certain

6 Spelling Check

1. courtroom
2. highway
3. England
4. eggshell
5. school
6. ear
7. cookbook
8. ashtray
9. kitchen
10. El Dorado

Answer: cheesecake

Answer Key for Book 4

Lesson 1

1 About the Reading

1. a. true   f. false
   b. false   g. true
   c. true   h. true
   d. false   i. false
   e. true   j. false

2. The person is putting a strain on his heart by makir it beat harder and faster.
3. 1,660,000 people in the U.S. die from heart disease.
4. Answers may vary.

2 The Human Body

1. artery
2. vein
3. nose
4. brain
5. elbow
6. bloodstream
7. nerve
8. ribs
9. lungs
10. spleen

3 Adding -er

1. dealer
2. reader
3. blender
4. printer
5. performer

1. trader
2. shaker
3. hiker
4. liner
5. believer

1. runner
2. drummer
3. bidder
4. flipper
5. patter

4 Syllables

1. book • case
2. win • ner
3. strong • ly
4. clut • ter
5. lo • cate
6. hope • less
7. nor • mal
8. for • give
9. cop • per
10. per • form

5 Brain Benders

1. kind
2. want something badly
3. a snob
4. full of pride
5. strongly moved
6. agree with your friend
7. insist on having your own way
8. teasing you
9. hurts your feelings
10. angry

Lesson 2

1 About the Reading

1. Baltimore
2. a reform school
3. the Boston Red Sox
4. Yankee Stadium
5. fifteen years
6. His legs gave out.
7. cancer
8. 53
9. Answers may vary. The reading suggests he lacked self-discipline and maturity — particularly as evidenced by the way he managed money.

2 Games and Sports

1. quarterback
2. outfield
3. yards
4. bases
5. squares
6. height
7. racket
8. paddle
9. checkers
10. dice

3 Words That Mean the Same

1. perform
2. car
3. brag
4. normal
5. gloomy
6. conceal
7. wrong
8. message
9. trousers
10. female

4 Word Opposites

1. conclude
2. edge
3. built
4. dull
5. normal
6. increase
7. restless
8. smooth
9. plump
10. brand-new

5 The Ending -er

1. buzzer
2. jumper
3. killer
4. learner
5. broiler
6. strainer

1. wiper
2. insider
3. outsider
4. invader
5. tuner
6. breather

1. digger
2. gunner
3. logger
4. jogger
5. skipper
6. snapper

6 Syllables

1. grāve • yard
2. dĭs • turb
3. wrăp • per
4. ĭn • quīre
5. ŭn • dĭd
6. tĕn • nĭs
7. brĕak • fast
8. fĭd • dle
9. păd • dle
10. trāin • ing

Lesson 3

1 About the Reading

1. *Concept* means a thought or idea about something.
2. They are afraid something serious has happened.
3. "A long time" can be anything from a few days to ten or twenty years.
4. They think "a long time" means thousands of years.
5. They think the person is rude or unfit for his job.
6. The Pueblo Indians begin something when they feel the time is right.
7. He had to wait until 2 a.m. for the dance to start.
8. Different groups of people have different concepts about time.
9. Answers will vary.

2 Time

1. spring, summer, autumn, winter
2. Tuesday, Wednesday, Thursday, Friday
3. dawn, noon, dusk, midnight (or *midnight* may come first)
4. New Year's Day, Easter, Fourth of July, Christmas Eve
5. second, minute, half-hour, hour
6. July, August, September, October
7. day, week, month, year
8. wristwatch, alarm clock, grandfather's clock, sun
9. free time, a normal working day, time and a half, double time

3 More about Time

1. steal
2. earned
3. save
4. waste
5. use
6. spent
7. lost
8. blown
9. lend
10. borrowed

4 The Ending -y

1. soapy
2. dusty
3. sandy
4. curly
5. bushy

1. breezy
2. wheezy
3. scary
4. nervy
5. greasy

1. peppy
2. potty
3. fatty
4. choppy
5. clammy

5 Syllables

1. wrĭst • watch
2. South • wĕst
3. clăm • my
4. short • cŭt
5. ŏb • jĕct
6. breath • less
7. rē • quīre
8. săd • ness
9. hōpe • ful
10. mĭs • trŭst

Lesson 4

1 About the Reading

1. 800,000
2. where it is cold or in salt water
3. Insects have six legs.

4. three
5. feelers
6. They help plants to grow by carrying pollen from one flower to another.
7. a. They serve as food for a number of animals.
   b. They return matter to the soil.
   c. They give us honey, silk, and wax.
8. a. Some bite.
   b. Some sting.
   c. Some carry diseases.
   d. They can mess up kitchens, etc.
   e. Some destroy crops.
   f. Some harm forests.
9. There are fewer insects in colder places.
10. There are so many of them that if they were larger they might overrun an area.

2 Name That Insect or Bug

1. bee
2. termite
3. ladybug
4. spider
5. tick
6. housefly
7. butterfly
8. grasshopper
9. ant
10. cockroach

3 Which Word Fits Best?

1. tick
2. huge
3. ocean
4. orange
5. fish
6. comfort
7. water
8. sand

4 Word Endings

1. speedy
2. rusty
3. silky
4. creamy
5. leafy
6. flowery

1. choosy
2. scaly
3. spongy
4. pasty
5. mousy
6. bony

1. baggy
2. Tommy
3. gummy
4. smoggy
5. floppy
6. sloppy

5 Syllables

1. cŏck • rōach
2. pīc • nĭc
3. ter • mīte
4. mouth • part
5. ĭn • sĕct
6. pŏl • len
7. flŏp • py
8. cŏn • cĕpt
9. out • look
10. ŭn • lĕss

Lesson 5

1 About the Story

1. dots
2. ten
3. one-third
4. can be unaware of what is happening
5. brain
6. We can be affected by things that we're not even aware of.
7. Subliminal advertising such as this can make us do things we might not do normally.
8. Ads may influence people to buy items they normally would not purchase.

2 Putting Sentences in Order

1. She checks the *TV Guide* to see what time the program is on.
2. She also reads what channel the program is on.
3. She turns on the set. (May also be #1)
4. She turns the knob to the right channel.
5. The picture is not clear at all.
6. She plays with the knobs to get a better picture.
7. The program turns out to be very dull.
8. She falls asleep on the couch.

3 Syllables

1. out • stand • ing
2. un • der • ground
3. yes • ter • day
4. but • ter • fly
5. Wash • ing • ton
6. com • mand • ment
7. grass • hop • per
8. per • form • er
9. re • mem • ber
10. a • part • ment

4 Working with Headings

Spending Time With Friends

Reading	Hiking	Playing Ball
Cooking	Talking on the Phone	Going to Night School
Making Things	Going to a Concert	Going out for Dinner

5 Words That End with-*y*

1. cooky
2. bunny
3. panty
4. battery
5. belly
6. muggy
7. brandy
8. moody
9. bully
10. gravy

Review: Lessons 1-5

1 Answer These Questions

1. vein
2. artery
3. Indian
4. Yankee
5. swamp
6. desert
7. termite
8. grasshopper
9. oxygen
10. carbon dioxide

2 Word Study

1. going on and off
2. a quarter
3. hero
4. George Washington
5. Baltimore
6. United States
7. tennis courts
8. meadow
9. museum
10. the American Southwest
11. gummy
12. flowery
13. insider
14. a jogger
15. Mother's Day

3 Words That Mean the Same

1. perform
2. underneath
3. meadow
4. locate
5. upper
6. concept
7. message
8. jogger
9. total
10. chat

4 Word Opposites

1. hero
2. townspeople
3. straight
4. cause
5. disease
6. exhale
7. prompt
8. scaly
9. baggy
10. aware

Lesson 6

1 About the Reading

1. false
2. true
3. true
4. true
5. true
6. false
7. false
8. true
9. false

2 Working with Headings

Solids	Liquids	Gases
1. chestnut trees	1. blood	1. air
2. ice	2. orange juice	2. carbon dioxide
3. rocks	3. water	3. oxygen
4. steel	4. wine	4. steam

3 Compound Words

1. starfish
2. moonlighting
3. moonshine
4. skyscraper
5. skylight
6. cloudburst
7. skyline
8. sunstroke
9. sunflower
10. suntan

4 The Ending -*ing*

1. spelling
2. crossing
3. drawing
4. coloring
5. coating
6. belonging

1. pleasing
2. mining
3. merging
4. boring
5. daring
6. carving

1. beginning
2. jogging
3. rigging
4. bidding
5. topping
6. matting

5 Confusing -*ing* Words

1. staring, starring
2. baring, barring
3. gripping, griping
4. hoping, hopping
5. filling, filing

Lesson 7

1 About the Reading

1. Ohio
2. February 11, 1847
3. Michigan
4. three months
5. Al
6. He wanted to see if his friend would fly when he passed a lot of gas.
7. She was angry that his teacher thought he was crazy.
8. He had caused a fire in the baggage car.

9. He could concentrate without being interrupted by a lot of noise.
10. a. light bulb
    b. phonograph
    c. moving pictures
11. 84
12. He spent so much time working that he didn't have much time for a family.

2 Compound Words
1. hourglass
2. padlock
3. dishwasher
4. handcuffs
5. boxcar
6. screwdriver
7. jackhammer
8. sandpaper
9. pacemaker
10. gearshift
11. airplane
12. mousetrap

3 Which Word Fits Best?
1. disease
2. part
3. knapsack
4. liquid
5. ears
6. dinner
7. state
8. stare
9. result
10. stage

4 Syllables
1. re • ceive
2. sky • line
3. dish • wash • er
4. wor • ship
5. rail • way
6. be • gin • ning
7. deaf • ness
8. com • pound
9. jack • ham • mer

Lesson 8

1 About the Story
1. the spoon
2. Italy
3. People carried a knife with them that was used for everything, including cutting meat.
4. A knife goes to the right of the dinner plate.
5. a. soup
   b. to cut meat
   c. meat
   d. two
   e. one
   f. cutting the salad
6. how we came to use knives, forks, and spoons.
7. Answers may vary.

2 The Last Word on Knives
The Johnson boys' table manners are so crude that they probably would not be invited to a fancy dinner party.

3 Food for Thought
1. potatoes
2. boiling
3. stew
4. deep frying pan
5. pound
6. berries (possibly oranges)
7. Italy
8. teaspoon
9. breakfast *or* picnic
10. Thanksgiving

4 Singular and Plural Words
1. singular
2. plural
3. plural
4. singular
5. singular
6. singular
7. plural
8. plural
9. singular
10. plural
11. singular
12. singular

5 One Knife/Two Knives
knives
lives
shelves
leaves
loaves
halves

1. life
2. loaf
3. lives
4. loaves
5. knives
6. shelf
7. half
8. leaf
9. leaves
10. knife
11. shelves
12. halves

Lesson 9

1 About the Reading
1. Children would rather act the way they want to rather than the way adults want them to act.
2. Answers will vary.
3. Answers will vary.

2 Which Word Does Not Fit?
1. ice cream
2. manners
3. release
4. dinner
5. beet
6. pockets
7. food
8. billionth
9. automobile
10. pacemaker
11. Huron
12. feet

3 Recipes
Fried Chicken
1. Put flour, salt, pepper and chicken in paper bag.
2. Shake until chicken is well coated.
3. Melt butter or fat in deep frying pan.
4. Brown chicken slowly until skin is crisp and golden.
5. Drain on paper towels.

Green Salad
1. Wash greens and throw away any stems.
2. Tear into bite-size pieces.
3. Chill greens in bowl until serving time.
4. Just before serving, pour ¼ cup dressing over greens.
5. Toss lightly until dressing coats leaves.

4 Singular and Plural Words
1. bubble
2. channel
3. concept
4. desert
5. effect
6. league
7. meadow
8. menu
9. message
10. pocket

1. batteries
2. children
3. heroes
4. museums
5. spiders
6. strawberries
7. tongues
8. waitresses
9. women
10. Yankees

5 More about Manners

1. d   5. d   9. c
2. a   6. b   10. Answers will vary.
3. b   7. b
4. c   8. d

Lesson 10

1 About the Reading

1. France and the state of Washington
2. 1947
3. The man in Washington saw nine discs, whereas the Frenchman had seen only one.
4. a. weather balloons.
   b. small meteors
   c. large hailstones
5. A group connected with an Air Force base in Ohio studies flying saucers.
6. It is hard for some people to imagine things they have not experienced for themselves.
7. Answers will vary.
8. Answers will vary

2 More about Meteors

piece, space, hot, shine

because, stars

200,000,000 entering, explode, heard

collected, outside

3 Choosing the Right Word

1. disc   5. related   9. record
2. morning   6. Earth   10. sunglasses
3. stony   7. cloudburst
4. sun   8. concept

4 Word Study

1. racket   5. tears   9. lying
2. use   6. racket   10. wind
3. wind   7. use   11. lying
4. wound   8. wound   12. Tears

Review: Lessons 1-10

1 Answer These Questions

1. star   5. the light bulb
2. gases   6. deaf
3. disc   7. Italy
4. reach the Earth 8. Thanksgiving

2 Word Study

1. worship   6. fork
2. drawing   7. Italy
3. crudely   8. tongue
4. inventor   9. whirling
5. medicine   10. record

3 Words That Mean the Same

1. enter   7. sloppy
2. dining   8. sudden
3. continue   9. beam
4. connected   10. tale
5. release   11. swirl
6. pretend   12. entire

4 Word Opposites

1. worried   7. swallow
2. daring   8. immense
3. release   9. bottom
4. skyscraper   10. lying
5. believe in   11. downward
6. sloppy   12. narrow

5 Syllables

1. pocket   6. cavemen
2. waitress   7. cranberry
3. Michigan   8. strawberry
4. medicine   9. atmosphere
5. America   10. Huron

6 Menus

Breakfast	Thanksgiving Dinner	Picnic
1. corn flakes	1. apple pie	1. hamburgers
2. oatmeal	2. cranberry sauce	2. ketchup
3. orange juice	3. dressing	3. pickles
4. poached eggs	4. sweet potatoes	4. potato salad
5. toast	5. turkey	5. ants

7 The Sound for *le*

little, middle, able, gentle, apples, bubble, gobble, Bible

struggle

single, double

table

Lesson 11

1 About the Reading

1. a. false   f. false
   b. false   g. false
   c. true   h. false
   d. false   i. false
   e. true   j. false
2. Answers will vary.
3. Answers will vary.

2 Changing the *y* to *i*

1. happier   happiest   happiness
2. lazier   laziest   laziness
3. lonelier   loneliest   loneliness
4. easier   easiest   easiness
5. moodier   moodiest   moodiness
6. busier   busiest   business

3 Word Endings

1. friendship	1. disagreement	1. deafness
2. worship	2. basement	2. loneliness
3. battleship	3. agreement	3. laziness
	4. statement	4. blindness
	5. apartment	5. happiness
		6. business

4 Silent Letters

1. gnat	6. fright
2. kneel	7. globe
3. wrench	8. sneeze
4. dumb	9. climb
5. fudge	10. misjudge

5 Happiness!

1. barber	6. February
2. Easter	7. happy
3. eighteen	8. moon
4. mammal	9. sign
5. knives	10. innings

Quote: Every human being is in some form
seeking happiness.

Lesson 12

1 About the Author

1. Holland
2. twenty-five
3. Hitler
4. kill all Jews
5. Six million Jews were dead by the end of the war.
6. World War II
7. They needed to take many clothes with them, but they didn't dare carry a suitcase.
8. It was a small attic in Mr. Frank's office building.
9. a. They were loaded into cattle trucks.
   b. There was only one place to wash for 100 people.
   c. There were not enough bathrooms.
   d. Men, women, and children all slept together.
10. the English radio
11. Answers may vary. By giving her diary a name, it became sort of a friend she could talk to.
12. Answers will vary.

2 Word Beginnings

1. bookworm	7. Everywhere
2. committed	8. backfired
3. homeless	9. downfall
4. cattle	10. remind
5. misjudged	11. concept
6. unlikely	12. doormat

3 Words That Mean the Same

1. basement	6. perhaps
2. inmate	7. truly
3. M.D.	8. excite
4. inflate	9. dozen
5. slaughter	10. depressed

4 Word Opposites

1. disagreement	6. depressed
2. attic	7. accept
3. fever	8. blindness
4. outskirts	9. North Pole
5. cheap	10. glance

5 Words That End in Hard or Soft g

Soft g		Hard g	
badge	gorge	beg	jog
binge	misjudge	brag	shrug
garbage	verge	egg	underdog

Lesson 13

1 About the Reading

1. Anne seems to have the most trouble with her mother. Her mother apparently criticizes her with words and looks.
2. a. Peter wanted to see a movie.
   b. Peter's father and Anne's sister wanted a hot, leisurely bath.
   c. Peter's mother wanted to eat cream cakes.
   d. Anne's mother wanted a cup of coffee.
   e. Anne's father wanted to see a friend of his. (Also the dentist wanted to see his wife; Anne wanted a home of her own and the chance to return to school.)
3. She was not in Germany when the war broke out.
4. She believes that people are really good at heart.
5. Answers may vary.
6. Answers will vary.
7. Answers will vary.
8. Answers will vary.

2 World War II

money, changes, history

fifty, wounded, armed

invaded, countries, bombed, declared

3 Cities, States, and Countries

Cities	States	Countries
1. Amsterdam	1. California	1. Egypt
2. Baltimore	2. Hawaii	2. Germany
3. Boston	3. Michigan	3. Holland
4. Detroit	4. Ohio	4. Japan
5. Rome	5. Washington	5. Spain

4 Word Endings
1. picture, nature
2. attic, picnic
3. foolish, selfish
4. cattle, terrible
5. swallow, meadow
6. total, chemical
7. manager, message, baggage
8. wilderness, kindness, sadness

Lesson 14
1 About the Reading
1. the camel
2. Asia and Africa
3. fat
4. seventeen
5. a. Its lids and lashes protect its eyes.
   b. Its nostrils can close, protecting its nose from sand.
   c. Its strong teeth can chew nearly anything.
6. twenty-five miles
7. one thousand pounds
8. a. Camels can carry cargo across the desert.
   b. Its hair is used to make cloth, blankets, and tents.
   c. Its skin can be made into leather.
9. It has a bad temper.
10. Answers will vary.

2 Compound Words
1. duckpin
2. pigtail
3. beeline
4. foxhole
5. mousetrap
6. snakebite
7. piggyback
8. dogwood
9. fishbowl
10. birdhouse
11. sheepskin
12. monkeyshines

3 Word Endings
1. bracelet, blanket
2. produce, reduce
3. America, Africa
4. channel, camels
5. curdled, paddle
6. narrow, borrow
7. affected, rejected, collected
8. heaven's, dozen, chickens, kitchen

4 Syllables
1. car • gō
2. cur • dle
3. shăg • gy
4. kīnd • ness
5. cŏn • fūse
6. thŭn • der
7. frēē • ly
8. at • tăck
9. Ger • man
10. of • fice
11. ĭn • māte
12. per • hăps
13. ŭn • păck
14. Hŏl • land
15. Ăm • ster • dăm
16. ō • ver • hang • ing

Lesson 15
1 About the Reading
1. a. southpaw   e. twenty million
   b. Italy   f. right-handed
   c. 1903   g. left
   d. hooker   h. oxygen

2. a. false   f. false
   b. true   g. false
   c. true   h. true
   d. true   i. false
   e. true   j. true

2 "Handy" Sayings
1. c   5. d
2. a   6. b
3. b   7. c
4. a   8. d

3 "Handy" Words
1. handlebar   6. handcuff
2. handball   7. handsome
3. handshake   8. handle
4. handbag   9. handy
5. handful   10. handpick

4 Singular and Plural Words
Singular	Plural
1. leaf	leaves
2. half	halves
3. employer	employers
4. ox	oxen
5. lash	lashes
6. deer	deer
7. diary	diaries
8. bicycle	bicycles
9. unit	units
10. cow	cattle

Review: Lessons 1-15
1 Answer These Questions
1. Adolf Hitler
2. 1945
3. Japan or Italy
4. Anne Frank
5. Holland
6. camel
7. Asia and Africa
8. fat
9. southpaws
10. twenty million

2 Word Study
1. throw it slowly
2. piggies
3. the United States
4. past
5. Yellow
6. breathing
7. start a fire
8. wet
9. solid
10. culture

3 Matching

1. Mr.   5. etc.
2. IOU   6. A.M.
3. Ms.   7. Dr.
4. Mrs.   8. B.C.

4 Matching

1. English   3. German   5. Dutch
2. French   4. Greek   6. American

5 Meet Ms. Brown

1. kindhearted   5. handicapped
2. lazy   6. moody, accepting
3. selfish   7. clumsy
4. foolish   8. confused, loneliness

6 Spelling Check

1. Holland   5. radio
2. Texas   6. dentist
3. truly   7. student
4. wages   8. Germany

7 Syllables

1. hand • cuff   9. fish • bowl
2. pro • tect   10. duck • pin
3. pig • tail   11. lone • li • ness
4. state • ment   12. un • com • mon
5. there • fore   13. wil • der • ness
6. de • press   14. mis • fit
7. bee • line   15. a • gree • ment
8. it • self   16. dis • a • gree • ment

Lesson 16

1 About the Reading

1. a   3. b   5. c   7. b   9. d
2. a   4. c   6. c   8. b   10. b

2 About the Reading

1. A living thing is badly hurt.
2. Hormones are released.
3. There is no pain.
4. The living thing becomes calm.
5. Death happens without a struggle.

3 The Ending -ly

differently   awfully
narrowly   nervously
suddenly   entirely
foolishly   strictly
mostly   promptly

1. narrowly   6. strictly
2. promptly   7. suddenly
3. entirely   8. mostly
4. nervously   9. awfully
5. foolishly   10. differently

4 The Ending -ly

1. easily   5. unluckily
2. bodily   6. speedily
3. busily   7. happily
4. greedily   8. clumsily

5 Compound Words

1. deadline   6. sunset
2. newsstand   7. neighborhood
3. overheard   8. lowdown
4. campground   9. jackhammers
5. freeway   10. outhouses

Lesson 17

1 About the Reading

1. 1856 to 1917
2. as a salesman
3. He collected diamond jewelry.
4. He planned to eat all the desserts on the platter.
5. His stomach rubbed against the table.
6. The doctors advised him to eat properly.
7. He thought that eating reasonable amounts of food would take all the fun out of eating.
8. He died in an Atlantic City hotel of overeating.
9. Answers will vary.

2 Food for Thought

1. Apple   6. dough (bread)
2. lemon   7. beef
3. chicken   8. honey
4. toast   9. crab
5. bread (dough)   10. Cheese

3 The Ending -ful

bagful   shameful
colorful   spiteful
delightful   successful
faithful   tearful
graceful   wishful
respectful   wonderful

1. colorful   7. tearful
2. Faithful   8. respectful
3. successful   9. shameful
4. wishful   10. delightful
5. spiteful   11. graceful
6. bagful   12. wonderful

4 Working with Syllables

1. vegetables   6. vanilla, chocolate, strawberry
2. oyster   7. restaurant
3. yogurt   8. spaghetti
4. doughnuts   9. menu
5. salad   10. breakfast

Lesson 18

1 About the Reading
1. false   6. false
2. true   7. true
3. true   8. true
4. false   9. false
5. false   10. false

2 More about Potatoes
writer

mountains, wheat, pieces, instead, bread

explored, Spain

brought, 1621, Ireland, settled

3 Where Would You Find It?
1. vines   8. purse
2. fork   9. piano
3. Italy   10. Holland
4. restaurant 11. ocean
5. bottle   12. stadium
6. jail   13. street
7. hotel   14. New England

4 The Ending -less
hitless   priceless
faultless   speechless
sugarless   strapless
pointless   treeless

1. sugarless   5. hitless
2. priceless   6. speechless
3. Strapless   7. faultless
4. treeless   8. pointless

Lesson 19

1 About the Reading
1. pints   6. large intestine.
2. small intestine. 7. What the person likes to eat
3. relaxed.   8. solid to liquid
4. waste.   9. glands.
5. makes food soft. 10. how food is digested.

2 More about Digestion
1. Teeth — break up food into small bits
2. Stomach — turns the food into a semi-liquid mass
3. Small intestine — digests the food
4. Large intestine — stores waste from food

3 Cause and Effect
1. The stomach has to work harder at churning the food.
2. It passes into the large intestine.
3. The person feels tired and upset.
4. The body can become diseased.

4 The Human Body
1. stomach   6. large intestine
2. glands   7. heart
3. lungs   8. muscles
4. liver   9. pancreas
5. small intestine 10. spleen

5 Word Endings
1. mentioned, digestion
2. Moments, agreement
3. continued, blue, tissues
4. settled, bottle, apple
5. pocket, blanket, racket
6. America, soda, saliva
7. handle, paddle, muscles
8. managed, message, cabbage
9. certain, curtains, mountain
10. ideal, hospital, chemicals

Lesson 20

1 About the Story
1. She was angry at him.
2. She was happy with him.
3. The young man has won her over with his charm and his soup.
4. He gives her the nail and tells her not to use it until she has nothing else to eat.
5. Answers may vary.
6. Nail soup, in this story, is a vegetable soup. The nail served only as a catalyst to obtain the other ingredients.
7. The young man is not a beggar. Granny willingly offered him the ingredients he needed for the soup.

2 May I Take Your Order?
1. a. $2.50
   b. $5.05
   c. $1.80
2. Iced tea is not available. (It's out of season.)
3. Probably you would try to talk a young child into ordering "Kid Stuff."
4. Answers will vary.
5. Answers will vary.

3 Same or Opposite?
1. same   9. opposite
2. same   10. same
3. same   11. opposite
4. opposite   12. opposite
5. same   13. opposite
6. same   14. same
7. opposite   15. same
8. opposite